Daniel L. Kohut

School of Music, University of Illinois

INSTRUMENTAL

MUSIC

PEDAGOGY

Teaching Techniques for

School Band and Orchestra Directors

Published By

STIPES PUBLISHING L.L.C.
204 W. University Ave.
Champaign Illinois 61820

Library of Congress Cataloging in Publication Data

Kohut, Daniel L
    Instrumental music pedagogy.

    Bibliography: p.
    1. Instrumental music—Instruction and study.
2. Bands (Music)—Instruction and study.   3. Conducting.   I. Title.
MT733.K59   785′ .07   72-10059

    ISBN 0-87563-664-0

CONTENTS

LIST OF CHARTS

PREFACE

This text is designed for the general practitioners of instrumental music: public school band and orchestra directors and instrumental teachers in training. Emphasis is placed primarily on instrumental performance problems and related pedagogy. Topics such as administration, recruiting, motivation, and related areas are not included, despite their importance, since this would merely duplicate published information already available.

In this text the elements of artistic performance are treated as items of foremost importance. In other words, fundamentals such as breathing, embouchure, and tone production are discussed as *means* toward the end—artistic performance. Consequently they emerge as supporting elements to our discussion rather than central issues in themselves. The main reason for this approach is essentially a pedagogical one. Pedagogical procedures and related performance practices should be judged on the basis of how effectively and efficiently they contribute to the musical result. For example, proper breath support is admittedly important in wind instrument playing, but in what ways does it influence the quality of a player's performance? How does it relate to tone quality and intonation? What is its effect upon phrasing and other aspects of musical expression? And if any of these are deficient, what is the real source of the problem and how does one go about correcting it?

Another feature of this text involves the author's desire to provide in-depth treatment to the major topics discussed. According to Highet, ". . . one cannot understand even the rudiments of an important subject without knowing its higher levels—at least, not well enough to teach it."[1] Too little knowledge can be dangerous, often resulting in misinterpretation of general principles as well as poor teaching of so-called advanced techniques. In-depth knowledge and understanding of important musical subjects are therefore considered essential to successful teaching, especially for the teacher of beginners whose quality of instruction largely determines his students' future success or failure as well as their initial musical progress.

This text also covers topics not commonly discussed in other publications of this type. These include learning to play by ear, jazz style and interpretation, and the teaching of music reading, including odd and changing meters. In addition, an effort has been made to summarize and interpret information from scientific writings and studies and relate it to specific pedagogical situations. Finally, the author felt the need for airing certain controversial issues such as stopping the tone with the tongue, tapping the foot in teaching rhythm, and the use of solfeggio in developing sightsinging ability.

The material in this text represents several years of formal study in music and educational theory, professional playing experience, personal research, and public school and university teaching experience at all levels. The text is not intended to be a substitute for formal music study nor does it replace the need for specialized study of each of the instruments. No book can fulfill these functions; it can only serve to supplement them. Nevertheless, it is hoped that this publication will be especially valuable to beginning instrumental teachers and teachers in training, and that it will also be useful in the continuing education of experienced school band and orchestra directors as well

ACKNOWLEDGMENTS

It has been said that few ideas expressed either verbally or in print are entirely original with the speaker or author. Most are simply a restatement of what others have said or written, or at least the basis for these ideas can be found in other sources. This is certainly true of this text. The author is indebted to numerous teachers, students, and colleagues whose stimulating ideas, helpful suggestions, and continued encouragement over the past eight years led to the final preparation of the manuscript. Thanks is also due to my wife, Maryann, and children, Michael and Laura, for their patience and understanding during the writing of the manuscript.

Daniel L. Kohut

[1] Gilbert Highet, *The Art of Teaching* (New York: Random House, Inc.), p. 13.

INSTRUMENTAL MUSIC PEDAGOGY

Chapter One

BASIC
PHILOSOPHICAL
CONSIDERATIONS

The primary purpose of this text is to discuss practical issues directly related to instrumental music teaching; discussion of philosophy is not to be a major concern. On the other hand, it is virtually impossible to divorce the two since philosophy, in its proper application, should serve as the underlying basis for pedagogical practice. The genuinely successful teacher not only possesses practical knowledge and experience of *how* to teach; he also has definite views on *what* should be taught and is able to explain *why* music should be taught in the schools. Particularly in this era of educational history, ignoring the latter can and has resulted in the elimination of music from numerous school systems.

A. OBJECTIVES OF MUSIC EDUCATION

A great deal has been written about goals and objectives in music education. Unfortunately, much of this literary effort has failed to emphasize viable reasons for teaching music. Primary justification frequently has been based upon extra-musical objectives such as development of mental discipline, promoting good citizenship, worthy use of leisure time, and the like. The major difficulty in applying these to music education is that mathematics, English, and other subject areas can also lay claim to these objectives; in fact, it can be argued that many other subjects fulfill such objectives far more effectively than music does. Furthermore, the proportionately higher cost of music instruction in comparison with other subject areas makes the justification of music even more difficult.

1

Another approach used to justify music in the schools is based upon the importance of developing man's aesthetic potential. According to Leonhard and House:

> Man is unique among all earthly living creatures in the extent and quality of his potential. He has physical, intellectual, ethical, and aesthetic potentials. If any aspect of his potential is neglected and underdeveloped, he never attains his true stature as a human being.[1]

Many music educators have long believed that aesthetic appreciation and understanding should be a prime aim of music instruction. During the past decade, however, aesthetic education, not only in music but in all of the arts, has become a topic of major interest in educational circles. This has fostered the publication of several books and articles along with increased discussion of this topic at educators' conventions. But to what extent has all of this influenced the direction of music instruction in the public schools?

Unfortunately, theory and practice seem to be at opposite poles in many school systems. Music as an art continues to receive minimal attention in those schools where it exists largely for its entertainment and public relations values. School administrators who use music programs primarily for these purposes, and music teachers who willingly allow this to happen, deserve to be chided for their neglect of educational responsibility. And then there are those programs in which top-quality performance alone seems to be the all-encompassing objective. Of what enduring value is it to play or sing a part perfectly unless one also acquires some understanding of the music itself? Performing a piece of music well does not in itself ensure aesthetic appreciation or understanding!

What are the answers to this dilemma? Eliminating performance groups in favor of allied arts and expanded general music classes has not proved to be the answer. Neither is it a matter of adding more hours of music instruction to the school schedule or instituting guitar and recorder study as part of the general music class, although each of these can contribute in its own unique way. Basically, it is a matter of music educators convincing themselves, their administrators, the students, and the community that music is a subject which merits serious study the same as any other basic subject. Music clearly deserves full standing in the curriculum and should be taught for its own sake. It should be justified primarily on the basis of its uniqueness as an art rather than its relationship to the other arts and its commonality with other academic

---

[1] Charles Leonhard and Robert W. House, *Foundations and Principles of Music Education* (New York: McGraw-Hill Book Company, 1959), p. 99. Used by permission of McGraw-Hill Book Co.

disciplines. Music is unique among other subjects in that it is the only subject where students can experience "musical thrills". This is the most fundamental justification for music's existence!

As a part of general education, music is unique in still another way. According to Leonhard and House:

> . . . Music is unique among the arts in lending itself to group participation. . . . Thus, music fits into the scheme of education more neatly than any other form of artistic endeavor and must perforce carry the major load of aesthetic education in all organized general education. Herein lies a major case for inclusion of music in general education.[2]

The other important issue is what types of music should be taught. Should the literature selected for study and performance include only so-called serious music by master composers? Do show music, avant-garde music, ethnic music, jazz, and youth music have sufficient musical and educational merit to be included in the total music education program?

In contemplating these questions, it might be well to consider first whether the prime objective of music educators is to teach the talented elite or the masses. If it is the latter, we should further consider that so-called "art music" has never been accepted by the masses; it has always existed for the elite few. If we believe that the masses should have access to "art music" and that education is the means to this access, then why is it that after several decades of music instruction in the schools we still cannot show any strong gains in educating the masses musically? This is not to say that some progress has not been made. There have been and continue to be some music programs in this country which deserve highest approbation for meeting valid and worthwhile musical and educational objectives. On the other hand, we are now in the midst of a great upsurge of interest in music amongst our youth for which music education per se cannot claim any real credit. Has our musical focus in teaching the masses been too narrow and conservative?

The topics and questions discussed here are not very pleasant or reassuring, but until such time when music educators are sincerely willing to come to grips with these basic issues, a large measure of their energies will continue to be directed toward entertainment and public relations. Music will continue to be an activity on an equal par with intramural sports, photography clubs, and the like. Under such circumstances, why shouldn't administrators consider it perfectly reasonable to drop music from the curriculum when financial crises arise? Or at very least, why shouldn't they feel justified in scheduling rehearsals after school along with all other extra-curricular activities?

In concluding this section, let us consider that educational objectives

---

[2] *Ibid.*, pp. 99–100.

as we know them are basically an invention of teachers, not students. As such, they represent what teachers believe to be important for the ultimate good of students. Since objectives tend to be teacher-oriented, this implies that students either do not know what is best for them or simply have no strong feelings on the matter one way or another. Both of these assumptions are open to serious question. Recent uprisings among the student populace have proved that a good many students do have strong opinions in this area, and it is time that more educators acknowledge this fact and decide how to deal with it intelligently.

Teachers need to reevaluate their role in the classroom. They need to realize that students, in the final analysis, really learn and retain best those things they sincerely want to learn. This does not mean that education should cater to the students' whims; it means that teachers have the responsibility to motivate, explain and illustrate not only *what* and *how* but also *why* certain knowledges and skills are important. Whitehead has said that "so far as the mere imparting of information is concerned, no school has had any justification for existence since the popularization of printing in the fifteenth century."[3]

B. OBJECTIVES OF INSTRUMENTAL MUSIC

How does the above relate to instrumental music and performing groups in general? First, directors need to acknowledge the unique strengths and limitations of the performance medium in meeting the objectives of aesthetic education. Performance alone does not necessarily provide optimum opportunity for teaching students about music, nor does it ensure that students will become intelligent consumers of music in later life; the thrill of performing in an ensemble is not the same as enjoying a piece of music for its own sake. Secondly, directors need to realize that aesthetic appreciation and understanding, along with developing performance discrimination for enjoyment in later life, are seldom the central reasons why students participate in performing groups. A student studies an instrument for its own sake, as a means toward getting to play in ensembles, and for the immediate enjoyment he receives from this activity. Even if a student never plays his instrument again after graduation, this does not mean that all of the time and effort devoted to instrumental practice and study has been wasted. The student who has experienced the thrill of performance will never again be quite the same person that he was previously. Young people need desperately to ex-

---

[3] Alfred North Whitehead, *The Aims of Education* (New York: Copyright 1929 by The Macmillan Company, renewed 1957 by Evelyn Whitehead), pp. 138–9.

perience beauty and express emotion through a discipline. These experiences, like all education, can never be taken away from them.

Even though instrumental music probably should not lay major claim to meeting the broad objectives of music education, it can open the door to aesthetic appreciation and understanding of music. Certainly instrumental teachers share a responsibility in this regard as do other music teachers; and in rehearsals in which musical style and other related elements are properly taught, a love and understanding of the music itself is often one of the major outcomes. Naturally, much depends upon the background and competence of the director. He need not be a composer, but he needs to be trained in much the same way as a composer. He needs to know the music inside out, its basic structure, materials, and concepts. Obviously this knowledge is also critical to the artistic success of his organization's performance.

One of the major reasons why instrumental music has flourished in the schools is the challenge it provides for students. No matter how well one learns to perform, there is always room for further improvement. The demands in mental and physical coordination in manipulating an instrument and reading music—sightreading in particular—are also undeniably great. A good performing group strives for A+ performance at all times. Also, consider the intense concentration and flawless accuracy demanded of the first chair player in a major symphony orchestra. Few professions require this type and level of excellence.

Should instrumental music exist primarily for the interested and talented elite, or should we strive to reach a much larger number of students? Instrumental music has always involved only a small minority of the total population in most schools. Not everyone is interested in studying an instrument, and not all those who express an interest have the desire or discipline to practice faithfully in order to be successful. Instrumental music in the schools, then, serves the musical needs of an elite few. Occasionally it also serves as an enrichment program for gifted, superior students who need to be challenged above and beyond their regular school work. On the other hand, the number of students participating in public school instrumental music would probably increase significantly if our offerings were expanded to include study of the guitar and piano, not to mention other, less popular, "social instruments". Since the piano in particular has such widespread appeal as a beginning instrument in this country, it is difficult to explain and justify its conspicuous omission from the instrumental offerings in the great majority of our public schools. (See Chapter Three of House's *Instrumental Music for Today's Schools*, for further discussion in this area.)

Some instrumental teachers believe that development of the ability to judge quality of performance should also be a major objective of instrumental study and instruction. The player who practices regularly in an effort to improve his playing presumably becomes increasingly more discriminating when he hears others perform. But how accurate is this assumption? How many students are actually aware of how they sound? How many really practice with specific objectives in mind and listen carefully to evaluate their overall results? In contrast, how many students merely "put in time" in home practice, pushing down valves, mechanically fingering the notes while listening with a deaf ear?

It is easy to criticize students, to blame them for their alleged carelessness and lack of musical sensitivity. But what about the teacher? Shouldn't he be held largely responsible for their musical achievement or lack of it? Is he capable of communicating proper concepts to his students? Is he able to motivate his students so that they are genuinely interested in learning to play at their best musically as well as technically? Most important, is he a good musician himself?

C. THE IMPORTANCE OF MUSICIANSHIP

Formulation of objectives, establishing minimum standards, curriculum design, testing and evaluation—all of these and other related topics are important to successful teaching. All first-rate teachers have definite objectives in mind and operate a well-organized program, even though these aspects of their teaching may be "behind the scenes" and not so readily observable. But all of these are a means to an end. They can never be of significant value to the teaching of music or any other subject without the presence of competent teachers who know their subject matter in depth and can communicate it effectively.

Most musicians agree that good musicianship is a vital requisite to success in music. But what constitutes good musicianship? How should it be developed? *Can* it be developed?

The word "musicianship" means a variety of things to different people. Most agree that it includes a person's ability to read music accurately, to sing or play with good tone quality and intonation, to perform technical passages with accuracy and finesse, etc. All of these are important, but the essence of musicianship is one's sensitivity to the expressive qualities of music, to the nuances of phrasing, interpretation, and style—in brief, all of those elements which make musical performance an art as well as a skill.

How does one develop musicianship that incorporates the more elusive qualities of musical expression? At the college level this is traditionally done in the applied studio, in large and small ensemble rehearsals, and in classes in conducting, theory, and music history. But much of this can be fruitless unless the prospective music teacher has above average intelligence and musical potential. Even when these criteria are met, much effort will be wasted unless students have intimate contact with good musicians and music literature of high quality. Concerning the latter, someone has said that musicians reveal their competence through the music they use. Good musicianship can hardly be developed through rehearsing and performing poor quality, synthetic music. Nor can it be developed by performing in groups which fail to achieve a high level of musical expressiveness in performance.

Hardly anyone will disagree with the above; and yet one of our major problems in music education today is still a lack of competent musicians who can teach. This may seem like a rash generalization, an oversimplification. After all, don't most music educators consider themselves to be competent musicians, competent enough to teach in the public schools, at least at the elementary level?

This raises the question of college admission and graduation standards. Public school students need music teachers who can communicate the expressive qualities of music as well as teach the mechanics of performance. They also need teachers who can separate the wheat from the chaff when selecting music for educational use, especially from among the flood of new compositions which hits the market each year. These facts are self-evident, and yet we still find far too many music teachers who have officially met all certification and degree requirements but whose level of musicianship is open to serious question. College and university music schools must be held accountable for graduates of their institutions who fail to meet adequate standards in these respects.

One aspect of musicianship not always considered in discussions of this type is that related to appreciation, understanding, and competence in various types of music including folk, jazz, youth music, show music and non-Western music. Again, colleges and universities should not neglect these areas by refusing to acknowledge their educational and artistic merit. Nor should they assume that these areas are common knowledge among their students. These types of music deserve to be studied as part of the total curriculum. If the curriculum does not allow for this, then the prospective teacher must assume personal responsibility for acquiring such information on his own time, to the extent that it is made available to him.

Let us assume, however, that the music teacher does possess the necessary level of musicianship needed to meet the requirements of his position. This does not ensure that he will become a superior teacher; but if he is not a good musician, his effectiveness as a teacher of music will be severely limited. Prospective teachers of music need to develop their musicianship to the highest possible level, and college and university music schools need to exert every effort to ensure that this criterion is fulfilled. At the same time, the teacher of music, once he is certified, must accept professional responsibility for continuing to learn, to attend concerts, and to perform after he leaves college. In a sense, college training is only the beginning of what needs to be a lifelong study of the art of music and the teaching of it.

In summary, it is the author's strong conviction that the primary objective of studying any instrument should be to develop musical sensitivity. Otherwise, the time and effort expended by both teacher and student results largely in mental and physical exercises which, by themselves, are rather pointless. Both teacher and student need to be able to understand and apply musical concepts in performance which will lead toward genuine musical experiences. This is the principal focus of this chapter and is the prime philosophical basis for all the chapters which follow.

D. THE IMPORTANCE OF EFFECTIVE HUMAN RELATIONS

To teach is to communicate. To teach effectively requires that positive human relationships be established between the teacher and his students. Possession of superior musicianship and knowledge of methodology is not enough. Students are first of all human beings and must be treated as such. In other words, good rapport between the teacher and his students is vital to effective teaching and learning.

In order to understand other human beings, one must first understand his own needs and inner desires. We all have biological needs such as food, shelter, and the like, but, more importantly, we need to recognize the various psychological needs we all share. Basic to all of the latter needs is the desire to feel important.

Psychologists have expressed this in varying ways. Some call it a craving to be appreciated; others explain it as the desire for recognition or even personal esteem. Regardless of the terminology used, the intent is the same: people want to be treated with respect. They thrive on honest praise and expression of genuine appreciation. They rebel against harsh, insensitive criticism and shun the person who is sarcastic and intimidating. Young students are no exception. They desire and deserve to be treated in the same way that adults like to be treated.

Someone has said that we should treat people not as they are but as we wish them to become. This has significant implications for teaching, especially with regard to student discipline. Positive reinforcement as opposed to indiscriminate criticism can also make the difference between enthusiastic, efficient learning and merely doing what one is told. Consequently, success in teaching, regardless of the subject, depends in large measure upon sound knowledge and application of the basic principles of effective human relations.

Learning to communicate effectively is important not only with students, but in our daily relationships with professional colleagues, parents, administration, and all others with whom we come in contact. Inability to get along with other people has been the cause of many professional failures in our society and therefore cannot be treated lightly. But since the subject is so complex, it will not be discussed further here. The reader is urged, however, to refer to the bibliography of this chapter for recommended references on this topic.

E. BASIC APPROACHES TO TEACHING

If one of the functions of an instrumental teacher is to help his students become more musical, he needs to be well versed in the area of methodology; he needs to know how to communicate viable musical concepts at both the general and specific levels. The following is a discussion of basic approaches directly related to instrumental music teaching.

For purposes of this discussion, there are two basic approaches: (1) teaching through demonstration, where students learn by imitating the teacher; and (2) analytical teaching, where individual performance results are analyzed and explained by the teacher in more or less scientific terms. Individual teachers are sometimes labeled as being basically of one or the other type. This does not mean that one approach is necessarily superior or inferior to the other; students can learn a great deal from both types of teachers. It is the author's belief, however, that the best teachers are those who incorporate both approaches into their style of teaching. The essential factor is how and when they use each of these approaches.

The first thing a student needs is an aural conception of how he should sound. Teachers sometimes have students listen to good recordings in order for them to gain proper performance concepts. While this can be helpful, it can never fully substitute for a live demonstration. Proper concepts are best learned through actually hearing the performer *up close* and observing as well as listening to him. Listening to a recording of a Mozart concerto can be helpful to a beginner, but only in a limited way; what he needs most is to have someone play the same tunes and exercises he is playing *right now!*

Despite the most sincere efforts of both teacher and student to teach and learn via the demonstration-imitation approach, some students will still not be able to execute certain techniques properly. Recourse to analytical procedures is then recommended. Also, a student started by another teacher who failed to emphasize proper musical concepts and playing techniques will probably need help in both areas. The teacher who inherits such a student must be prepared to analyze his performance deficiencies in two ways: (1) what he is doing wrong, and (2) how to change his playing so that positive results can be achieved quickly and effectively. In other words, the teacher needs to diagnose the performance ailment (where it is and what is causing it) and prescribe an appropriate remedy. This requires considerable knowledge and experience, as any "general practitioner" will verify. Ideally, the instrumental teacher is a competent general practitioner who not only knows how to solve a majority of his students' performance ailments but also knows when a specialist is needed and makes no hesitation in recommending a good one to his students.

The following section deals primarily with the pedagogical philosophies of Suzuki and Pestalozzi, which illustrate more fully the demonstration-imitation approach to teaching discussed above. Beginning with Chapter Two, the emphasis will be on the second basic approach to instrumental music teaching—analytical teaching.

1. Learning Through Imitation

Shortly after World War II, a major development in instrumental teaching began in Japan under the leadership of Shinichi Suzuki. Sporadic information about Suzuki's Talent Education program first became available in the United States during the early 1950s, based primarily upon personal accounts of Joseph Szigeti, Pablo Casals, and others who had visited Suzuki in Japan. But probably the greatest impact was made when Suzuki and several Japanese children appeared at the 1966 MENC convention in Philadelphia. The rest of the story is generally well-known.

What is Suzuki's secret? Can his approach be applied in this country? The questions are endless. Any significant change in educational practice traditionally invokes skepticism, and Suzuki's philosophy is no exception. Since one of his basic procedures is to teach children by rote, many music educators including some in his native country have expressed considerable doubt concerning the validity of his approach.

Many instrumental teachers in this country traditionally have viewed rote learning as having no place in the instructional program. Accordingly, some have also viewed classroom music as being essentially a waste of time when it involved considerable emphasis on rote songs. "Why don't general music teachers teach the students to read music?" has been a typical question. On the other hand, some instrumental teachers do advocate rote learning as an integral part of the early instructional program. According to Holz and Jacobi:

> . . . It is not at all important that youngsters be able to read musical notation. If children are allowed to learn melodies they know and love by ear, their first experiences will be more satisfying and interest in learning to play is more apt to remain at a high peak.[4]

Suzuki's approach, however, is not entirely original; the bases for some of his procedures are found in the pedagogical principles of Pestalozzi dating back over 140 years. The following is an outline of the "Principles of the Pestalozzian System of Music" as presented to the American Institute of Instruction in Boston in 1830:[5]

1. To teach sounds before signs and to make the child learn to sing before he learns the written notes or their names;
2. To lead him to observe by hearing and imitating sounds, their resemblances and differences, their agreeable and disagreeable effect, instead of explaining these things to him—in a word, to make active instead of passive in learning;
3. To teach but one thing at a time—rhythm, melody and expression to be taught and studied separately, before the child is called to the difficult task of attending to all at once;
4. In practicing each step of each of these divisions, until he is the master of it, before passing to the next;
5. In giving the principles and theory after practice, and as induction from it;
6. In analyzing and practicing the elements of articulate sound in order to apply them to music, and
7. In having the names of the notes correspond to those used in instrumental music.

The following discussion will show that Pestalozzi's principles and Suzuki's philosophy have much in common. But this does not make Suzuki's contribution to instrumental teaching any less significant. To him must go the credit for successfully applying these principles to the study of the violin. Nor can we afford to overlook his success in applying them in a meaningful, systematic way to the teaching of pre-school children. This type of pedagogy has been used sporadically in this country and elsewhere before, but this is the first time that literally thousands of children have been taught in this manner.

Suzuki recommends that young children first be exposed to good re-

---

[4] Emil A. Holz and Roger E. Jacobi, *Teaching Band Instruments to Beginners* (Englewood Cliffs, N.J.: Prentice-Hall, Inc., 1966), p. 67.
[5] Leonhard and House, *Foundations and Principles of Music Education*, pp. 52–53.

cordings played by fine performers. Once a child is ready to begin violin study, he learns to play through direct imitation; no written music is used. The basis for both of these principles is found in the Pestalozzian outline cited earlier, namely items 1 and 2.

When children first use their native language, they begin by speaking it. They learn primarily by imitating their parents. Later, after a relatively extensive vocabulary of words has been acquired, they learn to read the written symbols of their native language. Children normally are not expected to learn how to speak and read all at once. And yet in many school systems we try to teach children to play an instrument and learn to read music almost simultaneously!

If a child grows up in Mississippi, he learns to speak with a Mississippi accent. If he lives in New York, his accent sounds decidedly like that of a New Yorker. Much the same thing happens when a child imitates the tone, intonation, and phrasing of his teacher. If this is true, then the need for a superior musical model is obvious.

2. Playing By Ear

According to items 3 and 4 in the Pestalozzi outline, teachers should teach only one thing at a time, allowing the student sufficient time to master each item before moving on to the next. Suzuki advocates much the same thing. But think of how often these principles are violated in the so-called traditional method of teaching. The trumpet beginner, for example, is shown how to take a breath, form the embouchure, hold the instrument, and start the tone in a couple of lessons, and then has a method book placed in front of him. In addition to the complex fundamentals of playing the instrument—fundamentals of which he has only a very vague understanding—he is also asked to decipher the abstract symbols of musical notation. He looks at the exercise he is to play: the key signature is C major (no sharps or flats); the time signature is 4/4 (four beats in a measure; quarter note gets one count); the first note is G (fingered open), and is a whole note (gets four beats). Just before the student starts to play, the teacher also reminds him to use the tongue to release the tone and play with a big, full sound. "All right, here we go— one, two, ready, play . . ." The student surely has above-average potential, since he started the note on time and got the right pitch, but the teacher stops him before he is able to finish the first measure: "Your tone quality is horrible, it sags, it's lifeless. Support the tone more. Blow through the horn, etc., etc.," says the teacher. "Let's try again. . ."

The above is somewhat exaggerated but not entirely. The scene is far more typical than we might like to admit. Teachers repeatedly ask students to listen, to evaluate their playing. But how can they when the difficulties of mastering each new page in the book are such that they are literally forced to give full attention to reading the notation?

How many times have you had students come to class wanting to play a tune they learned to play by ear at home? And did you encourage them to do more of this, encourage others to do the same thing? Or did you merely concede to allowing the student to play his tune and then proceed directly to the really important task of the day, playing exercises from the book?

Perhaps you were afraid to place your stamp of approval on this type of playing for fear that the whole class might digress by spending their practice time playing by ear rather than practicing their assigned page in the book. But without realizing it, you probably missed many prime opportunities for teaching—*really* teaching—the most important elements of musical performance, elements such as beauty of tone, accuracy of intonation, musical style, and expression. Students have been known to study for years "out of a book" and still show little evidence of improvement in these areas!

It is the author's strong belief that students should be allowed to acquire reasonable command of their instruments through imitating the teacher and playing by ear prior to being introduced to musical notation. Once this is accomplished, the class can give the bulk of their attention to music reading when it is introduced. Learning to play by ear is not unnatural or necessarily difficult for youngsters, nor is there any real reason to feel that it is actually harmful or even undesirable. In fact, there is considerable evidence that the exact opposite is true.

It is perfectly natural for children to want to play tunes by ear. With a reasonable amount of practice they can also become quite proficient at it. Also, playing by ear is not necessarily a rare talent possessed by only a few individuals. Even though an individual teacher may consider it difficult, this does not mean that it will be difficult for his students. The real problem is mainly one of breaking with tradition, especially the way in which the teacher was taught. Are you willing to readjust your thinking and try a new approach to teaching, including eventually the teaching of jazz improvisation?

Let us assume that we decide to teach students to play by ear. We choose a repertoire of selected tunes, teach these to the class by rote, and assign them for home practice. We might even ask each student to prepare a "mystery melody" for the next lesson and have other students in the class try to guess the name of it. Once the class learns a piece in one key, a new starting note can be assigned requiring them to play it in a new key. With this approach it might be possible for students to learn to play reasonably well in F-sharp major (unless, of course, the teacher makes an issue out of how difficult this is supposed to be).

But sooner or later some hard realities must be faced: How long will it take before the class is ready to read music? How can they participate in band or orchestra if they cannot read music? If music reading is delayed for a whole semester or even one full year, does this mean that their reading ability will be stunted? Will they be able to adjust to the discipline of music reading, or will they merely try to fake their way through?

Experience has shown that none of the questions just raised should be cause for serious concern. The major factor is the teacher and his ability to adapt to and succeed in a new approach to teaching. Through experience, the teacher will learn when both the students and he are ready to begin music reading. The students will usually be ready to join the band or orchestra in a relatively short time after music reading is introduced. Time which may appear to have been lost at first is soon made up through the students' fast rate of progress. Not only are they able to devote more attention to the mechanics of music reading, but they should also retain their ability to listen to their performance results. This means they not only play the right notes at the right time but also play them with good tone. intonation, articulation, and musical expressiveness.

3. Conclusion

The key to successful music pedagogy is to stress music fundamentals, teach them one at a time in logical sequence, and teach them thoroughly.

The first and foremost fundamental is ear training. Students need to be taught from the very beginning the importance of listening to tone, intonation, articulation, and musical expression. Teachers who fail to do this can never hope to build a successful instrumental program or achieve valid musical objectives. Students need to be taught proper musical concepts. The teacher needs to be a good musician in order to make this possible.

The above is best accomplished through having students imitate the performance of their teacher while gradually learning to play by ear independently. Musical notation should not be introduced until the students have reasonable command of their instruments.

Learning to play by ear is not necessarily easy. As in learning anything well, it requires considerable practice and patience, and students need to be made aware of this important fact. The same is true for learning to read musical notation. In both instances the old adage of talent being 1 percent inspiration and 99 percent perspiration still applies. There are no secrets or easy shortcuts to becoming a fine performer.

Despite this, there are some who continually try to find an easier way, one which involves less time and effort. This is a noble objective so long as the end results are equally effective. Unfortunately, some teachers and students are much too shortsighted; they fail to see that what often appears to produce quick results usually creates numerous problems later. In the final analysis, such an approach proves to be a waste of time and effort rather than a saving of it.

This is not to say that teachers should not experiment and try new ways of doing things. Such an attitude would nullify a great deal of what has been proposed in this chapter; every teacher should strive to keep an open mind to new ideas which appear to have real merit. On the other hand, teachers with no established system or strategy for teaching music fundamentals often find themselves adrift in an ocean of methodology. When the pressure of performance is on, these teachers become victimized by the false god of rote teaching for its own sake and getting a first-division rating at contests, regardless of the cost in human time and energy. To prevent this, a thorough understanding of effective pedagogical procedures on the part of the teacher is necessary. The intent of the following chapters is to help meet this objective.

RECOMMENDED REFERENCES

Music Education Philosophy

Abeles, Hal, Charles Hoffer, and Robert Klotman, *Foundations of Music Education*. New York: Schirmer, 1984.

Elliott, David James, *Music Matters: A New Philosophy of Music Education*. New York: Oxford University Press, 1995.

Leonhard, Charles, and Robert House, *Foundations and Principles of Music Education*. 2nd ed., New York: McGraw-Hill book company, 1972.

Reimer, Bennett, *A Philosophy of Music Education,* 2nd ed. Englewood Cliffs, NJ: Prentice-Hall, Inc., 1989.

Swanwick, Keith, *Music, Mind, and Education*. London: Routledge, 1988.

Human Relations

Carnegie, Dale, *How to Win Friends and Influence People*. New York: Simon and Schuster, Inc., 1936.

Fleishman, Alfred, *Sense and Nonsense: A Study in Human Communication*. San Francisco, CA: International Society for General Semantics, 1971.

Kohut, Daniel L., *Musical Performance: Learning Theory and Pedagogy*. Champaign, IL: Stipes Publishing Co., 1992 (pp. 43-50, 135-141).

Schmitt, Sister Cecilia, *Rapport and Success: Human Relations in Music Education*. Philadelphia, PA: Dorrance and company, 1976.

Methods of Teaching

Gallwey, W. Timothy, *The Inner Game of Tennis.* New York: Random House, 1974.

Gallwey, W. Timothy, *Inner Tennis: Playing the Game.* New York: Random House, 1976.

Green, Barry with W. Timothy Gallwey, *The Inner Game of Music.* Garden City, NY: Anchor Press/Doubleday, 1986.

Kohut, Daniel L., *Musical Performance: Learning Theory and Pedagogy.* Champaign, IL: Stipes Publishing Co., 1992.

Maltz, Maxwell, *Psycho-Cybernetics.* New York: Pocket Books, 1960.

Schleuter, Stanley, *A Sound Approach to Teaching Instrumentalists.* Kent, OH: The Kent State University Press, 1984.

Stewart, M. Dee, collector and editor, *Arnold Jacobs: The Legacy of a Master.* Northfield, IL: The Instrumentalist Pub. Co., 1987.

Suzuki, Shinichi, *Nurtured by Love: A New Approach to Education.* Translated by Waltraud Suzuki, New York: Exposition Press, 1969.

Chapter Two

TEACHING
MUSICAL
NOTATION

Most experienced instrumental teachers agree that teaching musical notation is one of the most complex and challenging pedagogical problems facing the beginning teacher. The problem could be greatly reduced if only one standard procedure or solution were available. Unfortunately this is not the case. Individual teachers tend to have their own personalized methods, this diversity causing student progress to be retarded in some schools. For example, consider the frustration of the student who is taught one method one year only to find that a new teacher expects him to learn another method the next year. Both methods may be equally effective in themselves, but this is of little consolation to the student who must learn and relearn in order to please the teacher.

Mere acknowledgment of this dilemma does not excuse us from trying to seek practical, concrete solutions. Music students need to be taught to read music with the same proficiency that they read a book or novel. A music student who cannot read music properly is like a student of English who cannot spell or is unable to read a book intelligently: both are judged to be illiterate.

It is well known that students in some schools become very proficient in music reading while in other schools student reading achievement is often mediocre and in some cases very poor. While there are several explanations for this, it is the author's belief that student proficiency in music reading is largely proportionate to the quality of instruction provided. The teacher, therefore, is the primary limiting factor in most learning situations, not the students.

The quality of instruction received by students in their beginning years of study is especially critical to the success of any music reading program. When early instruction is neglected or misguided, future progress of the students is retarded. Until such time when students are taught to read music in a functional manner, their full potential as performers will probably never be realized. Instrumental teachers, therefore, should be prepared to teach music reading effectively regardless of the grade level they teach. It does little good for junior and senior high school teachers to blame the elementary teacher for allegedly doing a poor job. Every teacher needs to be prepared to take the student where he is and teach him precisely what he needs to know. Usually this requires at least a review of the fundamentals, and often concentrated drill of these fundamentals as well.

As an abstract system of symbols, musical notation is quite difficult for most youngsters, and it takes some of them a long time to master it. Even with superior students, some means by which the abstractions can be related to concrete concepts is necessary, and the means for achieving this goal should be as simple and direct as possible. There are many ways of going from New York to Los Angeles, and all open routes will eventually lead to one's destination, including a slow boat via the Panama Canal. But many of these routes have temporary blockages or involve detours which retard progress or understanding. Pedagogy should be an efficient means to an end, not an end in itself. For this reason, considerable time will be devoted in this chapter to comparing and evaluating various methods of music reading instruction, including foot tapping, time counting, and sight singing; two unique approaches, the BRIM Technique and the Beat Response Method, will also be discussed.

A significant portion of Chapter One was devoted to the merits of rote learning and playing by ear. Specific instructions on how to teach in this manner are included in this chapter, along with information on how to teach specific note values and rhythmic figures. The emergence of so-called odd and changing meters in program literature for school groups has, in recent years, been a source of concern to a number of school music teachers. This topic is discussed in the latter part of this chapter. Finally, attention is given to the subject of sightreading and how skills in this area can be developed.

A. BASIC PRINCIPLES AND METHODS
OF RHYTHMIC READING

Learning to read music accurately requires not only playing the right notes but also playing them *at the right time*. In order to do this, the performer needs to be able to "feel" given note values, rhythmic figures and patterns physically in order to play them correctly. Merely understanding their mathematical relationships and being able to intellectualize about them is not enough. Most instrumental beginners need a rhythmic crutch; they need to develop a feeling for rhythm through some concrete form of physical involvement.

1. Developing a Physical Feeling for the Beat

Some teachers rely exclusively on having their students count aloud. Beginning pianists, string players, and percussionists can count aloud easily enough while playing, but counting aloud is primarily a mental function, not a physical one. The question which remains is how the student will learn to "feel" the beat. Some educators point out that the physical activity of the string player's right arm and the movement of both arms in piano and percussion playing fills this need. But this argument is questionable, since this activity does not always involve feeling each downbeat. As long as the string player or percussionist plays successive quarter notes, he can feel the downbeats easily enough. If rests are substituted for some of the quarter notes, the situation is changed; since there is no physical motion during the rests, there is no feeling of the beat. The addition of eighth notes, dotted quarters, and sixteenth notes further obscures the sense of the downbeat.

The wind player, of course, cannot count aloud while playing. If he does not tap his foot, his only recourse is to count to himself. With beginners this usually results in their not counting at all. The teacher needs tangible proof that the student feels the beat. Foot tapping provides this evidence with wind players. The teacher can read the results of the foot; he cannot read the student's mind.

Some string teachers maintain that foot tapping creates problems in coordination; students become confused when trying to play upbow on a downtap of the foot and vice versa. If this is true, then a similar problem exists for trombone players (out-going slide against an upbeat of the foot), but trombone players seldom complain about this!

Choral teachers sometimes question the use of foot tapping in teaching rhythm. This is understandable since the choral student is seldom required to read rhythms as difficult as those required of the instrumentalist. When these teachers are asked to read portions of Stravinsky's *Petrouchka*, for example, or Marcel Bitsch's *Rhythmical Etudes*, their attitudes generally change. The need for feeling the beat through some physical means soon becomes self-evident. The need for considerable woodshedding of difficult rhythmic passages also becomes obvious.

A number of successful general music teachers have students tap their hands on their knees as a means toward feeling the beat. Others have the students pair off and tap the beat on each other's shoulders. There is nothing wrong with this, but the instrumentalist must rely on his foot since his hands are occupied in playing his instrument.

Authorities on etiquette point out that tapping one's foot while listening to music is in poor taste. Most music educators agree that foot tapping on a concert stage is distracting to an audience and can also adversely affect the overall tempo of a large ensemble. Others point out that students who have been taught to tap their feet will continue to do so regardless of when or where they perform. This may be true, but the author is not thoroughly convinced that teachers should repeatedly scold those students who find difficulty in "getting rid of the habit." Close observation of some highly respected, competent professional musicians and conductors will reveal that some of them also tap their feet in public—and we do not seem to be concerned about this!

Let us face the facts objectively. Performing intricate rhythmic patterns with accuracy and precision requires exacting physical coordination from every performer, regardless of his instrument. If this can be taught effectively without use of the foot or other means of physical involvement, then so much the better. Personal experience with beginners has proved, however, that foot tapping can be a valuable aid to learning when used correctly. The following discussion is offered to those teachers who either have not adopted a workable system of teaching rhythm or are dissatisfied with the results of their present methods.

Tapping the Foot

In teaching foot tapping, the most important things to remember are:

1. Students should be taught to tap the foot from the first day that music reading is introduced. They will usually respond to it easily and naturally at this time. Introducing it later often presents difficulties for both student and teacher.

2. Be sure the foot tap remains steady. Do not allow students to tap individually for each note as in ♩ ♩ ♩ ♫ . When this happens, the foot serves no useful purpose and ultimately does more harm than good. Use the foot to outline the downbeats and upbeats, not individual notes or rhythmic patterns.

3. Stress the importance of giving the upbeat as much duration and emphasis as the downbeat. Students often allow the foot to bounce up immediately after the downbeat, which destroys all feeling for division of the beat into two equal parts. Even though stressing the upbeat may seem superfluous when playing quarter notes and longer note values, its importance lies in the foundation it provides for "feeling" eighth and

sixteenth notes in simple time when these are introduced later. At that point, even the better students will probably encounter their first real difficulties. If not, then the dotted quarter-eighth note figure will surely prove to be challenging for most. In any case, proper stress on the up-beat as well as the downbeat from the very beginning will make these later rhythmic hurdles considerably easier to master.

Should students be taught to tap the toe or the heel? Actually, it makes little difference which method is used if the student is seated while practicing. Trying to tap with the toe while standing does tend to be awkward, however, and probably should be avoided if good playing posture is to be maintained. Since most wind and string teachers recommend a stance with the left foot slightly forward, tapping the heel of the right foot is recommended. In this way the student is less likely to disturb his stance or playing position.

The system of foot tapping outlined in Chart 1 has been used successfully by many instrumental teachers. Some preliminary comments

Chart 1

MARKING FOOTBEATS IN SIMPLE TIME

are in order, however, particularly as regards the marking of the arrows: Should the arrows be connected for quarter notes and longer note values (♩), or should they .be separated (♩)? Actually this is a rather minor point; but if one has to make a choice, use of connected arrows is preferred for the following reasons. First, connected arrows take less time to mark. Secondly, connected arrows also look neater and are therefore somewhat easier to read. Finally, connecting the arrows helps indicate duration, particularly in patterns such as ♩. ♪ . Otherwise, the two methods serve the same purpose.

A note of explanation is also due concerning the term "simple time" used in Chart 1 and the term "compound time" used in Chart 2. Simple time refers to meters such as 2/4 and 4/4 where the normal division of the beat is always two or multiples of two. (In 2/4 or 4/4, the division of the beat is two eighth notes; the subdivisions are four sixteenths and eight thirty-second notes.) Compound time, on the other hand, refers to meters such as 6/8 and 9/8, in which the normal division of the beat is into three and multiples of three. Here the division of the beat is three eighth notes; the subdivisions are six sixteenths and twelve thirty-second notes. Whenever a compound meter is played at a slow tempo (such as 6/8 in six beats per measure), however, it is treated the same as simple time.

When marking foot taps, students should be taught that each measure begins with a downbeat (downward arrow) and ends with an upbeat (upward arrow). If the measure ends on a downward arrow, this indicates that an error has been made somewhere and that the entire measure needs to be rechecked. This principle applies only to simple time, including slow 6/8 time, as shown in Chart 1.

The above system of foot tap marking is not usable in fast 6/8 and other compound meters, and a different system of marking is necessary. In Chart 2, three new methods of foot tap marking are shown. In Line 1, the player moves his foot down, slides it to the right, and brings it up on the third portion of the beat. Some feel that sliding the foot complicates things unnecessarily; these teachers choose to divide the regular upbeat into two parts (Line 2). Still others prefer to use the downward arrow only (Line 3).

Assuming the student has had an adequate drill in *slow* 6/8 meter, comprehension and execution of compound meters, regardless of the method used, should not present any great difficulties. The main thing the student needs to be aware of is where the downbeats occur. The method illustrated in Line 3 meets this criterion; it is also the least complicated pedagogically of the three and is preferred by the author for these reasons.

Chart 2

MARKING FOOTBEATS IN COMPOUND TIME

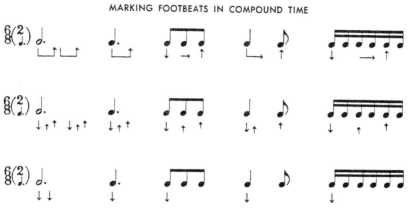

Hand Clapping

Some instrumental teachers use a down-up movement of the hands, corresponding to the down-up movements of the foot, as an additional aid in helping young beginners to feel the beat. In this method the hands are clapped together at the beginning of a note and remain pressed together throughout the duration of the note. During a rest the hands are separated but continue to move down and up in conjunction with the foot. Others feel that additional physical involvement through use of the hands is unnecessary. Experience has shown, however, that such an approach does have merit if introduced and used from the very beginning. Especially with students who appear to possess minimal rhythmic sensitivity, this method has frequently produced positive results in cases where all others have failed. Students who do not seem to need it, however, should discard it after the first few lessons.

Occasionally one finds youngsters whose coordination is so poor that learning to tap the foot, while simultaneously using the hands to clap rhythm, proves to be quite difficult. Others do not appear to need this type of training at all. Still others may insist they cannot use this method, that it confuses them. But it is the very rare individual who cannot be taught to coordinate his hands and feet in this manner. It may require extreme patience and perseverance in some cases, but the results usually more than compensate for the effort expended. Once foot tapping and/or hand clapping are no longer needed, they should be discarded like any other crutch. Their use during later stages of study should be limited to the study and practice of new and difficult rhythmic patterns. Pedagogy should not become an end in itself; it should serve as the *means* to an end.

2. Methods of Time Counting

Two aspects of time counting will be considered here: (1) how to count the basic beats in a measure, and (2) how to count the various divisions and subdivisions within each beat. Since various approaches have been used in both areas, this discussion will seek to compare and evaluate the pedagogical effectiveness of those methods most commonly used today.

Measure Counting, Note Counting, Beat Counting

EXAMPLE 1

Of the three methods of time counting illustrated in Example 1, measure counting is probably the one most often used and is also the one with which most readers will be familiar. This is not to say that everyone agrees that it is the best method. Some contend that since the composer is responsible for writing the correct number of beats within each measure of his composition, it is unnecessary for students to check continually the composer's intelligence by analyzing the number of beats in each measure. The answer to this is that students should be able to check the accuracy of their own knowledge of rhythmic notation and relative note values, not that of the composer. We assume the composer's competence; we can assume very little on the part of the student, regardless of what his background is reported to be.

Some teachers argue that measure counting is cumbersome, that students become confused as to whether the next count should be two, three, or four. Students presumably would be less confused if they used note counting—simply counting each new note or rest individually. Still others carry this a step further and suggest that the downbeats are the real items of significance. These persons advocate what is called beat counting (Example 1).

While note and beat counting may at first appear to be easier and more logical than measure counting, the latter proves to be more effective when divisions and subdivisions of the beat are first introduced. The student who in marking the counts ends up with only three and a half beats in a 4/4 measure immediately knows something is wrong. The measure counting system allows him to go back and easily recheck his work. Equally important is the fact that several measures' rest can be counted easily by counting 1-2-3-4, 2-2-3-4, 3-2-3-4, etc. The student who has learned to count 4/4 meter as 1-1-1-1 invariably becomes confused when trying to count several measures rest or when asked to rest for three beats and come in on the fourth. While some highly respected teachers prefer note counting and beat counting, use of these methods generally is not recommended.

Chart 3 illustrates the application of measure counting to the most common rhythms found in simple and compound time. Foot tap markings are included for the reader's convenience. The various rhythmic syllables used in this chart will be discussed in the following section.

Dividing and Subdividing the Beat

Chart 3

MARKING COUNTS IN SIMPLE AND COMPOUND TIME

Pronunciation of Syllables

e = ēē

+ = an

a = duh

Example 2 includes four types of rhythmic syllables. Notice that only the third type was used for simple time in Chart 3.

EXAMPLE 2

1 ta tu ta	1 a + a	1 e + a	1 ti te ta
(1)	(2)	(3)	(4)

In solfeggio, each pitch or scale degree, including chromatic tones, is assigned a different syllable. One therefore learns through practice to associate a *specific syllable* with a *specific pitch* (or scale degree if the movable *do* system is used). Use of the same syllable for more than one note except the octave would make the system confusing and illogical. The same principle should be applied relative to the use of rhythmic syllables; *different syllables* should be assigned to each *new rhythmic figure*. Use of the same syllables for two or more different rhythmic figures is confusing to the player and illogical pedagogically. And yet all too often we find teachers violating this principle. Example 3 illustrates the type of inconsistency and confusion which results when either the 1-*ta-tu-ta* or 1-*a-+-a* rhythmic syllables are used. Notice that the syllables are the same for both rhythmic figures.

EXAMPLE 3

1 ta	1 ta

1 a	1 a

Example 4 further illustrates the problem where the same syllable is used for different parts of the beat.

EXAMPLE 4

1 ta ta	1 a a
	or

On the other hand, if the 1-*ti-te-ta* or 1-*e-+-a* systems are used, no duplication of syllables exists and the student learns to associate *specific syllables* with *specific rhythmic figures* (Example 5). These systems are preferred over the first two for this reason.

EXAMPLE 5

```
1    ta      1    ti      1    ti   ta
   or            or            or
1    a       1    e       1    e    a
```

Advocates of the 1-*ti-te-ta* system point out that wind players already use tonguing syllables starting with the letter "t," so why not have them use rhythmic syllables which approximate those used in playing the instrument? Others question, however, whether *ti* and *te* really represent desirable concepts of throat opening for younger players. Actually, all four of the syllable systems described here can be taught successfully so long as the teacher has confidence in a given method and uses it consistently. On the other hand, there is little justification for using any system which is so needlessly confusing and/or inconsistent that it requires extra time for pedagogy alone. While both the 1-*ti-te-ta* and 1-*e-+-a* systems are judged to be acceptable, empirical evidence indicates that the 1-*e-+-a* system is the one most widely used. It is primarily for this reason that it is used in Chart 3.

The rhythmic syllables discussed above are intended for simple time. But it is in regard to compound time that the controversy concerning rhythmic syllables is probably greatest. Despite the fact that all of the systems listed in Example 6 can and have been used successfully, the important considerations are: Which method is most direct in its application and also the most consistent and logical in its basic structure?

EXAMPLE 6

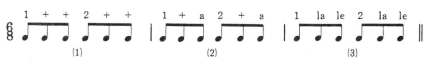

```
   1   +   +   2   +   +     1   +   a   2   +   a     1   la  le  2   la  le
         (1)                       (2)                       (3)
```

Methods 1 and 2 should be disqualified because the syllable "an" (+) is already used for counting rhythms in simple time. To duplicate its use in compound time creates several inconsistencies. One example of this is shown in Example 7.

EXAMPLE 7

```
      1     +  a  2  a                    1   +   a   2           a
   2
   4                                   6
                                       8
```

Teaching students to differentiate properly between ♪♫ — ♫♪ (3)

and especially ♩. ♩ — ♩ ♪ (3) is difficult enough. Why confuse the issue further by using the same counting syllables for each?

The rhythmic syllables used in Method 3 (pronounced *lah* and *lee*) are entirely different from those used in simple time, in order to give the student a means for clear differentiation between compound and simple time. Mere use of the 1-*la-le* method does not ensure that the student will be able to read rhythms in compound time automatically, but it does help him relate to a new system of unit beat division. For these reasons, the author prefers Method 3.

The above discussion involves information which presumably is well known to most experienced instrumental teachers. Two other methods exist that are not as widely known which merit consideration. One of these is the BRIM (BReath IMpulse) Technique originated by Middleton; the other is the Beat Response Method originated by Fitchhorn. The BRIM Technique is described in Middleton's University of Oklahoma doctoral thesis; Fitchhorn's method is outlined in his method book, *Practical Procedures in Sight Reading*, published by Henri Elkan. The following is a general discussion of the basic principles of each method.

The BRIM Technique

The BRIM Technique involves pulsating with the breath as in saying "ha ha ha ha." The abdominal muscles go through a sequence of tension and relaxation in order to create breath impulses in the tone. Wind players who have been taught to use intensity vibrato will recognize this as the first step in learning this type of vibrato. Middleton simply applies this approach to the teaching of rhythm for wind instrument beginners.[1]

In simple time, the student makes two pulsations on each beat which prepares him for division of the beat into two parts (Example 8).

EXAMPLE 8

Pulsations: 2   2   4   6   2   8

$\frac{4}{4}$ ♩ ♩ ♩ | ♩.   ♩ | o   ‖

Once eighth notes are introduced, the student is asked to pulsate at the rate of four pulsations per beat (Example 9).

---

[1] James A. Middleton, "A Study of the Effectiveness of the Breath Impulse Technique in the Instruction of Wind Instrument Performers" (Unpublished University of Oklahoma doctoral thesis, 1967), p. 3.

EXAMPLE 9

Pulsations: 4   4   2   2   2   2   6   2   8

In compound time, the division of the beat is three. Using the dotted quarter as the unit beat, the student pulsates at the rate of three pulsations for each beat. When eighth notes are introduced in 6/8 time, the rate of pulsations increases to six per unit beat.

This method aids the teacher in teaching proper breath support as well as in developing rhythmic ability, and also lays the foundation for developing intensity vibrato. Although this method already includes significant physical involvement on the part of the player, it is interesting that Middleton also recommends that foot tapping and time counting be used along with the breath impulse.[2]

It would appear that the most unique feature of the BRIM Technique is that of teaching proper breath support, since it is difficult to envision how students taught this method could avoid using the correct abdominal muscles in supporting the tone. Even though it is possible to introduce correct breathing procedures using traditional approaches during the first few lessons, getting students to apply them consistently thereafter is a much more difficult problem. Continued use of the BRIM Technique through at least the first year of study would appear to be a much more practical, effective solution to this problem.[3]

What happens when a student taught to use the BRIM Technique is asked to play a straight tone? According to Middleton, this is not a problem; students can play a normal, straight tone without any real difficulty when asked to do so. Also, students who do not experience the usual problems of rhythmic reading automatically become better sight-readers. Students who support the tone properly also learn to play with better intonation as well as improved tone quality. Finally, students not plagued with the usual rhythm and breathing problems can direct more attention to phrasing and musical interpretation, thus the BRIM Technique indirectly influences better quality musicianship.[4]

The Beat Response Method

Students should *see* the same thing, *feel* the same thing, and *hear* the same thing. All of this has no educational or habit formation value unless they *think* the same thing. Therefore they should first be taught to read

[2] *Ibid.*, p. 4.
[3] *Ibid.*, p. 8.
[4] *Ibid.*, p. 36.

orally and express the movements of the beat before they try playing the music on their instruments.[5]

The basic features of the Beat Response Method are: (1) use of foot tapping, (2) use of the right fist moving up and down in conjunction with the foot, (3) use of solfeggio, and (4) the use of a counting system which subdivides each beat in simple time into four parts. According to Fitchhorn, keeping time must become the responsibility of the students, not the director. This is accomplished through use of the right fist moving down and up for each beat in conjunction with the left heel, which he refers to as the "Auxiliary Director."[6] Regarding solfeggio, Fitchhorn points out that in the beginning it is not necessary that students be required to sing on pitch. Use of the syllable names in monotone while making the beat response ". . . invariably leads to singing the syllables with correct pitch."[7]

The Beat Response Method is based upon note counting rather than beat or measure counting. Precise duration of tones is controlled through use of two stylistic variations: One is the *staccato* or detached style (the one recommended in the beginning); the other is the *legato* style (introduced later). The *staccato* style provides for separation of notes by sixteenth rests. *Legato* style involves holding each note full value. Notice that both styles, illustrated in Examples 10 and 11, use a counting method which subdivides each beat into four parts. The pitch name in each case is assumed to be the tonic *do*.

EXAMPLE 10

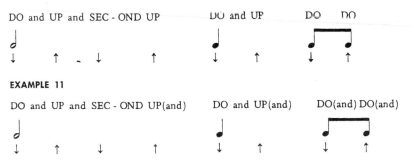

EXAMPLE 11

[5] E. J. Fitchhorn, taken from a personal letter to the author.
[6] E. J. Fitchhorn, *Practical Procedures for Sight Reading*, Teacher's Manual (Philadelphia: Henri Elkan Music Publisher, 1968), p. 3.
[7] *Ibid.*, p. 4.

Rests are counted by substituting the word "rest" for the syllable name. Additional topics including articulation, phrase rhythm and dynamics along with related methodology are discussed in the teacher's manual published along with the method book.

Although brief reference is made in the teacher's manual to use of the Beat Response Method in compound time, the method book itself consists entirely of simple time exercises and division of the beat into two parts. Sixteenth notes are used only in the context of 2/8, 3/8, 4/8 meter and *slow* 6/8 time, thus representing divisions rather than subdivisions of the beat.

B. BASIC PRINCIPLES AND METHODS OF SIGHTSINGING

1. The Importance of Pitch Training

The importance to French horn students of learning to "hear with the eye" is readily apparent. The same is true regarding string players, trombonists, and also players of valved-brass instruments. Woodwind players, on the other hand, can seemingly get by at first with minimal instruction in pitch recognition. But this assumption later proves to be false when woodwind players are expected to show evidence of improvement in tone quality and intonation. Quality musical performance requires much more than merely feeling the beat and using the correct fingering; it also depends upon the player's ability to listen, evaluate and improve the tonal aspects of his performance. Woodwind players are no exception. In fact, lack of adequate pitch training is viewed as a major reason why many novice woodwind players tend to play with such inferior tone quality and poor intonation.

Singers have no mechanical means for approximating their pitch and have to rely entirely upon the ear; consequently, they have to develop a good sense of relative pitch and this usually involves considerable time and effort. The latter also applies to instrumentalists. Like other fundamentals of performance, relative pitch should be introduced as soon as the student has a need for it. The need arises as soon as the student begins reading music. He needs to learn to "hear with the eye" so that he can learn to reproduce written pitches with reasonable accuracy. In succeeding months and years this ability should be improved to the point where he is able to play with beatless intonation as well as meet the needs of "musical meaning," to be discussed in the next chapter.

2. Singing with Letter Names or Numbers

Ideally, the first lessons received by an instrumentalist will be either private lessons or class lessons of like instruments or at least instruments all pitched in the same key. This allows students to sing pitches using letter names, which is highly recommended since it helps students associate a given written pitch with a specific fingering on their instrument. But in a heterogeneous class consisting, for example, of one flute, two clarinets, an alto saxophone, and perhaps a trombone, unison singing of letter names will not work, since each player will have different written notes in his part.

With the number system, where the numbers one through eight are used to identify the eight tones of a major or minor scale, students learn to associate specific degrees of the scale with specific numbers. Some teachers prefer to use numbers rather than letter names for sightsinging purposes right from the start, since this system allows all players, regardless of the pitch designation of their particular instrument, to sing together in unison.

The number system is useful so long as the rhythms are relatively easy, the tempo reasonably slow, and only a few accidentals are present. But once the rhythms become more complex and the tempo faster, enunciation of individual numbers, especially the two-syllable number seven, becomes increasingly more difficult. Add to this several accidentals as in "sharp three" or "flat four" and the system becomes quite unwieldy. Solfeggio, which uses single syllables for all accidentals as well as for diatonic scale degrees, emerges as the best system, encompassing all types and speeds of music at all stages of student development.

3. Solfeggio

Solfeggio originated in Europe with Guido of Arezzo in the eleventh century and reportedly is still in popular use on that continent. In the United States it also has its strong advocates in certain schools, while other schools tend to ignore its existence almost entirely. That solfeggio is less effective or more difficult than the use of letter names or numbers has yet to be proven, but some teachers insist that the latter methods are easier. Actually, the real reason is perhaps due to that old adage: We tend to teach the way we were taught, not how we were taught to teach. While this may be the path of least resistance, it is not always a sound one pedagogically.

There are two types of solfeggio used in this country and abroad:

fixed *do* and movable *do*. With the fixed *do* type, *do* is always the pitch of C; the diatonic and chromatic tones above C always retain their assigned syllables regardless of the key signature. Many arguments can be made in favor of this method from a theoretical point of view, but the prime reason why it is not entirely practical with heterogeneous instruments is the same as that discussed earlier regarding the use of numbers: instrumentalists playing diversely pitched instruments will have different written notes in their music, and thus the resulting solfeggio syllables will be different. In the movable *do* system, *do* is always the tonic of the key in which the music is written. All diatonic and chromatic tones above the tonic are figured in relation to *do* or tonic of the key; consequently they are different for each key.

Movable Do Syllables in Major Keys

Most beginning band method books begin with Concert F as the starting note implying the key of Concert B-flat, thus the Concert F is sung on the syllable *sol*. After this, most method books usually descend diatonically in major to Concert B-flat, a fifth below. The syllables for this descending tetrachord are *sol, fa, mi, re, do*. Example 12 indicates the syllables to be used in singing the Concert B-flat scale.

EXAMPLE 12

do   re   mi   fa   sol   la   ti   do

If the concert key is B-flat major, the written scale for cornet and clarinet, for example, will be in C major. C will be *do* but will sound a Concert B-flat when actually played on the instrument.

EXAMPLE 13

Cornet or Clarinet

do   re   mi   fa   sol   la   ti   do

Chromatic notes require use of new syllables which are derived from related diatonic notes (Example 14).

EXAMPLE 14

		Sharp Chromatics			Flat Chromatics
Diatonic		*Chromatics*	*Diatonic*		*Chromatics*
do	=	di (dee)	re	=	ro (row)
re	=	ri (ree)	mi	=	me (may)
fa	=	fi (fee)	sol	=	se (say)
sol	=	si (see)	la	=	le (lay)
la	=	li (lee)	ti	=	te (tay)

Example 15 illustrates the application of all the syllables to a Concert C chromatic scale, ascending and descending.

EXAMPLE 15

do di re ri mi fa fi sol si la li ti do

do ti te la le sol se fa mi me re ro do

Movable Do Syllables in Minor Keys

There are two basic approaches to syllabification used in minor keys. One is based upon the parallel minor-major key relationship, the other on the relationship of the relative minor to the major key or scale.

The parallel minor approach is where the tonic or first note of the minor scale is called *do,* the same as in the parallel major key. The chromatic flat syllable *me* is used for the third scale degree and appropriate chromatic syllables are used for the sixth and seventh scale degrees, depending upon whether the minor scale exists in its natural or harmonic form. Example 16 illustrates a C major scale along with its parallel minor in harmonic form.

EXAMPLE 16

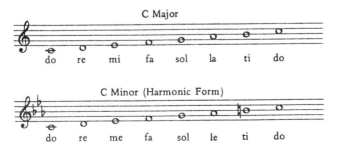

C Major

do re mi fa sol la ti do

C Minor (Harmonic Form)

do re me fa sol le ti do

Had the melodic form of the minor scale been used in Example 16, the diatonic syllable *la* would have been used for the sixth scale degree rather than the flatted chromatic *le*. Also, the descending melodic minor in its natural form would involve the syllables *do te le sol fa me re do*.

The relative minor approach utilizes the syllables of its relative major scale. The first or tonic note of the relative minor begins on *la* which is the sixth degree of the relative major scale (Example 17).

EXAMPLE 17

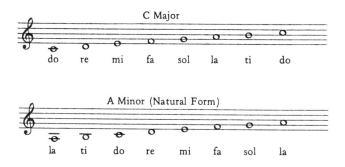

C Major

do   re   mi   fa   sol   la   ti   do

A Minor (Natural Form)

la   ti   do   re   mi   fa   sol   la

Although both systems have been used successfully, the author prefers the parallel minor approach, as seen in Example 16, for the following reasons: (1) Since the natural form of the minor scale is probably used less often in music played today than either the harmonic or melodic forms, the use of a solfeggio system based primarily upon the natural minor scale is difficult to justify. (2) Students taught to use the movable *do* system, where the tonic note of the key and the syllable *do* are always the same in major, naturally want to apply the same principle to minor keys as well. Learning the relative minor approach, on the other hand, requires adjusting to a significantly different usage of the basic syllables. (3) Students using the relative minor approach must also cope with new chromatic alterations whenever the harmonic and melodic minor forms are used. In the parallel minor approach, students are faced only with adding chromatic alterations to the basic syllable system they have used all along in the major key. (4) Finally, the real problem in learning minor scales is developing sensitivity to the tonality. Relating the minor scale to its parallel major utilizes the pedagogical principle of relating the unknown to the known. Students soon learn that the basic feature of all forms of minor scales is their flatted third. Alteration of other specific notes depends upon the form of minor scale used.

C. SPECIFIC PEDAGOGICAL PROCEDURES

Student success in music reading and enjoyment of musical performance depends greatly upon the quality of instruction received during the early years of study. The young teacher, therefore, should select and refine a proven system of music reading pedagogy and apply it consistently thereafter. Regardless of the specific system used, the important things to remember are:

1. *Experience should precede theory.* Musical performance should be introduced first through rote processes in which students imitate the teacher. Children should learn to "speak" the language of music *before* they try to read the symbols of musical notation.
2. *The system used for teaching music reading should be functional.* Students need to learn how to visualize and solve their own reading problems from the very beginning. They must learn to think for themselves! Otherwise the teacher may be forced to teach all musical notation by rote.
3. *The same system of music reading pedagogy should be used throughout the school system.* This is essential in order to prevent confusion and wasted effort for students who change schools or teachers from year to year. Admittedly this is a difficult problem to solve. Primarily it requires a music department head who can encourage or guide his faculty toward mutual cooperation so that this goal can be realized on a day to day basis. Presumably such cooperation is possible only when the pedagogy adopted is one that can fully stand on its own merits.

1. Ear Training Through Imitation

Item one—experience should precede theory—will be used as the basis for this discussion. First, the teacher plays some short, simple rhythmic patterns on a single pitch and the students imitate by playing the same patterns back to the teacher (Example 18).

EXAMPLE 18

Such ear training should be introduced as soon as the students can produce their first tone. Rhythms played inaccurately the first time should be repeated by the teacher, preferably at a slower tempo, until the students can reproduce them correctly, or else a different, easier pattern should be substituted.

As soon as the class learns two notes, melodic as well as rhythmic imitation is possible. Example 19 gives examples which can be used with a beginning clarinet or cornet class whose pitch vocabulary includes the written notes E, D, and C.

EXAMPLE 19

Beyond this, new notes along with new and varied rhythms in various meters of two measures or more may be introduced as the students' capability and the teacher's creativity allow.

As soon as possible students should be taught to play several familiar tunes by rote. The following list is suggested as a starting point. Other melodies should be added, including current popular tunes familiar to the students in the class.

Suggested Songs to Help Develop Musicality
for the Instrumental Beginner[8]

1. Indicate starting tone for each song when assigned.
2. Emphasize tone, intonation, articulation, and musical expression in student's performance.

3-Note Songs	Hot Cross Buns
	At Pierrot's Door
	Mary Had a Little Lamb (simplified)
5-Note Songs	Go Tell Aunt Rhodie
	Lightly Row
	Jingle Bells
	Mary Had a Little Lamb
	Theme from Finale of Tchaikovsky Symphony No. 4
6-Note Songs	Twinkle, Twinkle Little Star
	Baa Baa Black Sheep
	Are You Sleeping (Frère Jacques)
	London Bridge
	A Tisket A Tasket
	This Old Man
	Polly Wolly Doodle
	America

[8] Used with permission of Carl Wickstrom.

Do-to-Do Songs	Long, Long Ago
	Row, Row, Row Your Boat
	Joy to the World (Begins on a descending major scale.)
	Marine's Hymn
	The First Noel
	Swanee River
Sol-to-Sol Songs	Old MacDonald
	Little Jack Horner
	Clementine
	Yankee Doodle
	Jolly St. Nick
	O Christmas Tree
	Hark! The Herald Angels Sing
	On Top of Old Smoky
	America the Beautiful

The tunes in the preceding list should be taught by having students learn only one or two measures at a time before going ahead. Difficult passages should be repeated several times, very slowly if needed, until all pitches and rhythms are played correctly. Then go back and try to play the entire section without stopping, and eventually the entire tune. Once the entire tune can be played with reasonably good intonation, tone quality, articulation and musical expression, it should be practiced in other keys as well. This will further aid the student in developing his sensitivity to intervallic distances and tonality as well as increasing his awareness of the other musical elements mentioned earlier.

There is no need at this point for students to know about rhythmic note values or letter names of the notes; this information is irrelevant at this stage. It becomes important only *after* the students have been introduced to actual musical notation.

The author wishes to emphasize that a rote approach to *music reading* is definitely not advocated. Students need to be taught to analyze and solve their own rhythm problems when actually reading music. In the type of rote learning advocated here, the students do not use any music; the emphasis is entirely upon listening and actually learning to play by ear.

2. Learning to Tap, Clap, and Count

Measure counting, as it applies to a four-beat measure in simple time, is recommended along with foot tapping. Hand clapping is also suggested as an optional teaching aid. The downbeats are identified by number counts and downward arrows. The upbeats are counted "an" indicated by plus signs and upward arrows.

Before introducing the class to actual rhythmic notation, have them execute the following steps one at a time. This is to ensure thorough understanding and accurate execution of the system itself before applying it to specific note values.

1. Have the class stand up without instruments and move the right heel down and up in steady rhythm at approximately ♩ = 60 . Be sure the upbeat gets as much time duration as the downbeat.
2. With the hands in a clasped position, have the class move both hands down and up corresponding to the movement of their heels.
3. Finally, add the counts 1 + 2 + 3 + 4 +. Do not allow the class to rush the tempo. Emphasis on the upbeat as well as the downbeat will help prevent rushing and provide the basis for feeling divisions and subdivisions of the beat when these are introduced later.

Next, the written formula as shown in Example 20 should be illustrated on a chalkboard for use in class and a copy distributed to each student to be taken home. Before having the class read the note values shown, the instructor should demonstrate, *at a slow tempo,* how to tap, clap and count each individual note value. Then have the class repeat each one several times, slowly, before going on to the next. Be sure the class knows exactly what to do and how to do it. Leave nothing to the imagination!

EXAMPLE 20

Counts:

Foot Taps:

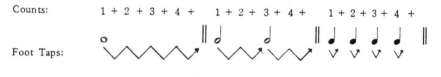

3. Understanding Note Value Relationships

Students may understand that in 4/4 meter a whole note gets four beats, a half note gets two beats, and a quarter note gets one beat, and yet may still be unable to apply this knowledge successfully in a performance situation. The reason is that they have little or no concept mentally or physically for note value relationships; they do not see the relationship of the whole note to the quarter, or the whole note to the half note, in terms of duration or comparative speed. The problem can be solved in part through visual illustration, as in Chart 4. This information should also be included on the copy of the written formula mentioned earlier so that students can easily refer to it during home practice sessions.

Students also need to "feel" note value relationships *physically* through actually doing them. This can be accomplished by having the class tap, clap and count a series of quarter notes immediately followed by a series of half notes, this followed by a series of whole notes and back again to quarter notes. Finally, these note values should be mixed at random either by pointing to a specific note value written on the chalkboard or calling it out by name (Example 21).

EXAMPLE 21

The speed of the beat should be slow enough so that students can execute the notes correctly while maintaining a steady tempo. The class should also understand that the beat remains constant; the only variable is the length or duration of the notes.

Young teachers trying to use this method for the first time may seriously question its practicality. If they have difficulty in executing it themselves, they may find it especially difficult to envision a group of inexperienced youngsters learning to do it. Initial failure is not the fault of the method, nor is it usually due to lack of ability on the part of the students. The problem often lies in the manner of presentation, the usual mistake being that the tempo set by the teacher is much too fast. Try a slower tempo and the chances for success should increase greatly.

Remember that considerable repetition is usually required when teaching youngsters to do something they have never tried to do before. Re-read the presentation given earlier, being especially certain to demonstrate the method clearly by doing it at a slow tempo in front of the class. Teach the students to tap, clap and count, introducing each item one at a time, and maintain a tempo of $\quarternote$ = 60 or slower if necessary. As soon as class facility allows, the tempo should be increased.

Once the class is able to tap, clap, and count with reasonable success, this knowledge should be applied directly to the instruments. Using the foot to establish a steady beat beforehand, each note value introduced should be played in series on a single pitch followed by random permutations (mixed combinations) of the same at the instructor's direction. The pitch used is arbitrary although it is usually easiest to use either the principal tuning note or the first note learned on their instrument.

It is not too soon to have the class practice following a conductor's beat including *rubato* and dynamic contrast. With the class playing a series of quarter notes, vary the tempo by conducting *accelerando* and *ritardando* to make the class more flexible and to add interest to the lesson. While learning to play with a steady beat is very important, try to avoid giving students the false impression that all music is played at the same tempo throughout.

As soon as students can tap, clap, and count the notes and corresponding rests discussed thus far and are able to execute them on their instruments, they are ready to start almost any standard beginning method book. Those who have reasonable command of their instrument through having practiced playing by ear first will find learning to read musical notation to be relatively easy. The temptation to rush through the first few pages should be avoided, however. Tone, intonation, tonguing, bowing, and other aspects of musical performance need to be properly emphasized. Otherwise much of the effort expended in learning to listen via the "ear approach" will be wasted.

4. Introducing Specific Note Values and Rhythmic Figures

Eighth Notes

Few students find any great difficulty with the longer note values discussed earlier. Real problems usually emerge when the division of the beat is first introduced. Example 22 illustrates the marking of counts and foot beats for a series of eighth notes in simple time.

EXAMPLE 22

Eighth notes should first be related to quarter notes. Whole and half notes should be mixed in later for more complete understanding. The class should also be told that in 4/4 meter the quarter note gets one beat, each eighth note gets half a beat, and that eighth notes are twice as fast as quarters but the speed of the foot tap remains the same. Having the students tap, clap, and count while the instructor plays a series of eighth notes often proves to be quite helpful.

Sixteenth Notes

Example 23 illustrates the marking of counts and foot beats for a series of sixteenth notes. This is derived from the 1 + 2 + method of counting eighth notes.

EXAMPLE 23

The above should be introduced by again relating the known to the unknown, i.e., sixteenth notes are twice as fast as eighth notes, each sixteenth note gets one-fourth of a beat, etc. Play a series of eighths followed by sixteenths and go back again to eighths. Also mix in a series of quarter notes for better comprehension of note value relationships.

Unequal Subdivisions

Because of their more complex nature, unequal subdivisions are usually more difficult for youngsters to comprehend than equal subdivisions such as a series of sixteenth notes. Use of the tied equivalent helps relate these to the equal subdivisions already understood by the class (Example 24).

EXAMPLE 24

The Dotted Quarter-Eighth Note Figure

Students who have found little difficulty in understanding and executing units, divisions, and subdivisions of the beat will probably encounter their first major stumbling block in the dotted quarter-eighth note figure. Several method books introduce this figure through *America* and most students play it correctly simply because they play it by ear. Eventually the student must learn how to sightread this rhythm in a new, unfamiliar piece of music through some form of independent analysis. The first step is to relate the known to the unknown (Example 25).

EXAMPLE 25

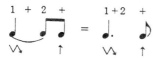

Older students who understand mathematical fractions may find the following rule helpful: "A dot after a note means add half again the value of the note." It should be explained that this rule applies to the half note as well as to the quarter. Later, when the dotted eighth-sixteenth note figure is introduced, all three dotted note values should be discussed and related to each other.

The Dotted Eighth-Sixteenth Note Figure

This figure is often played incorrectly in terms of both rhythm and musical interpretation. Students usually play the sixteenth too soon, and consequently the figure loses its musical crispness. In an effort to solve this problem, three pedagogical solutions are offered (Example 26):

EXAMPLE 26

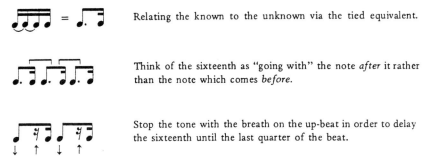

Relating the known to the unknown via the tied equivalent.

Think of the sixteenth as "going with" the note *after* it rather than the note which comes *before*.

Stop the tone with the breath on the up-beat in order to delay the sixteenth until the last quarter of the beat.

Students usually play the above figure incorrectly because of their failure to subdivide the beat properly both mentally and physically. "Guessing at" the dotted eighth-sixteenth figure usually results in the following (Example 27):

EXAMPLE 27

$$\frac{2}{3} + \frac{1}{3} = 1 \text{ beat} \qquad \frac{3}{4} + \frac{1}{4} = 1 \text{ beat}$$

instead of

Syncopations

The tied equivalent again serves as a valuable tool in allowing easier comprehension by the student (Example 28).

EXAMPLE 28

The Eighth Note Triplet

The eighth note triplet, although used in simple time, has its true basis in compound time. As a rhythmic division of the beat into three parts rather than two or four, it is called a "borrowed rhythm." The counting system recommended is 1-*la-le* 2-*la-le*, the same as in compound time. Use of mnemonic aids in teaching the triplet is also recommended, the details of which will be discussed in a later section.

The Quarter Note Triplet

The quarter note triplet in *alla breve* (Example 29, measure 1) presents no great problem since it involves the division of *one beat* into three parts. The same figure in 4/4 meter (Example 29, measure 2) is quite difficult for the novice, since he must learn to play three notes equally over a span of *two beats.*

EXAMPLE 29

Although the quarter note triplet can be and frequently is taught by rote, relating the known to the unknown can prove helpful (Example 30).

EXAMPLE 30

The 6/8 example above should at first be practiced very slowly in six beats per measure, gradually increasing the tempo until there are two beats per measure. The final result should be the desired one—three equal notes in two beats. Students who are unsuccessful at first should tap, clap, and count the rhythm slowly before trying to play it again.

5. Introducing Alla Breve and Compound Time

For many young teachers, the teaching of *alla breve* and 6/8 meter in particular tends to be a major hurdle. But anything new tends to be difficult at first. Ample time and drill are necessary before new techniques can be understood properly. Too often, youngsters are not given sufficient time for such understanding to take place, for what appears simple to the teacher is very complicated to the student.

Some teachers also tend to forget that learning to play in *alla breve* and compound time usually presents a greater challenge in terms of finger technique in addition to the problem of learning new note-value relationships. When a piece is played up to tempo, the notes go by much faster and the student may find himself struggling to maintain the pace. The problem in such cases, therefore, is not so much a music reading problem as it is one of technical dexterity.

Regardless of why a student may be experiencing difficulty with *alla breve* and compound time, it is important to remember that considerable slow practice on the part of the student and patience on the part of the teacher are required in order for both to be successful. In striving toward this objective, the following procedures are recommended:

1. Have the student practice the *alla breve* exercise slowly in regular 4/4 meter until he can play it accurately.
2. Increase the speed gradually in 4/4 until he reaches the "breaking point"—that point where it becomes uncomfortable to tap the foot four beats per measure or for a conductor to beat time in four.
3. Have the student continue to *think* four beats per measure mentally but ask him to tap his foot only on beats one and three.
4. Finally, explain that in *alla breve* the half note rather than the quarter note gets one beat. Have the student tap, clap, and count the piece or exercise using two beats per measure, to ensure proper understanding. Then go back and have him play it up to tempo, thinking two beats per measure, one beat per half note.

In introducing fast 6/8 meter, essentially the same procedure is recommended as with *alla breve*. The exercise should be practiced very slowly at first, in six beats per measure. The speed is then increased through the "breaking point," at which the transition from six beats to two beats per measure is made. Construction of a chart of note-value relationships in both *alla breve* and fast 6/8, similar to Chart 6, is also recommended.

Relating fast compound time to simple time (known to the unknown) is also helpful in initial instruction of compound rhythms. Many method books have used this approach, which is worthy of consideration (Example 31).

EXAMPLE 31

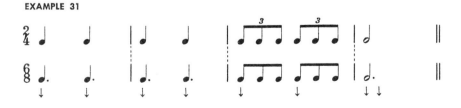

6. Mnemonic Aids

Words used to define specific rhythmic figures (such as "part-ners" for a duplet) are called mnemonic aids. These aids provide a means for mental association in much the same way one associates a specific solfeggio syllable with a specific pitch or scale degree. Any word can be used as long as its total number of syllables and its stress pattern fit the rhythmic figure it is designed to represent. Use of familiar words, names of local cities, students' names, etc., is recommended to help add interest to the lesson (Example 32).

EXAMPLE 32

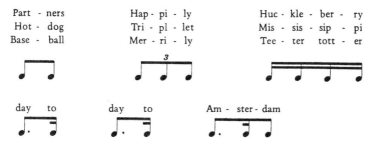

D. ODD METERS

Although odd meters and changing (mixed) meters have been an integral part of the contemporary music scene for the past several decades, their emergence in the repertoire for school music ensembles has been relatively recent and on the whole rather limited. Various reasons for this paucity have been advanced by individual music educators. One of the more common arguments is that music publishers tend to shy away from publishing music which is new and different, presumably because of their fear that it will not sell. Others place the blame upon contemporary composers for what they interpret to be a lack of interest in writing for public school groups.

The above allegations seem to be without basis, however, if we stop to realize that odd meters are not peculiar to twentieth-century composition. Tchaikovsky used 5/4 meter in the so-called "three-legged waltz" of his Sixth Symphony. Odd meters were also used as far back as the Baroque period, as the score of Handel's *Rinaldo* will reveal. To blame today's composers and publishers for the dearth of certain types of literature is also, for the most part, an empty argument, since publishers and composers will continue to produce inferior music only so long as music educators persist in buying it. When music educators convincingly prove via the purchasing medium that they want more contemporary music which uses odd meters, publishers will surely exert every effort to provide it.

There was a time when teachers were without any published instructional materials for the study of odd and changing meters. Publication of the *Odd Meter Etudes* and *Odd Meter Duets* by Everett Gates, available for all instruments, has helped fill this void. Also published are the percussion studies, *Mixing Meters* and *Reading Can Be Odd* by Joel Rothman. It is hoped that this trend toward more odd meter materials will continue.

Some teachers still insist that students find odd meters difficult because they are simply unnatural. When such meters are introduced for the first time to older players via musical notation, this argument may appear to be true. Let us not forget, however, that contemporary jazz, rock music, and television commercials abound with odd and mixed meters, and that consequently most of today's students already "feel" these types of meters and rhythms. Perhaps it is the teacher, rather than the students, who really needs to develop a "feel" for them.

When odd meters are introduced properly, beginners find them no more difficult than any other *new* meters. Careful explanation coupled with adequate drill is needed if they are to become an integral part of the students' metric vocabulary. Once this is accomplished, however, the only problem remaining is the teacher-conductor's ability to feel the rhythmic pulses and to conduct meters such as 5/8 and 7/8 accurately and with assurance. The purpose of the following discussion is to help the teacher understand odd meters better, along with providing methods for teaching them effectively.

1. Organization of Beats

In simple meters such as 2/4 or 4/4, consecutive eighth notes are organized rhythmically in groups of two. In compound meters such as 6/8, they are organized in groups of three. Odd meters, on the other hand, consist of diverse combinations of rhythmic groupings. For example, 5/8 can be grouped as $2 + 3$ or $3 + 2$. 7/8 can be any combination of $2 + 2 + 3$ or $4 + 3$ (Example 33).

EXAMPLE 33

How do we know which combination the composer had in mind? As a rule, this is most easily determined by the rhythmic organization of the notes. The first measure of Example 34 indicates 4 + 3; the second measure is 2 + 3 +2.

EXAMPLE 34

There are instances where the organization of beats is not so obvious (Example 35). One answer is for the player to listen to the phrasing of the other instruments. Another is to follow the conductor's direction. Once the conductor decides how he intends to conduct the measure, the player simply takes his cue from him.

EXAMPLE 35

The easiest type of odd meter, of course, is one in which a given rhythmic combination is established and maintained throughout the piece. An example of this is a combination of 2 + 3 used consistently in each measure in 5/8 meter. If 3 + 2 combinations are also mixed in at random, this makes the reading process more difficult. Fortunately for the player, random mixing of rhythmic combinations is not as common as consistent use of the same combination throughout the piece.

Unequal rhythmic combinations are not unique to meters using odd numbers such as five and seven; such groupings are also possible in 6/8 and 9/8 meters. For example, 2 + 2 + 2 is possible in 6/8 and 3 + 2 + 2 + 2 or 4 + 3 + 2 and their various permutations are sometimes used in 9/8. 8/8 meter also provides several interesting possibilities such as 2 + 3 + 3, 4 + 2 + 2, and 5 + 3.

2. Tapping the Foot

Learning to feel the beat physically is as important in studying odd meters as it is with more traditional meters, perhaps even more so. In odd meters as in compound time, the important item is the downbeat of the foot; the upbeat is secondary. Example 36 illustrates use of the unequal foot tap along with recommended time counting procedures.

EXAMPLE 36

3. Methods of Time Counting

The method of counting used generally depends upon the tempo. If the tempo is slow, as in slow 5/4, measure counting (1-2-3-4-5) normally is used. In a tempo such as fast 5/8, beat counting is recommended. If the rhythmic grouping is 3 + 2, the player will count 1-2-3 1-2; if the grouping is 2 + 3, he counts 1-2 1-2-3.

Counting 1-2-3-4-5 in a 3 + 2 rhythmic combination usually makes no more sense than counting 1-2-3-4-5-6 in fast 6/8—both are awkward. One-and-duh-two-and or one-and-two-and-duh could be used, but beat counting using numbers exclusively is preferred since the count of one at the beginning of each rhythmic group helps establish the slight downbeat accent desired in odd metered music.

4. Use of the Metronome

A major pitfall for advanced players is an almost instinctive desire to make the irregular beats of odd metered music conform to the regular pulsations of simple or compound meters. A specific example is where the player hesitates after the fifth eighth note in 5/8 meter so that the result sounds like 6/8 (Example 37).

EXAMPLE 37

One method of alleviating the above problem is to use the metronome at a very slow speed from the start. If the foot taps each count of one, this will help establish the consistency of the smaller rhythmic units along with developing a physical feeling for the unequal basic beats in the measure.

As the tempo of odd meter music is increased, the tendency toward making errors of the type just described increases. Here the metronome can be an invaluable aid. The speed of the metronome should be increased very gradually along with the student's ability to play the passage accurately. Eventually, the metronome should be turned off to see if the student can play without it. Assuming his practice with the metronome has been of sufficient quantity and quality, the student should soon feel as comfortable with irregular beats as he does with regular beats in simple or compound time. It simply takes time and correct practice.

E. CHANGING OR MIXED METERS

The composer who desires to change frequently the basic pulse or rhythmic accent of his music can use changing or mixed meters to accomplish this objective. This need not necessarily involve odd meters; a measure of 2/4 followed by a measure of 3/4 followed by a measure of 6/8 constitutes an example of mixed meter. In contemporary works, however, typical use of mixed meter will include odd as well as more traditional meter signatures (Example 38).

EXAMPLE 38

In Example 38, the eighth note is the basic unit, the speed of which remains the same from one meter signature to another. The novice performer and teacher sometimes fail to realize this, tending instead to make all of the rhythms in Example 38 conform to a quarter note unit (Example 39).

EXAMPLE 39

There are instances in mixed meter where the basic unit does not remain the same from one measure to the next. Usually the composer will indicate the rhythmic relationship of the measures to each other (Example 40).

EXAMPLE 40

A frequent error made by the novice is to perform the passage as
$\downarrow = \eighthnote$, resulting in slow 6/8 rather than fast 6/8. Marking in the downbeats combined with slow metronome practice can help alleviate the
problem.

1. The Significance of Measure Accent

Regardless of whether the meter signature is 2/4, 3/4, or 6/8, the first
count or downbeat of the measure is normally played with a slight accent
referred to as measure accent. This is especially true in the Viennese
waltz, where the downbeat receives considerably more emphasis than
beats two and three. If the composer chooses to alter this principle, he
accomplishes this by use of accent symbols or *sfz* markings (Example 41).

EXAMPLE 41

The above can also be accomplished through use of mixed meters.
Since the *sfz* markings coincide with the measure accents, some might
argue that the version given in Example 42 is preferable to that in Example 41.

EXAMPLE 42

2. Aids in Marking Individual Parts

Experience has proved that some examples of odd meters are almost
impossible to read without including extra markings in the part to help
the performer decipher the passage. In meters such as 13/8 one might
best forget the time signature and think only of downbeats and rhythmic
groupings (Example 43).

EXAMPLE 43

Some composers increase the confusion with unusual notation (Example 44). Some written indication of where the conductor's beats will fall becomes a necessity.

EXAMPLE 44

F. DEVELOPMENT OF SIGHTREADING ABILITY

The primary key to the development of superior sightreading ability is a solid background in music reading fundamentals, particularly in the area of rhythm. This has been the principal focus of this chapter, and there is no real substitute for learning to feel the beat, its divisions and subdivisions in order to solve one's own rhythmic problems. The student who continues to have rhythm problems cannot possibly become a good sight reader. So long as he is preoccupied with rhythm, he can hardly be expected to give adequate attention to fingering, intonation, phrasing, tone quality, or articulation. In this context, it might be argued that mastery of rhythm is the key to development of general musicianship.

1. The Importance of Scale and Arpeggio Practice

Many teachers diligently prescribe scale and arpeggio practice for their students, especially when these are included in the method book, but not all teachers or students are fully aware of *why* scales are supposed to be so useful. One answer is that scale and arpeggio practice helps develop sightreading skills. The experienced sightreader eventually learns to read extended rhythmic patterns rather than isolated notes and rhythmic figures. The same is true concerning the reading of melodic passages; students who have learned to play diatonic, whole-tone, and chromatic scales along with scales in thirds and straight and broken arpeggios in at least the principal major and minor keys will find that they are able to read extended melodic passages with much greater ease than those who have not. Practice of scales can result in other positive outcomes as well. These will be discussed in detail in Chapter Seven.

2. Transposition at Sight

Orchestral brass players learn to transpose as a matter of necessity, and occasionally jazz and pit orchestra musicians are required to do some on-the-spot transposition in order to meet the unique demands of their performing situations. Other players, however, tend to shy away from practicing transposition since they see no practical need for it. The author wishes to propose that there is a good reason why every musician should have some experience in transposing: to improve his ability to sightread. Transposition at sight requires the player to concentrate considerably harder on reading the music than if he plays it as written. Also, consider how the player reacts when he transposes a note or two incorrectly. He learns to listen and to be more aware of the pitches he is producing; performance becomes less mechanical and more sensitive. Some of this aural sensitivity should transfer when he goes back to playing the written notes.

Transposition at sight is not easy; it too requires practice and experience, but it can be mastered in a relatively short length of time if approached logically and systematically. At first, relatively easy pieces should be used with the interval of transposition restricted to either a whole step up or a whole step down (half steps, thirds, and other more difficult transpositions should be saved until later). The teacher should not expect too much too soon and should not do too much transposition all at once; a little bit done at each rehearsal will ultimately achieve better results than long, sporadic sessions.

3. The Importance of Sightreading Experience

Actual experience in sightreading is, of course, essential to becoming proficient in this area. Probably the best type of sightreading experience is that of playing new music in ensemble situations. When practicing alone, it is all too tempting to stop repeatedly in a new piece of music and go back to work out difficult passages. A limited amount of this kind of practice is excellent and highly recommended, but playing with a group is far more desirable since it forces the performer to read ahead in order to keep his place. There is no substitute for this type of experience, as veteran professionals will testify. One cannot really learn to play the game by spending most of one's time alone warming up in the bullpen.

Also important is the size of the ensemble in which one acquires his experience. Large ensembles such as band and orchestra can offer good sightreading experience, but very often the band clarinetist and orchestra violinist, in particular, find it all too easy to let someone else in the section "carry the load." Small ensembles with only one person on a part probably provide the most valuable type of sightreading experience. The player finds himself with no one to lean on; he must play his part or else it is not played at all. The ideal chamber group for this purpose has four to twelve players, but duets or trios can also be quite beneficial. Two or three persons can usually schedule a session quite easily, and every player should be encouraged to purchase at least a few collections of duets and/or trios specifically for such occasions.

Exactly what can the student expect to learn from ensemble sightreading sessions? As was pointed out earlier, a major benefit is that of learning to read ahead without losing one's place in the music. The player should also learn to look ahead especially when playing long tones. Eventually he will learn through experience to perceive larger rhythmic patterns rather than single rhythmic units. Once he is able to do this, he is well on his way to becoming a good sightreader.

G. CONCLUSION

The purpose of this chapter has been to analyze and compare various methods of teaching musical notation along with outlining related pedagogical procedures recommended for teaching school musicians. It is hoped that new teachers will feel sufficiently equipped to cope with a majority of the reading problems encountered in a practical teaching situation as a result of studying the material presented here, and that experienced teachers will have discovered several new approaches worthy of trial.

Music reading ultimately involves far more than simple comprehension and execution of rhythm and pitch symbols, of course. Performers need to know how to interpret rhythmic patterns stylistically and to understand how pitch fits into the melodic, harmonic, or contrapuntal fabric of the work being performed. The study and interpretation of jazz rhythms and style is still another topic in itself. All of these areas will be discussed in Chapter Five, Phrasing and Interpretation.

RECOMMENDED REFERENCES

American School Band Directors Assn., *The ASBDA Curriculum Guide.* Pittsburgh, PA: Volkwein Bros., 1973.

Holz, Emil, and Roger Jacobi, *Teaching Band Instruments to Beginners.* Englewood Cliffs, NJ: Prentice-Hall, Inc., 1966. (Chapter 10)

LaButa, Joseph A., *Teaching Musicianship in the High School Band.* West Nyack, NY: Parker Publishing Co., 1972. (Chapter 3)

Pizer, Russell, *Administering the Elementary Band.* West Nyack, NY: Parker Publishing Co., 1971. (Chapter 3 and pp. 177–183)

Robinson, William C. and James Middleton, *The Complete School Band Program.* West Nyack, NY: Parker Publishing Co., 1975.

Chapter Three

TONE QUALITY, INTONATION, AND BLEND

It has often been said that a good tone is a player's greatest asset. Whether this is entirely true or not is immaterial. The important thing is that possession of a good tone is, without a doubt, very important to every performing musician and deserves high priority in his training and development.

In order to produce a good tone, it is essential that the student first have a valid concept of what a good tone sounds like on his instrument. It is even more important that his teacher possess this concept. In the case of the school band and orchestra director, this means not only being able to identify a good tone on many diverse instruments but also possessing the knowledge and ability of how to teach proper tonal concepts effectively. To some this seems like an impossible task, but it can and has been done successfully by many teachers.

Ideally, the instrumental teacher should be able to demonstrate a good tone on all of the instruments, but in actual practice this seldom happens. Except for the major instrument and a few strong minors, the average teacher has his students rely upon recordings, live performances, and, when possible, private lessons with specialists in order to gain good tonal concepts. Recordings and live performances, however, are useful only as supplementary aids; the teacher still must be able to analyze the students' tonal problems and recommend solutions for improvement.

How does a teacher describe a good tone on an instrument that he cannot play himself? Assuming that he possesses a good concept of tone for the instrument being taught, he might proceed in teaching it as follows:

"Your tone needs to be brighter and more intense. Support the tone more, use a stronger reed, make the embouchure more firm, or whatever is needed. Try again on third space C . . . fine, that's better. Now see if you can open the throat more as in *oh* and use the same amount of breath support as before . . . good try, but now the tone is too open. Try once again and think *ah* . . . ah, that's much better. Now support the tone more . . . excellent, that's it, that's the idea. Now let's go back and try the whole passage . . ."

The above does not, of course, include any unique secrets on how to teach tone quality. What it does emphasize is that the teacher must know exactly what he is after tonally and also how to get it. Knowing how to get it clearly requires specialized knowledge of all the instruments as well as knowledge of basic fundamentals which apply to the various instrument families and larger instrumental groups. There are times, therefore, when analytical teaching offers the only recourse. This is particularly true with regard to the teaching of tone by the general practitioner of instrumental music.

The issue involving the French school of tone versus the German versus American, etc., will not be discussed in this chapter. Since the topic is largely subjective in nature, probably no amount of discussion could ever result in conclusions acceptable even to a large minority. Instead, emphasis will be placed upon tonal development as it relates to ensemble color, intonation and blend.

Poor intonation is considered by many to be the most persistent and frustrating problem encountered in school instrumental ensemble performance. Because of this there is a tendency among some teachers to spend the bulk of the lesson or rehearsal time chiding students about poor intonation while neglecting the usual source of the problem—poor tone production. When this happens, neither intonation nor tone quality improves to any significant degree. Emphasis on good tone production should be given first priority. When this is done, many of the more common intonation problems will automatically disappear.

No one likes to be guilty of playing flat in relation to other players. For some reason, flatness makes the tone sound dull and lifeless, even to the layman's ear. On the other hand, playing a bit sharp in a solo passage appears to give the tone more life and brilliance. The soloist who plays sharp intentionally, however, is using the easy way out at the expense of the other players. If more brilliance is actually needed, the solution should be sought through improving the basic quality of the player's tone, not through synthetic means.

Some teachers insist that tone quality and intonation are basically inseparable. This is true to a great extent. The performer who fails to focus (center) his tone properly will seldom possess good intonation or tone quality. The wind player who continually plays on the top side of his tone will likely produce a tone which is excessively bright and thin and a pitch which is sharp. If his embouchure is too relaxed or his breath support lacking, the tone will tend to be dull and the pitch flat. Achieving proper ensemble blend with tones deficient in these respects is also out of the question, thus it can be said that tone quality, intonation and ensemble blend are inseparable.

Any thorough study of tone quality, intonation, and blend requires discussion of a wide array of acoustical and musical fundamentals as well as instrumental techniques. For this reason, the reader is urged to review first the outline of this chapter in the table of contents so as to obtain a sense of perspective regarding the sequence of topics to be covered. A preliminary reading of the conclusion of this chapter is also recommended.

The first topic in this chapter deals with general principles of musical acoustics. While this is not a primary practical concern, a general understanding of these principles is necessary as background information to the other topics which follow. Eventually, the reader should also study the reference books on acoustics, tuning, and temperament listed in the bibliography so as to acquire a more comprehensive understanding of these subjects.

A. GENERAL PRINCIPLES OF MUSICAL ACOUSTICS

The weakest link in the entire chain of music education is the lack of knowledge and understanding of the simple facts of musical acoustics; no phase of musical performance has been so sadly neglected as the study and practice of musical intonation and harmony.[1]

The study of musical acoustics forms the scientific basis for music. It includes the harmonic series, the various tuning systems, and analysis of tonal color. Over the years there has been a tendency among some musicians to shy away from study in these areas. Some feel that such information is entirely theoretical, has little to do with the practical aspects of musical performance, and therefore should be left to the mathematicians and philosophers. Others feel that music is an art, not a science, and that any attempt to study it from a scientific standpoint negates its aesthetic essence. Such attitudes are indeed unfortunate since acoustical knowledge can be significantly helpful in understanding and solving many of the problems related to ensemble intonation in particular. Instrumental teachers would do well to obtain as much knowl-

[1] William Stegeman, "The Art of Music Intonation," Part I, *The Instrumentalist* (May, 1967), 61.

edge as possible about musical acoustics in order to improve the performance of their groups.

Recent research by Stegeman has revealed that few students are able to recognize and correctly tune simple unisons and octaves when asked to do so with a variable pitch tuning device. Also, few students are able to tune a major triad properly, and the vast majority are oblivious to the presence or absence of beats.[2] These areas of ignorance are not limited to students:

> Few indeed are the music directors who can recognize and tune accurately intervals and chords in natural as well as tempered harmony and know how to use each to best advantage. It seems that this should be a requisite for anyone teaching and directing music ensembles.[3]

Part of the problem stems from a lack of practical research and pertinent written materials from the past in the areas of tonal analysis, intonation and related acoustical phenomena. Lacking these, theoretical assumptions and empirical knowledge frequently have served as the primary bases for applied pedagogy. The recent work of a few dedicated individuals, however, has greatly expanded our knowledge in these areas, though many questions remain to be answered.

A major purpose of this section is to relate the findings in these areas to specific, practical, pedagogical situations. It is hoped thereby that teachers of instrumental music may find this information immediately helpful in improving the intonation of their groups without the need for researching the entire topic themselves. This is not to say that further study is not recommended; on the contrary, careful study of the materials cited in the bibliography of this chapter is strongly recommended.

1. The Harmonic Series

The harmonic series is a series of tones whose frequencies are in the ratio of 1:2:3:4., etc. This series is also called the overtone series and the "chord of nature." Strictly speaking, the first harmonic is the fundamental generator or first partial but not the first overtone. Harmonic number 2 is the first overtone, harmonic number 3 is the second overtone, etc. (See Chart 5.)

The harmonic series directly affects tone quality, intonation, and ensemble blend. Every musical tone contains not only a fundamental pitch but also a series of overtones (exact multiples of the fundamental fre-

[2] *Ibid.*
[3] *Ibid.*

Chart 5

THE HARMONIC SERIES⁴

* Black notes indicate pitches which are flat in relation to equal temperament.

Ratio	Interval Name	Interval Distance in Cents	Interval Distance in Cents in Equal Temperament	Difference in Cents Between Two Intervals
1:2	Perfect 8ve	1200 C-C	1200	0
2:3	Perfect 5th	702 C-G	700	2 sharp
3:4	Perfect 4th	498 G-C	500	2 flat
4:5	Major 3rd	386 C-E	400	14 flat
5:6	Minor 3rd	316 E-G	300	16 sharp
6:7	Minor 3rd	267 G-B♭	300	33 flat
7:8	Major 2nd	231 B♭-C	200	31 sharp
8:9	Major 2nd	204 C-D	200	4 sharp
9:10	Major 2nd	182 D-E	200	18 flat
10:11	Major 2nd	165 E-F#	200	35 flat
11:12	Minor 2nd	151 F#-G	100	51 sharp

quency) of varying quantity and strength. Weakness or absence of certain overtones can result in a dull, lifeless tone. Strong relative intensity of certain overtones, on the other hand, can cause the tone to be excessively brilliant or even harsh in quality. Overtones, therefore, determine the tonal color of given musical tones.

When two tones sounded simultaneously are out of phase (out of tune) with each other, the ear perceives periodic pulsations in the sound which we refer to as beats. In Example 45 this phenomenon is illustrated through use of a sine wave diagram.

EXAMPLE 45

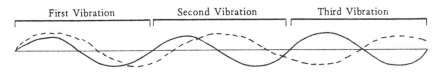

First Vibration   Second Vibration   Third Vibration

⁴ Used with permission of Everett Gates.

Note in Example 45 that tone no. 1 (solid line) and tone no. 2 (dotted line) begin together but become progressively further apart with each successive vibration. By the end of the third vibration, the two tones are completely out of phase. At this point the two tones actually cancel out each other, resulting in momentary silence. The ear does not normally hear an actual break in the sound but instead perceives a decrease in loudness which we call a pulsation or beat.

Some teachers and players assume that beats are *entirely* the result of the fundamental pitches being out of tune; but in fact, the overtones also contribute to the bad intonation. Stauffer provides us with an illustration of this principle (Example 46).

EXAMPLE 46[5]

M 3   P 5

In the first measure of Example 46, the fifth partial based on the C fundamental is also the fourth partial of the E fundamental. In the second measure, the third partial of the C fundamental is also the second partial of the G fundamental. In both cases, beats resulting from the out-of-tune partials as well as the fundamentals contribute to the "out of tuneness" perceived by the ear.

Examples 45 and 46 also serve to illustrate how beats affect ensemble tone color and resonance. In a chord scored for full band or orchestra, the upper partials of lower-voiced instruments and the fundamentals and lower partials of upper voiced instruments are literally entwined and enveloped by each other. When intonation problems occur creating beats between fundamentals of the upper voices and the upper partials of the lower voices, this results in a degree of cancellation of certain partials. This manifests itself in a decrease in the richness of the combined ensemble tones.

Concerning instrumental performance specifically, the harmonic series (Example 47) is especially important to the brass player since it determines every interval produced in any given valve combination or slide position on his instrument. The student brass player, with the exception of the French hornist, normally uses the second through the eighth partial of the harmonic series. The fundamental pitch or first partial is not

[5] Donald W. Stauffer, *Intonation Deficiencies of Wind Instruments in Ensemble* (Washington, D.C.: The Catholic University of America Press, 1954), p. 9, fig. 3.

considered part of the practical playing range except for the occasional pedal B-flat written for trombone in works such as Clifton Williams' *Fanfare and Allegro.* Trumpet players sometimes practice fundamentals (pedal tones), however, in an effort to improve their upper range. (Performance of pedal tones requires an open throat which is necessary in order to produce high tones properly.) Advanced brass players with good high ranges frequently play above the eighth partial.

EXAMPLE 47

The specific series of tones in Example 47 happens to be the open series (no valves) for F horn. As can be readily seen, the player of a single F horn must frequently use the ninth partial and above in order to play beyond fourth line D. The harmonic cluster above the seventh partial creates acute problems in pitch placement, and the need for the B-flat side of the double horn becomes obvious. On the B-flat horn, the open harmonic series is a fourth higher than on the F horn. This reduces pitch placement problems in the top area of the staff, as seen in Example 48, which illustrates the open series for B-flat horn.

EXAMPLE 48

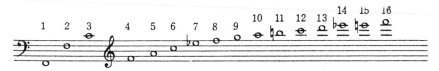

The harmonic series is important to musicians in still other ways. String players use harmonics (overtones) in actual performance. Woodwind players depend upon the harmonic series to extend the fundamental range of their instruments by overblowing at the octave and (in the case of the clarinet) at the twelfth and other intervals. The harmonic series also serve as a basis for orchestration of vertical sonorities. A typical chord for full band or orchestra is usually voiced with an octave, fifth, fourth, etc. in ascending order, paralleling that of the harmonic series. Some musicians even suggest that the harmonic series is the basis for Western music. Note in Examples 47 and 48 that the major and minor scales and triads along with other scales and triads can be derived from this series of tones.

2. The Four Basic Tuning Systems

The subject of tuning and temperament has intrigued musical acoustic-ians throughout recorded history. Of all the various systems of tuning which have evolved, the Pythagorean, just (diatonic), mean-tone, and equally-tempered systems of tuning have received the greatest amount of attention within musical circles and will be discussed briefly here.

In approximately 550 B.C., Pythagoras established a tuning system derived from the perfect fifth. Since this system includes a perfect fourth and pure major second as well as the perfect fifth, it was usable through-out the Middle Ages. The Pythagorean major third is quite sharp, how-ever, and this created intonation problems once harmonic music came into prominence. (The Pythagorean third is 22 cents higher in pitch than a pure third, a difference of approximately one-quarter of a half step.)

The problem of the sharp third of the Pythagorean system led to the establishment of mean-tone tuning, which is derived from the pure major third. This system was in vogue from about 1500 to 1750 and was first discussed by the Spanish theorist Salinas. Although organs in Bach's time were tuned to this system, it could not be used satisfactorily in keys with more than three sharps or flats, primarily because the fifth is flat.

Just or diatonic tuning is derived from the harmonic series or "chord of nature." Since it has both a pure third and perfect fifth, this system would seem to be a panacea to the problems inherent in Pythagorean and mean-tone tuning. But the just system has two sizes of whole step, a fact which creates intonation problems in harmonic (chordal) music.

Equal temperament did not receive attention in Europe until about 1650. It is a tuning compromise in almost all respects: the octave is divided into twelve equal parts, with the unison and octave being the only pure intervals. It is used today for pianos and other fixed-pitch in-struments and also serves as the tuning basis for the Stroboconn. Further-more, twelve-tone composers depend upon it entirely. Since it allows free modulation to all keys, it reportedly inspired Bach to compose the *Well-Tempered Clavier*, although not all authorities agree on this point.

3. Achieving Good Intonation

When we speak of "good intonation" today, what does this really mean? According to *The Harvard Brief Dictionary of Music*, intonation means "the degree of adherence to correct pitch."[6] But what is correct pitch? Do we mean Pythagorean, just, mean-tone, or equal-tempered

---

[6] Willie Apel and Ralph T. Daniel, *The Harvard Brief Dictionary of Music* (Cam-bridge, Mass.: Harvard University Press, 1960), s.v. "Intonation."

pitch? The desirability of equal temperament for fixed-pitch instruments is obvious. Some teachers also feel it is also the most *practical* solution for wind and string instruments. Others take great issue on this point, arguing that equal temperament definitely is *not* the most desirable type of tuning for artistic wind and string performance.

String players often contend that they use Pythagorean tuning. This makes sense if we consider that the open strings of the violin, viola, and cello are tuned in perfect, beatless fifths, which are also the basis for Pythagorean tuning. (Good string players normally avoid tuning their open strings to the piano because its fifths are slightly flat.) Also, string players almost always play sharped notes higher in pitch than flatted notes, except when playing with a piano. They even finger them differently. On the violin, for example, G-sharp in the staff in first position is fingered with a high third finger on the D string; A-flat, however, is fingered low fourth finger on the same string. This is in line with Pythagorean tuning, in which sharped notes are always higher in pitch than flatted notes.

It would seem, therefore, that string players tend to favor Pythagorean tuning, but only insofar as melodic performance is concerned. Since Pythagorean tuning is not practical in harmonic music, it is probable that string players actually use the pure intervals of just intonation in chordal sections. Due to the ease of making minute adjustments in pitch, the string player can tune each melodic interval or note in a chord to precisely the pitch desired.

Concerning wind instrument intonation, there are some who advocate the same types of tuning standards as for string instruments. Others maintain that this sort of thinking is unrealistic, since it is doubtful that the average listener could ever tell the difference. Still others point out that if the average performing group could easily meet the requirements of equal temperament, most of its intonation problems would probably vanish. Stegeman maintains, however, that there is a definite difference between the sound of pure and tempered intervals. Artist wind and string players consistently deviate from equal temperament in their performance when not required to play with a fixed-pitch instrument such as the piano. Also, ". . . it is not uncommon for vocal soloists in a melodic sequence to deviate as much as a quarter tone or more from tempered scale frequencies."[7]

Piston reinforces Stegeman's view:

> . . . Composers recognize equal temperament by free use of enharmonic equivalents and chromatic harmonies. But, paradoxically, we do not find in this system the standard of correct pitch, or the guide to that fine

[7] Stegeman, "The Art of Music Intonation," Part III, *The Instrumentalist* (September, 1967), 69–70.

intonation we so admire in the best string or wind playing. . . . One seeks rather an intonation nearer that of pure intervals and perhaps even more an underlining of musical meaning, which is closely tied traditionally to tonal feeling, the sense of key. . . . The term musical meaning is employed here as referring to the body of melodic, rhythmic, and harmonic patterns, that has, like language, come to possess through usage a common ground of meaning. . . . Notes having melodic tendency are customarily given a slight exaggeration in pitch, in the direction of that tendency.[8]

Piston further states that in experiments where sound waves were photographed on microfilm, marked changes in pitch occurred as each player replayed a new piece of music. This was presumably due to each player's acquiring a keener sense of the relationship of his tones to the other parts and also understanding the musical meaning of each phrase better with each successive playing.

Piston also discusses one of his own experiments where a string bass player was asked to hold a low A-flat while two different chords were played at the piano:

. . . The first chord consisted of the notes F, B-flat, D, so that the A-flat was identified as the seventh of the dominant seventh chord in the key of E-flat. As such it would have a strong downward tendency. The second chord was E, B, D. This sounded the dominant seventh chord in the key of A, so that the low A-flat was now heard to be really a G-sharp, with a strong upward tendency. When the second chord was played the bass player was clearly seen to move his finger by an appreciative amount up the string. . . .[9]

According to Piston, it was the change in the *musical meaning* of the A-flat (a G-sharp was implied) which caused the bass player to adjust the pitch higher for the second chord.

Stegeman states that the only reason why equal temperament was developed in the first place was so that keyboard and other fixed-pitch instruments could play in all keys and harmonies with equal and tolerable tuning results. Pythagorean, just and mean-tone tuning do not allow free modulation to and from any key. Equal temperament, which is a "precisely controlled mistuning" of all intervals except the octave, allows free modulation without inducing intolerably poor intervals in certain keys or chords. Because of the rapid decay in volume of tones produced on the piano and keyboard percussion instruments, the equal-tempered compromise can be accepted without our being unduly disturbed by it. But on the organ as well as on string and wind instruments, which are capable of sustaining tones at full volume throughout the duration of a

[8] Walter Piston, *Intonation and Musical Meaning* (pamphlet published by C. Bruno and Son, Inc., New York, 1963), pp. 3–4.
[9] *Ibid.*, p. 5.

given tone, the presence of beats can be offensive to sensitive ears. This is particularly true if the players' early training has been aimed toward appreciation of beatless intonation. In these situations it becomes desirable to adjust the pitch away from tempered intervals so that optimum intonation results are possible.[10]

The first step in meeting the above objective is to concentrate on producing the best tone possible. Use of a stroboconn and devices such as the Johnson Intonation Trainer can serve as valuable supplementary aids. The most important phase of one's training, however, is actual playing experience in ensemble—learning to listen, to adjust, to give and take with other players. On individual, isolated intervals and chords all beats should normally be eliminated. With respect to *musical meaning* as discussed by Piston, however, the following generalizations may be applied:

1. Diatonic half steps should be played close together. In a major scale, for example, the pitch of the third and seventh degrees should be raised slightly so that they lean toward the fourth scale degree and the octave. In a harmonic minor scale the third and sixth should be lowered slightly and the seventh raised slightly in order to emphasize their melodic tendencies.

2. In a major chord the third should be raised slightly to emphasize major tonality. The third in a minor triad should be lowered to emphasize minor tonality.

3. In chords with an added seventh, the seventh should be raised or lowered depending upon the next chord in the progression. When the voice leading involves half steps, the pitch of the first note should be altered so that harmonic tension is increased.

When these principles are applied in performance, there may be times when beats are clearly audible in chords of great tension moving to a strong resolution. This is desirable, for a beatless chord, although rich in quality, can be somewhat static. In any case, players who develop acute pitch sensitivity in these basic areas should then be able to deal with most other problems in intonation which may arise. At its highest level, good intonation is an integral part of sensitive musicianship. It is hoped that musical sensitivity is the focal point toward which all musical instruction is aimed.

B. ACOUSTICAL PROBLEMS IN
INSTRUMENT DESIGN AND MANUFACTURE

If Pythagorean tuning is desired in melodic performance and just intonation is preferable in harmonic music, what system shall the instru-

[10] See note 7 above.

ment manufacturer use in designing a wind instrument? The most practical system to use is, of course, equal temperament. Use of Pythagorean, just, or mean-tone tuning would require fifty or more notes per octave in order for the player to play comfortably in all keys; since this is not practical, wind players must learn to alter the pitch of individual notes away from tempered intonation as needed to meet the particular melodic or harmonic requirements of a specific solo or ensemble passage.

Even though equal temperament is the most practical tuning system to use, no one has yet been able to produce a practical wind instrument which was perfectly in tune throughout with equal temperament or any other tuning system. The major obstacle is the natural harmonic series, which predetermines the pitch of every tone above the fundamental pitch. The fifth, seventh, and, to some degree, the sixth partials of the harmonic series do not match the pitches of corresponding notes in equal temperament. Thus every wind instrument necessarily consists of a variety of compromises in intonation as well as other factors.

Benade states that every time an instrument maker redesigns an instrument to improve the loudness, intonation, or ease of playing, the tone quality is altered.[11] This happened in the case of the Boehm flute, and it exists in today's organ as compared to the Baroque organ, which was tuned to the mean-tone scale. To improve one factor at the expense of all of the others is obviously not the answer. Some sort of reasonable balance must, of necessity, be maintained.

In order to achieve reasonably good intonation while maintaining proper balance with other factors, different instrument makers use different solutions. These efforts meet with varying degrees of success. One answer for teachers and performers has been to identify specific makes of instruments which represent the best overall quality in basic design and to limit one's purchases to those particular instruments. Instruments which have poor tone quality or possess bad notes not commonly considered faulty on other makes of instruments should not be purchased. The objective is to find instruments so designed that they require minimal adjustment by the player in order to be played in tune. Moreover, not all instruments made by the same manufacturer are equal in quality. Some variation inevitably exists, and in some instances the variation may be considerable. The only sure method of identifying a quality instrument is to put it to a practical playing test. Ideally, each instrument should be played and carefully checked by a specialist before purchase. While this may not be practical for all instruments, it should be a matter of policy with expensive instruments such as the bassoon, tuba, oboe, bass and contrabass clarinets, saxophones, and double horns. Since these

---

[11] Arthur H. Benade, "On the Tone Color of Wind Instruments," reprinted from the *Selmer Bandwagon*, No. 59 (1970), published by the Selmer Division of the Magnavox Company.

instruments are usually purchased by the local school system, the director will want to be sure that good ones are purchased. Otherwise he may be obliged to accept the negative consequences of owning poor quality instruments for many years to come.

While having a specialist try out an instrument prior to purchase seems like a direct, simple solution, even this poses some problems. First, it is improbable that any two players will prefer exactly the same type of instrument. Some prefer a resistive instrument with less resistance in the mouthpiece and/or reed, while others prefer a rather free blowing instrument with which they use a more resistive mouthpiece and/or reed. Secondly, different styles of playing also influence the type of equipment a given performer may need or prefer. Teachers and students need to consider all of these factors, especially the importance of proper balance of resistance, when purchasing wind instruments.

1. Brass Instruments

Deficiencies of Valve Combinations

Manufacturers of valved brass instruments continue to seek improved solutions to the intonation problems created when two or more valves are used in combination. If the first valve is built so it is perfectly in tune, this results in poor intonation when it is used in combination with the second or third valve or both. For example, when the 1-2-3 combination is used, the combined length of tubing is much too short, causing the pitch to be quite sharp.

Some manufacturers compromise by making the first valve slightly flat, so that when it is used in combination with the second or third valve or both, none of the combinations will be extremely sharp. Stauffer states that ". . . a more or less happy medium is arrived at by building *all three valves* slightly flat so that the couplings (valve combinations) will not be too sharp."[12] Such flattening of the individual valves should not be excessive, however. Since the individual valves and the 1-2 and 2-3 combinations are used much more often than the 1-3 and 1-2-3 combinations, improving the latter at the expense of the former is self-defeating. (See Stauffer, Chapter IV, for further details.)

The pitch of individual notes can be altered by lipping the note up or down as needed. If the note is quite out of tune, however, lipping it in tune becomes increasingly difficult and in some cases impossible. At very least, excessive lipping will result in very poor tone quality. Here again, instrument makers have devised various solutions to the problem. One of

[12] Stauffer, *Intonation Deficiences*, p. 38.

these is the thumb trigger found on cornets and trumpets, which is used primarily for lowering the pitch of the sharp 1-2 valve combination. Another is the third valve slide ring which lowers the pitch of the sharp 1-3 combination and the very sharp 1-2-3 combination. Both of these allow for optimum intonation without sacrificing tone quality, and are recommended as standard equipment for any cornet or trumpet purchased today.

Another solution used by one manufacturer is that of a trigger mechanism for the main tuning slide. While this solution may seem ideal, it is only as effective as the individual player's ear. A professional might learn to use it to great advantage, but experience has shown that in the hands of inexperienced student musicians the intonation results can be disastrous. Not only does the novice tend to overcompensate but, more importantly, he may never learn to focus his tone properly. Extending the tuning slide for a high note being pinched sharp by the player may alleviate the intonation problem but not the tone, embouchure, and/or breath support errors which are usually the real sources of the problem.

Problems Related to the Harmonic Series

Since the fifth, seventh, and eleventh partials of the natural harmonic series are flat in relation to equal temperament, all brass players must learn to deal with them accordingly. The fifth partial is only 14 cents flat and can be lipped up easily enough in most cases. The seventh partial is 33 cents flat, which is quite out of tune; consequently brass players cannot use this partial and must substitute other fingerings. (See Example 49, which shows the fingering substitution used by a trumpet player to avoid the flat seventh partial.)

EXAMPLE 49

fingering: 0   0   0   0   0   0   1*   0

*When the first valve is used, this makes this B-flat the eighth partial of a harmonic series built on B-flat in the bass clef.

The trombonist, who possesses a potentially perfect wind instrument in regard to intonation, need not resort to lipping out-of-tune partials on his instrument; he need only adjust the slide up or down as a string player adjusts his finger on a string to alter the pitch. The only exception is the fifth partial in first position which is D above the staff. Some trombones come equipped with a spring inside the casing near the mouthpiece allowing the player to play a "sharp first position" and thereby raise the D sufficiently. On trombones without this spring, the player must either lip up the D or use flat fourth position. A-flat above the staff, the seventh partial in first position, generally is not used; this A-flat is usually played in third position as the eighth partial of an A-flat fundamental.

According to Stauffer, the third and sixth harmonics may also be slightly sharp on brass instruments. The greatest offender is the sixth partial or G on top of the staff on trumpet and cornet and F above the staff on trombone and baritone.[13] Players should listen carefully and lip these partials down as needed.

Stauffer also mentions that some manufacturers reportedly have tried raising the pitch of the flat fifth partial only to find that this increased the sharpness of the sixth partial.[14] This fact re-emphasizes the necessity for a compromise in pitch which will allow the player to get all of his notes in tune with reasonable ease—not perfect intonation on some and very poor intonation on others. Wind players do not need instruments that are perfectly in tune, but rather instruments with compromises which will allow them to be played in tune with minimal adjustment required of the player.[15]

"A peculiar flaw of the overtone series exists in many baritones that is rarely found in any other type of brass instrument," Stauffer points out. This flaw is a significantly flat second partial which is the lowest written open tone on the instrument. The tones most affected by this problem are low B-flat, A and A-flat. This creates a particularly severe intonation problem on three-valve instruments between low B-flat and B-natural, since the B-natural is normally fingered with a 1-2-3 valve combination which tends toward extreme sharpness.[16] This flat second partial, coupled with the usual discrepancies associated with the fifth and sixth partials, makes the problem of intonation on the baritone horn a most frustrating one. In an effort to solve the problem, some manufacturers have added a fourth valve which transposes the harmonic series down a fourth allowing the player to avoid some of the larger, out-of-tune valve combinations. In addition, the fourth valve extends the range of the baritone horn and tuba down from low E to the pedal B-flat.

The problem of out-of-tune partials is not limited to the open-valve

13 Stauffer, *Intonation Deficiencies*, p. 47.
14 *Ibid.*, p. 48.
15 Philip Farkas, *The Art of French Horn Playing* (Evanston, Ill.: Summy-Birchard Company, 1956), p. 17.
16 Stauffer, *Intonation Deficiencies*, pp. 62–63.

series alone; it exists on all of the various single valves and valve combinations used. The only difference is that since each valve or valve combination has its own unique pitch deficiency, the resultant intonation of given partials may either be better or worse depending on a given set of circumstances. For example, C-sharp in the staff on trumpet fingered with a 1-2 valve combination is the fifth partial of a harmonic series based on an A fundamental. Since this valve combination tends to be sharp, this counteracts the inherent flatness of the fifth partial (C-sharp in the staff); thus the player finds this note reasonably well in tune without having to lip it very much. On the other hand, the trumpet with a very flat first valve will find the fourth line D quite difficult to lip up to pitch. Since this D is the fifth partial of the first-valve B-flat series, the flatness of this partial coupled with the flatness of the first valve makes the problem of pitch adjustment twice as difficult. This again points up the need for selecting an instrument with valves that are built only *slightly* flat.

The following information is based primarily upon the author's personal teaching experience. Not everyone will agree with all the generalizations made; the author admits he has altered his own opinions on more than one occasion in light of new evidence. It is important, nonetheless, that instrumental teachers adopt some systematic approach toward solving specific problems in intonation. Otherwise, the tendency is to teach primarily by instinct, "stabbing in the dark," hoping to achieve success in one's own unique, frequently unscientific manner.

Bad Notes

The "bad notes" listed in Chart 6 are those which are most often out of tune on most makes of brass instruments. Every brass instrument will, of course, possess its own unique intonation deficiencies. The final answer lies in checking one's instrument with a stroboscope and adjusting the pitch of individual notes in ensemble as needed.

Chart 6

BRASS INTONATION CHART

Methods of Alteration:

1. Alternate Fingerings	5. Use of Fourth Valve
2. Thumb Trigger	6. Tuning Slide Trigger
3. Third Valve Slide Ring	7. Use of Right Hand in
4. Varying Lip Tension	The Bell

(*continued on following page*)

Chart 6 (cont.)

Name of Inst.	Bad Notes	Methods of Pitch Alteration
Trumpet		1 2 3 4 6
French Horn		1 4 7
Trombone		1 4
Baritone Horn		1 4 5
Tuba		1 4 5

*Bad notes on three-valved baritones and tubas only. Use 4th valve instead of 1-3, 2-4 instead of 1-2-3, on four-valved instruments.

Valve Combination Characteristics:

1 2 3 — Extremely sharp	2 3 — Moderately flat
1 3 — Very sharp	1 2 — Moderately sharp

1. Methods of alteration numbers 2, 3, and 6 are available only on the trumpet; number 5 is presently limited to baritone horn and tuba; number 7 is used by the French horn only. Methods 1 and 4 are available to all the brasses and are used by all.

2. Open valve tones are in tune except for the fifth, seventh and eleventh partials, which are flat. The harmonic series based on each of the valve combinations contains similar flat partials.

Methods of Pitch Alteration

Trumpet-Cornet: Probably the most frequent alternate fingering used on the trumpet as well as other three-valved brass instruments is the third valve alone instead of the sharp 1-2 combination. The use of other alternate fingerings for improving intonation on individual notes becomes a matter of experimenting toward a solution of a specific pitch problem. An example is the flatness of the trumpet or cornet's fourth line D. If the note is very flat and a young player simply cannot lip this note up sufficiently, the 1-3 combination can be substituted for the single first valve.

The 1-3 combination will usually be slightly sharp on the D and will need to be lipped down somewhat, but this is much easier than lipping up a very flat D fingered with the first valve alone. The 1-2 combination can also be used similarly to solve the problem of a very flat open E in the fourth space.

The more valves used to play a given note, the greater the resistance to tonal response; some brass teachers argue against using the larger valve combinations for this reason. But one must make a choice: poor intonation or ideal response. In ensemble the choice necessarily must be in favor of improved intonation. Experience has also proved that any problems in response experienced at first soon vanish after the player has had sufficient time to adjust to the new fingering.

Trumpets and cornets equipped with a thumb trigger on the first valve slide can easily lower the sharp 1-2 combination through proper use of this device. Those equipped with the third valve slide ring, theoretically, can deal with the deficiencies of the 1-3 and 1-2-3 combinations in similar fashion. This would seem to solve most all of the significant intonation problems on these instruments, except for the fact that easy, efficient operation of the third valve slide ring is not always possible, particularly with young beginners. Chenette agrees with this and further points out that asking young students to lip down continually or in any way "bend" the notes is not a desirable solution either. Instead, the third valve slide should be pulled out about half an inch and left there. Although this will make the E-flat and A-flat low in pitch, they should still be tolerable—in any case, much more so than the sharp C-sharp and D. The E-flat and A-flat are used much less often in the beginning stages than the C-sharp and D; in fact, most beginning trumpet books do not introduce the E-flat until the ninth or tenth lesson. Later, the following rules may be applied: "In keys of two or more flats, push the third valve slide in; otherwise, leave it out one-half inch." In the key of B-flat, both the D and E-flat are important notes; "Compromise here by pulling the slide one-quarter of an inch."[17]

On the other hand, some trumpet teachers feel that beginners can and should be taught to use the third valve slide ring right from the start so that they will automatically consider it an integral part of the 1-3 and 1-2-3 fingerings. The ring itself should be carefully adjusted so that the player learns to push against it with the fingernail of the third finger rather than inserting the finger past the first joint. The valve slide can be lightly buffed by a repairman if it does not move easily. A light coating of toothpaste on the valve slide can also sometimes provide better lubrication than vaseline or other substances normally used for this purpose.

French Horn: The intonation problems inherent in large valve com-

[17] Ed Chenette, "Use That Third Valve Slide," *The Instrumentalist* (October, 1967), 30.

binations on the trumpet apply equally to the French horn. But because of the large variety of fingerings available on the double horn, the player can often bypass the larger combinations by switching to the other side of the horn and thereby use a fingering that is better in tune.

The player can also vary the pitch of individual notes with his right hand in the bell; lowering the pitch of sharp notes by cupping the palm of the hand inward slightly would seem to be the easiest solution. But the reader is reminded that most intonation problems can be better solved by checking to see that the tuning slides and valve slides are properly adjusted. Beyond this, alternate fingerings and some lipping should solve the great majority of the horn player's intonation problems.

Trombone: The trombone is inherently a perfectly tuned wind instrument, but this presupposes that the player also is "well tuned." Any note can be easily brought perfectly in tune through minute adjustments of the playing slide but this rarely happens unless the teacher repeatedly and emphatically insists that this actually be done. Suggestions such as, "touch your finger against the bell to find fourth position" may be helpful in some cases with beginners, but such a crutch should not be used too long. Just as in using tape on the finger-board of a violin to help the beginner find "the right spot," such aids are frequently used for too long, with the result that the student becomes almost completely dependent upon these "crutches" at the expense of ear training. The student eventually must learn to listen carefully to the pitch itself and make appropriate adjustments based on what he hears, not what he sees or feels.

Experience has shown the following tendencies among young trombonists to be the most common: Third position is played sharp and fourth is flat. E-natural in the staff in second position is often played out too far. Young students with short arms also tend to play low B and C high in pitch.

Baritone Horn: Several years ago McMillen and Roth developed a device called the MP Tuning Mechanism. This was essentially a tuning slide trigger similar to that developed by the same manufacturer for the trumpet. (Refer to the earlier section on trumpet-cornet where this device is discussed.) More recently, the addition of a fourth valve to the regular three valves has been employed as a panacea for the baritone's intonation problems. Boosey and Hawkes, Besson, Getzen, and other instrument manufacturers employ various designs and approaches in regard to the fourth valve. The author will not attempt to explain or evaluate the specific characteristics of all these makes and models; instrumental teachers are urged to seek the advice of specialists in these matters and to consult literature on the subject available from various manufacturers.

Tuba: According to William Bell, "Having found an instrument with good open tones and one on which the first, third and fourth valve slides can be manipulated with the left hand, there should be no excuse for playing any note out of tune [on the tuba]."[18] Given these conditions, good intonation or the lack of it on the tuba is largely determined by the competence and experience of the player.

2. Woodwind Instruments

Bad Notes

The "bad notes" listed in Chart 7 are those most frequently out of tune on most makes of woodwind instruments. Every individual woodwind instrument will, of course, possess its own unique intonation deficiencies. The final answer lies in checking one's instrument with a stroboscope and adjusting the pitch of individual notes in ensemble as needed.

Chart 7

WOODWIND INTONATION CHART

Methods of Alteration:

1. Varying Lip Tension
2. Alternate Fingerings
3. Amount of Reed in Mouth

4. Finger Shading
5. Jaw Movement
6. Rolling Embouchure Hole

Name of Inst.	Bad Notes	Methods of Pitch Alteration Used
Flute		1 5 ⑥
Oboe	* Forked F	1 ③ (4)
Clarinet		1 2 ④
Bassoon		1 ②③ (4)
Saxophone		① 2

(continued on following page)

[18] William Bell, *A Handbook of Information on Intonation* (pamphlet published by the Getzen Co., Inc., Elkhorn, Wis., n.d.), p. 1.

Chart 7 (cont.)

1. All bad notes listed usually are sharp.
2. Circled numbers denote *primary* method of pitch alteration used by specific instruments.
3. Numbers in parentheses denote methods which conceivably could be used but are seldom employed in actual practice.
4. Varying lip tension is a method available to all woodwind players. The more tension, the sharper the pitch, and vice versa.
5. Alternate fingerings are available on all woodwind instruments as a means toward pitch adjustment of individual notes. The bassoonist is especially fortunate in this regard because of the unusually large number of fingerings at his disposal.

Methods of Pitch Alteration

Flute: When the embouchure hole is rolled inward, more air is directed downward into the hole, thereby lowering the pitch. Rolling the embouchure hole outward causes more air to be directed across the hole, which raises the pitch. It is recommended that this be accomplished by lowering and raising the head rather than by rolling the flute in and out with the hands. To lower the pitch of the "bad notes" C-natural and C-sharp, the head is "ducked" downward slightly; to raise the pitch of flat notes, the head is lifted slightly. This method is actually easier than rolling the flute with the hands and is also less likely to disturb the embouchure.

Another method of pitch alteration is that of moving the jaw. Pushing the jaw forward causes more air to be directed across the hole, which raises the pitch; drawing the jaw back causes more air to be directed down into the hole, which lowers the pitch. (For further information, see Edwin Putnik's *The Art of Flute Playing*, pp. 10–11.)

Experience has shown that the primary sources of intonation problems in flute playing are poor breath support and/or a tense embouchure. Students often sound flat because of inadequate breath support and some compensate by tensing the lips excessively to raise the pitch (brass players are equally guilty of the same problem). The usual result is a thin, pinched tone which sounds especially sharp because of the lack of resonance and the insufficient quantity of fundamental in the timbre spectrum. Students should be taught to rely primarily upon proper breath support in order to keep the pitch up, not excessive lip tension.

Another error made by young flutists is to leave the first finger of the left hand down when playing D and E-flat in the staff. This lowers the pitch and obscures the tone by injecting the fundamental pitch of the instrument. Since the flute is particularly susceptible to being played with incorrect fingerings by student musicians, special effort should be made to ensure that the student has a reliable fingering chart and uses it faithfully.

Oboe: The oboist's primary method of pitch alteration is that of altering the amount of reed in the mouth. The more reed in the mouth, the sharper the pitch; the less reed in the mouth, the flatter the pitch. This method of pitch alteration is accomplished by rolling the lips in and out in order to vary the amount of reed in the mouth at any given moment. To lower the pitch of third space C, the player should take less reed in the mouth.

The forked F on some makes of oboes tends to be sharp in pitch and stuffy in quality. Adding the E-flat key will usually alleviate both the pitch problem and the fuzziness of the tone.

Clarinet: The primary method of pitch alteration recommended for the clarinet is finger shading. On B above the staff the clarinetist should lower his left hand second finger over the second finger hole until the note is in tune. On C above the staff the first finger should be lowered over the first finger hole until satisfactory intonation is achieved. Consistency in finding the right spot with either finger is not easily accomplished, and considerable practice is required for the procedure to become second nature. Changing to a new instrument means that the fingers will need to be re-oriented to its unique pitch deficiencies, of course, including the amount of finger shading needed in order to achieve optimum intonation.

Other notes which may require finger shading are low D and A. The throat tones, which traditionally have been maligned as being out of tune, normally should not require finger shading or any other type of pitch alteration so long as the barrel joint is properly adjusted in the initial tuning process. An especially stuffy throat register B-flat can be cleared up, however, by using either the side key fingering or by adding the second and third fingers of the left hand (over their respective tone holes) to the regular B-flat fingering. The latter fingering may be flat on some clarinets, however, limiting its use in exposed passages.

Since the clarinetist has considerable room for adjusting his pitch downward, why not simply lip down the sharp high B and C? Actually, this is just what is needed in the case of a player who is biting the reed. But one can lip down only so far without the tone becoming flabby, particularly in the upper clarion register. Finger shading, on the other hand, allows the player to lower the pitch without sacrificing tone quality and is preferred over excessive lipping for this reason.

One reason why high C-sharp is played out of tune by many clarinetists is that they tend to bite the reed. (This topic will be discussed in detail later in this chapter.) Another reason is the use of incorrect fingering. High D through high G should be played with the right hand little finger E-flat key down. This E-flat key *should not* be used on high C-sharp, despite the fact that high C-sharp is the first note of the altissimo register which extends through high G and above; since this note is the exception, some players erroneously or carelessly use the E-flat key on this note along with all the rest, causing the pitch to be sharp. Special attention to proper fingering in this register from the very beginning is important, lest bad habits become engrained which will be difficult to break later.

Bassoon: Alternate fingerings and the amount of reed in the mouth are the bassoonist's primary methods of pitch alteration. To lower sharp notes such as F-sharp and G in the staff, the jaw should be dropped down and back more than usual, which decreases lip tension as well as the amount of reed in the mouth. Careful selection of a reed of proper strength and use of adequate breath support on notes which tend to be flat are also important. (See Spencer's *Art of Bassoon Playing*, p. 15, for a detailed analysis of bad notes on the bassoon and the reasons why they exist.)

A fair share of the bassoonist's pitch problems, as with the oboist, can be directly attributed to a faulty reed. A soft reed can cause the pitch of fourth line F to be very unstable with the tone quality being quite thin and unfocused. In fact, many reed deficiencies can be diagnosed specifically by the pitch and tonal characteristics of certain notes. (See Spencer's *Art of Bassoon Playing*, p. 32.)

All of the sharp notes on bassoon listed in the Woodwind Intonation Chart can be lipped down. In slower passages, when technique will allow, the left hand little finger C-sharp key may be added to lower the pitch of third space E-flat. For fourth line F-sharp, some teachers recommend that the so-called "alternate F-sharp," fingered with the *little finger* of the right hand, be used; the right hand *thumb* F-sharp key should be used primarily for the *low* F-sharp. These fingerings usually provide the best intonation for both F-sharps.

Due to the extraordinarily large number of fingerings available on the bassoon, most players will find at least one fingering for each note which will provide good intonation. As with all instrumentalists, the problem is not so much *how* to play a note in tune, but *being aware* that certain notes are in fact out of tune and require adjustment *by the player!*

Saxophone: The two worst notes on all saxophones are the D in the staff and A above the staff. The D is the first note using the thumb octave key; the A is the first note employing the *second* octave key (an automatic key located opposite the high F key). Both of these notes are unstable tonally and tend to be sharp as a result of the compromise problem inherent in the placement of all octave and register keys on woodwind instruments. Pitch and tonal stability both improve as one moves away from these two notes.

The saxophonist's primary method of pitch alteration is varying lip tension. Unlike the clarinetist, lip tension serves the saxophonist very well since he has much more flexibility in varying the pitch with this method. Some advocate venting and closing various keys in order to bring certain notes in tune. (For further information on the latter, see Colwell's *The Teaching of Instrumental Music*, p. 246.)

Mechanical Adjustment of Bad Notes

Mechanical adjustment of bad notes means simply retuning the instrument, where possible, so that it can be played in tune more easily without the need for excessive "doctoring" of the pitch by the player. But assuming the instrument has been tested and selected by a specialist before purchase, shouldn't this mean it is as well in tune as it can be? The answer is usually no. The author's experience has been that even a carefully selected professional model woodwind instrument can often be improved in pitch through careful, discriminate adjustment. In the case of the average woodwind instrument owned by most school musicians, the possibilities for improving intonation through adjusting pad height and altering tone hole size are often quite numerous.

The first step is to check each note on the instrument against a stroboscope and record the pitch deviations on a chart, preferably one similar to Chart 8. Next the chart should be examined carefully to determine which octaves (twelfths on the clarinet) have the same direction of pitch deviation. For example, if both G's on the saxophone are sharp in pitch, some mechanical adjustment can alleviate the problem. If, on the other hand, one G is sharp and the other is flat, there is little, if anything, that can be done.

Adjusting Height of Pads

When a key on a clarinet or saxophone opens too far, the pitch will be sharp. Putting a thicker piece of cork underneath the key concerned will decrease the distance it travels and thereby lower the pitch somewhat. Care must be taken that the key is not lowered too much or else the tone will become stuffy and possibly too flat as well. In each case the note(s) in question should be rechecked with a stroboscope to determine any need for further adjustment.

Occasionally, the first finger C-key pad on the flute tends to open too far causing undue sharpness of C-sharp in the staff. Putting a thicker cork under the C-key will decrease the opening of this pad and lower the pitch. The same is sometimes true for the bell tones C and B on the clarinet. In such a case, the key causing the problem should be adjusted to the optimum height without lowering the pad so much that the tone becomes stuffy.

The problem of proper pad height is especially critical on the saxophone, where the top half of the instrument frequently sounds very sharp from the keys' opening too far. Assuming the player's embouchure support is correct (blowing the mouthpiece alone should produce A-440 on the alto saxophone), these pads should be checked with a stroboscope and lowered until optimum intonation is achieved.

Finally, too great an opening of the octave or register keys can also create unnecessary intonation problems. Decreasing the distance between the tone holes and the respective octave keys on saxophone or oboe can improve the pitch of D and A on the saxophone and E and A on the oboe. (In each case these are the first notes on these respective instruments which require use of one of the two octave keys.) On the clarinet, a register key which opens too far can cause sharpness on B and C above the staff. A rule of thumb is to try inserting a five-cent coin between the register hole and the register key pad. If the coin fits snugly in between, the opening is satisfactory. If the coin fits loosely, the register key should be bent down until the coin fits snugly.

Altering the Size of the Tone Hole

Let us assume that a strobe check reveals that the pitch of *both* A's on an oboe is consistently sharp. If the pitch discrepancy is slight, then the pitch of both A's can be lowered slightly by applying two or more coats of fingernail polish inside the next lowest tone hole on the instrument. By decreasing the size of this tone hole, the resistance to the air emitted through this hole is increased and the pitch is thereby lowered slightly. (Clear rather than colored nail polish is recommended; if too much nail polish is applied, it can be easily removed with nail polish remover.)

To use another example, if low D and A above the staff on a clarinet are both *slightly* sharp, fingernail polish can be applied in the third finger hole to lower the pitch somewhat. If the pitch of both tones is *appreciably* sharp, then use of friction tape or thin cork strips is recommended. These may be glued in place with pad or cork cement to the *top side* of the tone hole (the side of the hole nearest the mouthpiece or reed). This creates the effect of increasing the distance between the top end of the instrument and the specific tone hole involved, as if the tone hole had been drilled at a point lower down on the instrument.

Next, let us assume that the pitch of *both notes* cited above proves to be slightly flat. In this case the distance between the top of the instrument and the open tone hole needs to be decreased. This can be accomplished by wrapping a piece of fine sandpaper around a pencil or smaller, similar object and sanding against the *top side* of the tone hole. Care should be taken to ensure that too much wood is not sanded away, by frequently checking with the stroboscope.

All of this may seem very logical and quite simple but experience has shown that when the bottom note is sharp, the corresponding note in the second octave or register will often be flat or vice-versa. As a specific case in point, low D on clarinet is usually sharp but the A a twelfth above is most often flat. Decreasing the size of the third finger hole to improve the sharp low D can be done only at the expense of making the A above the staff still flatter. The solution to the problem lies elsewhere, presumably in altering the size of the instrument's bore at some given point. A few competent, experienced repairmen are able to ream the bore successfully at a specified point, but this is at best a risky undertaking. Instruments with severe deficiencies of this sort should not be purchased.

The above problem may also be due to a faulty mouthpiece, in which case replacement of the mouthpiece may alleviate much of the deficiency. Past experience has shown that severe sharpness of high B and C along with sharpness in the altissimo register of the clarinet can sometimes be alleviated by changing to one of the hard rubber barrels made by Lee Springer of Chicago. The Springer barrel also darkens the tone somewhat in the top range of the clarinet, a fact which is considered to be a special asset to the concert band clarinetist. This latter characteristic cannot be easily determined during a single testing period. Rather it is suggested that the player use the Springer barrel consistently for at least one week, and then go back and try the regular barrel; he will then be better able to decide whether there is an actual difference in resistance and resultant tone quality or whether it is an aural illusion. (The same might also be said with respect to trying a new mouthpiece or brand of instrument as well as a "new style" reed.)

While tuning adjustments such as those described are admittedly time-consuming, the improvement in intonation will usually serve as ample reward for the effort expended. If a repairman or specialist teacher knowledgeable in these matters is available nearby, it is recommended that students be sent directly to that person. But experience has shown that the number of qualified and interested persons who can do this type of work is relatively small, and it therefore behooves the teacher to do much of this work himself.

3. Register Intonation Deficiencies

Woodwinds

The purpose of Chart 8 is to generalize the pitch tendencies of woodwind players and their instruments via graphic illustration. No absolute claim is made as to specific pitch tendencies of any note on any instrument; this is impossible because of the many variables found in different makes of instruments and in players with diverse training and playing experience. It is hoped, however, that the chart may serve as an aid toward helping the teacher be aware of *what to listen for*. Understanding some of these principles and applying them *from the very beginning*

Chart 8

WOODWIND REGISTER INTONATION

should eliminate a large share of student problems which usually require repetitive remedial work in the later stages of study.

The horizontal lines above or below each chromatic scale represent the mean or in-tune pitch. The plus sign above the horizontal line represents sharpness; the minus sign represents flatness. The pitch tendencies indicated are those where the basic or "number one fingering" is used. It is assumed that the student, unlike an experienced musician, is using very little if any lipping in order to improve the intonation. Through careful listening and appropriate "doctoring" of the pitch, most of the intonation deficiencies shown can, of course, be eliminated eventually.

As seen in the chart, all upper registers tend to be sharp except the oboe's. In order to keep the pitch down, the player's throat should be kept as open as possible without harming the tone quality. Biting and excessive embouchure tension should also be avoided. (This is especially important with regard to the *upper* register of the bassoon and saxophone.) The player should also be sure that the jaw is down and the throat open, and should be especially conscious of supporting the tone properly lest it go flat, especially in soft passages.

Players sometimes try to improve a dull, flat tone by pinching it up with the embouchure rather than relying, as they should, on proper breath support to maintain proper pitch and resonance. This seems to be particularly true of flutists and brass players. Much of the flattening of the oboist's upper register is due to soft reeds as well as lack of adequate breath support. Use of the Stroboconn can be a significant aid in helping alleviate such problems.

Upper register intonation is of special significance, since this is where bad intonation tends to be the most painful to the average listener. This is based on the idea that the presence of beats becomes increasingly more disturbing as one goes higher in the tonal spectrum; as one goes lower the presence of beats is relatively less bothersome. This is not to say that out-of-tune playing on the string bass, for example, is to be tolerated any more than poor intonation on the piccolo. We recognize the importance of accurate intonation with low-voiced instruments, particularly with respect to setting the pitch standard of vertical sonorities. At the same time, how many of us prefer to hear poor intonation in the upper registers of the clarinet or bassoon, for example, in contrast to poor intonation in the bottom ranges of these instruments?

All extreme low registers tend to be flat, except on the saxophone and bassoon. On the flute much of this problem can be corrected by firming the upper lip and using more breath support. Oboists also need to rely on more support and more firmness of embouchure, but the pitch of the oboe in its bottom register may still tend to remain somewhat flat. (Close listening to professional oboists in live performance and on recordings will demonstrate that even they on occasion find it difficult to solve this problem.) In such a case the other players may need to adjust their pitch a little more in order to alleviate ensemble pitch problems.

Clarinetists frequently pull out at the bell to get B and C in the staff down to the correct pitch level. This also flattens the low E and F, which already tend to be flat. Many clarinetists are willing to live with this inequality, however, since low E and F are used very infrequently as compared to the B and C in the staff.

Bassoonists and saxophonists can combat the sharpness of their bottom registers by relaxing the embouchure more than usual. The bassoonist can also try to use as little reed in the mouth as is reasonably possible to further lower his pitch.

An interesting corollary exists between the first and second registers of each of the woodwinds. In the case of the bassoon, for example, notice how the notes in the first register tend to possess intonation deficiencies just opposite to those in the second register. This gives us an idea of some of the problems faced by woodwind instrument manufacturers when they try to design instruments which will play reasonably well in tune throughout the playing range. Since the same tone holes are used for playing two or more different pitches, some compromise becomes necessary in order to achieve reasonably good intonation for all the tones using basically the same fingering. A major factor contributing to this problem is the compromise which is necessary when trying to decide where the octave or register key hole is to be placed. (For further details see Stauffer, *Intonation Deficiencies*, pp. 80–83.)

Brasses

All lower registers of brass instruments tend to be sharp. On valved brasses this problem results from the necessity of using the inherently sharp large valve combination in the lower range. The only exception to this is the tuba where the player may sometimes relax the lips too much in an effort to get the low tones to respond accurately. When this happens, the pitch of the lowest tones may tend to be flat despite the inherent sharpness of the valve combinations.

The low E and F on trombone are also played sharp occasionally, especially by younger players with a short arm reach. But intonation in the low registers of brass instruments is seldom a significant problem in most performance situations. The most predominant problem is that of playing the upper register in tune. Too small an aperture (opening between the lips), closing the throat too much, excessive mouthpiece pressure and lack of proper breath support all contribute individually and collectively to the production of a thin, pinched tone accompanied by sharpness in pitch. Curling too much lower lip inward and clenching the teeth are additional sources of difficulty to be reckoned with.

Diagnosing and solving these problems is not easy. The best solution is to try to prevent their ever taking place. Teachers should be especially careful to avoid exploiting the upper ranges of young brass players. Arrangers are also occasionally guilty of doing this, in instances where most of the band parts are relatively easy except for a high first cornet part. Music of this type is best passed over for the time being and attempted later when the players' embouchures are able to meet the demands of high register performance.

Another reason for poor intonation in the outer ranges is that students have not learned to listen carefully. Students would undoubtedly be less prone to develop incorrect performance habits if only they realized their negative effects beforehand. This is another prime example of why the rote approach (playing by ear) can be so valuable in the beginning stages. Teach the student *what to listen for!* Teach the musical concept first. A good embouchure, for example, can be meaningless unless the student has some reasonable idea of what kind of tone he is trying to produce.

Finally, wind instruments which are not properly swabbed out and otherwise kept clean and free of sediment will invariably play out of tune with themselves. Accumulation of foreign matter inside the bore of both the instrument and mouthpiece and open tone holes on woodwinds affects intonation far more than most players realize. Periodic inspection of each player's instrument is therefore strongly recommended, not only for reasons of sanitation and checking the mechanical condition of the instrument, but also for purposes of intonation.

4. Bad Notes on String Instruments

Assuming that the open strings are in tune, "bad notes" per se simply do not exist on string instruments. String *players,* like wind players, are the major cause of intonation problems. Experience has shown the following tendencies to be prevalent among string students:

1. Young string players seldom play sharped notes high enough or flatted notes low enough. Since string players need not be confined to the limitations of equal-tempered tuning, they should strive to emphasize rather than minimize the pitch direction of accidentals. The third and seventh degrees of the scale should be treated likewise. While playing along with a piano may be helpful in the beginning, this crutch should not be used too long. It is true that most orchestra directors would be elated if only their string players could meet the requirements of equal-tempered tuning as it exists on the piano. But why not aim toward more ideal pitch discrimination? The author sees no valid reason why students' ears should be conditioned to equal temperament over the course of several years of public school instruction when a better alternative is available.

2. The violin F on the top line of the staff is frequently played quite sharp. Students simply do not get the first finger back far enough to play the F in tune. Check the player's hand position and make sure that the wrist is straight and the palm of the hand is down.

3. Notes on violin and viola fingered with the fourth finger are usually played flat. In passages where the specific tone color of the fingered tone is required, one has little choice but to get it in tune and use it. But with young string players, whenever the use of a fingered tone is optional, the open string is usually recommended for public performance. Use of the fingered tone is recommended *after* sufficient practice has made it more acceptable to the ear!

4. Fourth finger notes on cello and string bass are apt to be played flat. Check to see that hand positions are correct. In fact the majority of severe intonation problems in string playing are usually due to poor left hand position.

5. When the starting note of a composition requires use of the third or fourth finger, prepare the pitch beforehand by *lightly* plucking the string in diatonic fashion until the correct spot is located. Then the player is all set to play the first note in tune.

6. The use of crutches such as tape on the fingerboard to aid young players in finding the right spot is a source of considerable debate among some teachers. But as with foot tapping, there is nothing really objectionable about it unless teacher and student depend upon it too heavily and for too long a period. The teacher is urged to use his good judgment in these matters and employ such aids to the extent that they actually help the student without doing harm to his future development.

The student will derive little value from knowing all of the "bad notes" on his instrument unless he has learned how to finger these notes and uses them frequently either in group rehearsal or in home practice. The same applies to all general knowledge concerned with intonation and other fundamentals as well. In the beginning, the fact that the note is three beats long is immaterial if the student has not yet been introduced to music reading. Such information is usually important to the student only if he can use it immediately. The teacher should present musical facts in a relevant, logical sequence, relating the known to the unknown and then applying it in a practical, musical context.

C. OTHER OBJECTIVE FACTORS AFFECTING TONE QUALITY AND INTONATION

1. Standard Pitch

History shows that the pitch of A has changed considerably over the years. During the Baroque period it varied from what we know today as first space F-sharp to third space C-sharp. Mozart's piano in 1780 was tuned to a standard of B-422. In 1858, the French government established the pitch of A at 435 vibrations per second.[19] The present inter-

[19] Fredrick Dorian, *The History of Music in Performance* (New York: W. W. Norton & Company, Inc., 1942), pp. 319–20.

national tuning standard, adopted in 1939, is A-440. Pottle's research reveals, however, that the Boston Symphony under Munch used A-444 as the basis for tuning.[20] The pitch of A, therefore, has continued to rise since the Baroque and there is no real assurance that it will not continue to do so in the future.

Today's instrument manufacturers reportedly build wind instruments so that they will play *best in tune* at a tuning standard of A-440. When a conductor chooses a tuning pitch such as A-444, this creates severe intonation problems for wind and keyboard percussion instruments. The problem of tuning to a higher pitch standard cannot be successfully solved simply by shortening the main tuning slide, the barrel joint or head joint; the design of the entire instrument must be altered. This means shortening valve slides as well as tuning slides on brass instruments and retuning individual tone holes on woodwind instruments. Keyboard percussion instruments also require major alteration of a similar nature.

Excessive readjustment in order to meet the requirements of a lower pitch standard such as A-435 also creates severe intonation problems for wind and keyboard percussion instruments. The intonation of some notes on wind instruments will be changed much more than others. Notes adversely affected will be so severely out of tune that no amount of "lipping" can correct the problem.[21] Again the only real solution for both keyboard percussion and wind instruments is to rebuild them so they can meet the needs of this lower pitch standard.

In order to achieve best intonation most easily, close adherence to A-440 is strongly recommended. It is the author's conviction that a significant amount of the poor intonation found among school groups is caused by directors who either are indifferent to maintaining a consistent pitch standard or else carelessly rationalize the need to tune higher than A-440. In either case the intonation problems created are such that even professional players cannot cope with them. Indiscriminate deviation from A-440 should therefore be avoided if one is ever to expect reasonably good intonation from student musicians.

2. Temperature

A wind instrument which is cold will sound flat in pitch. Conversely, a wind instrument exposed to high temperatures will sound sharp. Some believe that this is due primarily to expansion and contraction of the

[20] Ralph R. Pottle, "Factors in Boston Symphony Tuning," *The Instrumentalist* (March, 1960), 108–9.

[21] Jody C. Hall and Earle L. Kent, *The Effect of Temperature on the Tuning Standards of Wind Instruments* (Elkhart, Ind.: C. G. Conn Ltd., 1959), p. 3.

material of which the instrument is made. But according to Stauffer, such expansion-contraction has only a slight effect upon wind instrument intonation. The real explanation lies in the temperature of the air inside the bore of the instrument. Cold air is dense, with its molecules close together; this offers added resistance to the air blown through the instrument and lowers the pitch. Warm air, on the other hand, is less dense, with its molecules farther apart, thus allowing the air to travel through the instrument with relatively less resistance. Since the air travels faster in this case, the pitch goes higher.[22]

On the other hand, fixed-pitch instruments such as the marimba, chimes, bells, celesta, and xylophone are affected somewhat by contraction and expansion caused by changes in temperature, but the pitch change which actually results is relatively small. The pitch of these instruments remains fairly constant in fluctuating temperatures.

Metal instruments warm up and cool off faster than instruments made of wood; therefore, a longer period is required for the pitch to stabilize on a wooden instrument such as the oboe than on a metal instrument such as the flute. Also, instruments with large bores and long tubing warm up considerably slower than instruments with smaller bores and shorter lengths of tubing. In the case of the tuba, for example, laboratory tests have shown that at temperatures less than 80 degrees, fifteen to twenty minutes of warmup has been necessary in order to stabilize the intonation.[23] Since the tuba sets the standard of tuning for vertical sonorities in the band, the intonation of the tuba section should be checked fairly often and readjusted accordingly throughout a rehearsal or performance.

In order for a wind instrument to play in tune at A-440, today's manufacturers specify that the external temperature should be 72 degrees Fahrenheit. If the temperature deviates from 72 degrees, this affects the overall pitch level of the entire instrument, as can be seen in Chart 9. Notice also that the pitch deviation of larger instruments such as the tuba is much greater than that of smaller instruments such as the flute and oboe.

Chart 9 also shows that the mean deviation of a full wind band at a temperature of 95 degrees is only 20 cents, or one-fifth of an equally tempered half step. But conductors sometimes believe the pitch deviation at such high temperatures to be much greater, and consequently allow their ensembles to tune higher than they should. This in effect is an indiscriminate deviation from standard pitch. Intonation problems of individual wind instruments are thereby increased, not to mention the

[22] Stauffer, *Intonation Deficiencies*, pp. 25–26.
[23] Hall and Kent, *Effect of Temperature*, p. 3.

wide discrepancy which inevitably results between keyboard percussion and the wind instruments as separate groups.

Chart 9

**THE EFFECT OF TEMPERATURE
ON TUNING OF WIND INSTRUMENTS[24]**

The normal condition of tuning is A-440 vib. per sec. at 72° Fahrenheit. A rise of 1° F. in external air temperature increases the pitch of:

	Cents
Flute and oboe	0.5
Clarinet	0.7
Cornet and Trumpet	0.9
French Horn and Trombone (Bassoon)	1.0
Euphonium and Baritone	1.1
Tuba	1.2
Organ Flue Pipes	1.8
Mean of Full Wind Band	0.9

TABLE FOR TEMPERATURE RANGE FROM 72° to 95° BASED UPON THE MEAN OF THE FULL WIND BAND WITH FIXED PITCH IN-STRUMENTS

Temperature in Degrees, Fahrenheit	*Frequency of A in Cycles per sec.*	*Scale Setting on Stroboconn-cents*
72°	440.00	0.0 cents
73	440.23	plus 0.9
74	440.46	1.8
75	440.68	2.7
76	440.92	3.6
77	441.15	4.5
78	441.37	5.4
79	441.61	6.3
80	441.83	7.2
81	442.07	8.1
82	442.29	9.0
83	442.52	9.9
84	442.75	10.8
85	442.98	11.7
86	443.22	12.6
87	443.43	13.5
88	443.67	14.4
89	443.91	15.3
90	444.14	16.2
91	444.37	17.1
92	444.60	18.0
93	444.83	18.9
94	445.06	19.8
95	445.30	20.7

[24] From the Conn Vocational School *Repair Manual*, section 2, p. 36.

Since manufacturers specify a temperature of 72 degrees Fahrenheit for ideal tuning and intonation, special attention should be given to the average temperature of the rehearsal room and concert halls where performing groups play. This is particularly important when wind instruments are being used together with fixed-pitch instruments such as the marimba, chimes, bells, celesta, and xylophone. Since the pitch of these instruments remains fairly constant in fluctuating temperature, consistency should be maintained in the pitch standard and in the *temperature of the room* where concerts are given.[25]

If all temperature-intonation problems ceased to be troublesome after the initial warmup, the difficulty of maintaining good intonation would be greatly reduced. But mean temperatures vary from concert hall to concert hall, from one season to another, and from one part of the country or the globe to another, not to mention the inevitable fluctuation of temperature between the beginning and end of a single concert or rehearsal. It is therefore highly important that students be properly informed about the effect of temperature change on the overall tuning of their individual instruments. They should further realize that tuning is something which one must continue to check and recheck throughout a rehearsal or concert. Frequent reminders and *insistence* on positive results by the director will help students avoid a careless or indifferent attitude toward this important "fact of life" of performance.

3. Changes in Dynamics

Most wind instruments tend to go sharp in *fortissimo* passages and flat in *pianissimo* ones. The pitch deviation of the clarinet and saxophone, however, is just opposite. In band situations where the single reeds comprise a large share of the total instrumentation, this discrepancy can be an especially frustrating one.

In *pianissimo*, the pitch of all the brasses, the flute, and the double reeds tends to go flat. Frequently this problem is due to lack of proper breath support. Players need to be reminded to maintain adequate breath support even though the quantity of air being used is smaller. Conscientious practice with a stroboscope can also help the player recognize his problem and provide him with a concrete means for evaluating his progress in solving it.

In *fortissimo*, the pitch of all the brasses, the flute, and double reeds tends to go sharp. Keeping the embouchure firm and practicing with the stroboscope while playing *crescendos* and *decrescendos* can help. Reed

[25] Ralph R. Pottle, "Temperature and Tuning," *The Instrumentalist* (February, 1966), 51.

players, however, should also check the quality of their reeds, since poor reeds are often the major source of the problem.

A special technique employed by some oboists in controlling pitch deviation is that of the lip *diminuendo.* Since the pitch of the oboe tone tends to go flat when tapering a delicate *diminuendo,* oboists can roll the lips out onto the reed gradually until the reed tip is completely covered by the lips and can no longer vibrate. Breath pressure is kept constant, thereby maintaining the pitch level; the lips create the *diminuendo.* (See Sprenkle's *The Art of Oboe Playing* for further details.)

Flutists experience much the same problem as do oboists in executing delicate *diminuendos.* A technique used by some flutists is to push the butt joint forward slightly with the right hand. This causes increasingly more air to strike the right side and outside portions of the embouchure plate until finally the tone is cut off completely. Breath pressure remains constant throughout, keeping the pitch up.

What about the clarinet and saxophone, which tend to sound sharp in *pianissimo* and flat in *fortissimo?* Some teachers recommend that players of these instruments should simply relax the embouchure when playing softly and make it progressively more firm as the dynamic level is increased. This is good advice so long as the embouchure is not relaxed excessively. Too much relaxation of the embouchure usually results in very poor tone quality and should be avoided. But how does one resolve this conflict of poor tone versus poor intonation in pianissimo playing on single reed instruments? The answer lies mainly in the type of reed used, which is the topic to be discussed in the next section.

4. Reeds

The usual analysis of reed quality is: the harder the reed, the sharper the pitch; the softer the reed, the flatter the pitch. Also, soft reeds tend to sound thin and nasal while hard reeds tend to sound stuffy and harsh. But too little knowledge can be a dangerous thing. Misinterpretation of these generalities has proved to be a source of misguided teaching in far too many cases. The student needs to know exactly what a good reed feels like when he blows it. This can only be taught in a live, either private or class, lesson by a teacher who himself knows the answer. The best we can do here is to try describing in words the characteristics of a good reed and how to adjust reeds so that they meet these criteria.

What is a good reed? A good reed is one which: (1) blows freely with good resonance; (2) is playable at all dynamic levels from *pianissimo* through *fortissimo;* (3) has good response to the attack in all playing ranges, even in *pianissimo;* (4) has good pitch stability and tone quality throughout the playing range; and (5) feels comfortable to the player. Each of these criteria will be discussed in detail in the following subsections.

Initial Steps in Reed Selection and Adjustment

There are various factors involved in the selection of good reed cane, including the length and size of its grain, its basic color, etc. Since detailed discussions of these matters are available in other publications, they will not be treated here. This discussion will center on details not commonly discussed elsewhere.

While selection of good cane is important, actual blowing of the reed is the real test of its potential. This should be done only after the reed has been properly soaked, preferably in water. Single reed players can use a small water glass filled high enough to cover the reed vamp (scraped portion). Double reed players can use an aspirin bottle or other small bottle so that only the vamp is immersed in water.

How long should reeds be soaked? Experience is the best teacher. Single reeds that are insufficiently soaked will be wrinkled at the tip, and double reeds will leak air around the sides. Single and double reeds which are soaked too long will become waterlogged and hard to blow. Probably the best approach is to let several reeds soak for approximately one minute or less and then try blowing one. If it appears to be properly soaked, all of the others should be removed immediately from the water glass.

Does the reed blow freely, does it have good response to breath pressure and produce a firm, resonant sound? If it meets all of these criteria, then the reed has good potential and can probably be adjusted so that it plays reasonably well in a minimal amount of time. If it does not play well, this does not necessarily mean that it should be discarded, although some reeds can never be made to perform satisfactorily. The answer is to determine quickly why a given reed fails to respond properly when it is first blown.

A major reason for poor reed response on the clarinet and saxophone is that of reed warpage. The back of the reed needs to be as flat as possible in order to create the best possible vacuum against the mouthpiece when the reed vibrates against it. If one side of the reed curves away from the mouthpiece, causing air to escape, the reed will not blow freely and the tone will sound stuffy. To alleviate this problem, the back of the reed should be sanded with silicon carbide watersand paper, number 400A or finer, until it is reasonably flat. A sheet of this paper may be taped to a piece of plate glass to ensure a flat sanding surface. A piece of Scotch tape should also be attached to the underside of the reed tip to avoid damaging it during the sanding process. Use of this technique alone will improve the playing qualities of more reeds in a box than any other single technique of which this author has knowledge.

There are two methods for testing a clarinet or saxophone reed to see if the underside is flat. One is to cover the back opening of the mouthpiece and suck the air out through the mouthpiece tip until the reed "sticks" against the mouthpiece lay. A reed which is relatively flat on the underside will remain in place for at least three seconds or more before "popping away" from the mouthpiece. A warped reed will leak air around the sides, making it difficult to create a good vacuum between the reed and mouthpiece.

Another approach is to coat the back of the reed liberally with water or saliva and lay it against a piece of plate glass slightly larger than the reed itself. By turning the glass over one can see if both sides of the reed lie flat against the glass by searching for air bubbles between the reed and the glass. The presence of air bubbles on either side indicates reed warpage and exactly where it exists. Frequently both sides will be warped. The back of the reed should then be sanded until good response is achieved.

Oboe reeds usually have goldbeater's skin around the lower half of the reed cane to prevent air from leaking around the sides. If the reed fails to blow freely, absence of this material may be the source of the problem. Students often loosen the skin through careless handling, causing it to fall off and be lost. Teaching students to grasp the cork section rather than the lower blade section of the reed when removing it from the instrument will help avoid this problem as well as avoid the strong possibility of damaging the reed cane itself.

After the reed has been properly soaked, double reed players should blow the reed alone to see if it will produce a good, healthy "crow," a sound consisting of many varied pitches produced simultaneously. A reed which does not blow freely or does not produce any sound at all is probably too hard. One which vibrates at only one pitch is usually too soft. Hard reeds should first be checked for leaks by covering the bottom end with a finger and blowing air through the tip. If the check is positive, then the reed needs to be scraped. Soft reeds should be cut off at the tip to raise the heart of the reed, this followed by thinning the reed tip until good response is restored.

After this comes the matter of breaking in reeds properly. Here again the reader is advised to consult other publications for detailed information. However, there is one item related to this topic which will be mentioned here—waterproofing the reed. There are various ways of doing this. Some advocate rubbing the vamp with the thumb nail; others use Dutch rush and some even use talcum powder to close off the open pores of the reed. The author prefers to use silicon carbide paper, the same type that was recommended for sanding the underside of the reed. Whichever method one chooses to use is actually secondary. The important thing is that the reed be somehow waterproofed so that saliva absorption by the reed pores is held to a minimum. Otherwise the reed will soon lose its resiliency and no longer respond properly. A reed which has been properly waterproofed will last much longer than one which has not. Some such reeds have been known to play well after six months or more of use. If the player is to spend considerable time adjusting each reed so it will play properly, he might as well finish it off so that it will last for a while.

Achieving Proper Resistance

One often hears that a certain teacher or player uses and recommends soft reeds while another uses hard reeds. This type of categorization is inappropriate as well as confusing, since no good player really uses reeds which he considers soft or hard. He uses reeds which are of *proper resistance* to meet the requirements of good musical performance.

The amount of reed resistance that an individual player needs depends upon a variety of factors including the mouthpiece, instrument, the make and type of cane used, and the type of playing he does, as well as his own unique physical makeup. Generally speaking, a mouthpiece with a small tip opening requires harder reeds. The wider the tip opening, the softer the reed should be in order to respond well. Variation in the distance between the point where the reed leaves the mouthpiece lay and the mouthpiece tip also affects basic reed strength, particularly tho thickness of the sides and the heart of the reed. In addition, if the bore size of the mouthpiece, barrel, and/or instruments tends to be smaller than normal, the resulting greater resistance of these factors will probably require a reed of lesser resistance. Conversely, if the mouthpiece, barrel, and instrument offer minimal resistance, compensation will need to be made by increasing the reed's resistance. The answer then is one of achieving *proper balance* among all of the factors involved.

How does one determine if *his reed* is of proper resistance? This is done by checking the ability of the reed to vibrate freely in a *crescendo* from *pianissimo* through *fortissimo*, and then by checking its pitch and tonal stability throughout the range of the instrument. Primary discussion here will be devoted to the reed's dynamic range; detailed discussion of pitch and tonal stability will follow in a later subsection.

Checking a reed to see if it will vibrate freely at all dynamic levels should be done on a note of least resistance such as third line B on oboe, open G or the throat tones A or B-flat on clarinet, fourth line F on bassoon, and open C-sharp on saxophone. A reed which closes up before reaching the peak of a good *crescendo* is too soft and should be clipped at the tip in order to increase its resistance. After it is clipped it may need to be thinned at the tip in order to restore good response.

A reed which fails to vibrate properly at a *pianissimo* level is probably too heavy at the tip and should be thinned down until it responds easily. After this is done, the reed may feel soft and require clipping at the tip to increase its overall resistance. The critical factor in reed adjustment, therefore, is to maintain proper balance between all aspects of the reed's structure. One adjustment to improve one aspect of the reed's vibrating qualities usually requires adjustment in another area in order to restore proper balance. Proper balance is achieved when all five of the characteristics of a good reed mentioned earlier are achieved.

Youngsters often tend to choose the path of least resistance. Whether this be in reference to homework, eating spinach, or preferring soft reeds and easy-blowing instruments, youngsters tend to share the same basic characteristics. Paradoxically, students sometimes assume that a reed is too hard when actually it is too soft. For example, a player who uses proper breath support and tries to blow a soft reed beyond *mezzo forte* may find that the reed closes and refuses to vibrate. The problem is not one of the reed being too hard, but too soft. This problem can be easily solved by clipping the reed or changing to a reed of greater resistance.

Adjusting the Tip for Good Response

Relatively few clarinet and saxophone students use reeds which are too hard, since it is an easy and inexpensive matter merely to change to a softer reed if desired. Double reed players, however—oboists in particular—are more apt to use hard reeds. In doing so they fail to achieve good response in *pianissimo* and find great difficulty in playing softly. The explanation for this is that as a reed is being broken in, the cane expands each time it absorbs additional moisture. While it does contract somewhat after being allowed to dry, it never returns to its original size. This causes the reed tip to become increasingly heavier, which makes good response at a soft dynamic difficult. The solution lies in acquiring a reed plaque and a sharp reed knife, then very carefully scraping both blades of the reed tip until the reed again responds easily.

How thin should the reed tip be? It should be thin enough to respond properly even at the softest dynamic level. To those students who require a more concrete explanation, the reed tip should be approximately the same thickness as the edge of a piece of typing paper. The comparison can be made by placing the thumb and index finger on either side of the reed and on the typing paper to serve as a background so that the edges can be more easily seen with the eye. While not a precise method, it appears to be helpful to some. Those interested in scientifically accurate measurements may wish to purchase a dial indicator which can be used to measure reed thickness in micrometers at any given point of the vamp.

Another cause of poor response and stuffiness is reed imbalance, the most critical area being that nearest the reed tip. Sometimes the imbalance can be identified on single reeds simply by looking at the reed against a strong light. Reed imbalance not easily seen with the eye on double reeds can be checked by looking at the tip opening to see if it is evenly shaped. With single reeds, each side of the reed can also be checked by applying pressure with the index finger against the underside. (See Opperman, *Handbook for Making and Adjusting Single Reeds,* for further information.)

Achieving Good Pitch and Tonal Stability

The major reason why so few oboe and bassoon reeds sold commercially are acceptable is that most of them have had too much of the heart or center scraped away. This means that the reed can never possess good pitch or tonal stability. If one must rely on commercial reeds, only those with a heavy center should be purchased. Such reeds can then be thinned at the tip and balanced at the sides until they are properly adjusted to meet the requirements of good performance.

A frequent problem with some makes of commercial clarinet and saxophone reeds is that the sides of the reed in the area nearest the tip are too thin. This causes the tone to be excessively edgy or bright which in turn creates problems in tonal blend in ensemble. Such reeds as well as those lacking sufficient heart should be avoided.

Some teachers recommend buying the hardest reeds available and working them down to proper strength or resistance. Others prefer to buy medium to medium hard reeds, clipping the tip along with other needed adjustments until the reed is brought up to a proper resistance level. Both approaches can be successful, and neither one is necessarily recommended over the other; the individual should experiment and decide which works best for him.

The reader is cautioned, however, that excessive clipping of the reed tip on clarinet or saxophone may result in the reed vamp becoming too short for proper reed response and vibration. When this happens, the vamp should be lengthened by scraping off enough bark at the back of the vamp so as to return the vamp to its desired length. This is determined by comparing the length of the vamp to the length of the mouthpiece window (opening against which the reed is attached). Ideally, the length of both should be the same. Sometimes the reed will still perform satisfactorily if its vamp is a little shorter than the mouthpiece window. But if it is quite short or too long, reed response will be poor.

The primary factor, therefore, which determines whether or not the reed will have good pitch and tonal stability is the thickness of the heart or center section and the distance it extends toward the reed tip. A reed which is properly proportioned in these respects can be played up to pitch easily without any need for excessive biting and will produce a tone with good center or core and maximal resonance. It will also tend to focus in on a mean pitch and stay there. This greatly reduces the need for relaxing and tightening the embouchure to compensate for pitch deviation resulting from changes in dynamic levels.

How can one tell if a reed has good pitch and tonal stability? First, check its ability to withstand the test of air pressure from *pianissimo* through *fortissimo* on a note of least resistance. (A reed with insufficient heart will not produce a full, resonant *fortissimo*.) Secondly, play a scale in the top register of the instrument and listen to both the pitch and tone quality. If it is necessary to bite the reed in order to maintain a good center or core to the sound and to keep the pitch up, then the reed is lacking sufficient heart. In both cases, the reed should be clipped until good pitch and tonal stability are achieved.

The reader is cautioned that in learning to play a reed of the type advocated here, the muscles of the embouchure must be allowed to develop *very gradually and naturally* in order to be able to control the reed properly. The younger player who immediately attempts to play reeds that are as resistant as those used by his teacher will find his endurance measurably decreased and will probably resort to biting the reed in order to control it. The latter should be avoided. With proper development of the embouchure, there should be no teeth marks or cuts on the inner lip, nor should there be excessive fatigue after a normal period of playing. The answer is to increase reed resistance very gradually so that the reed feels only slightly harder than it did before. Once it feels normal again, the reed resistance should again be increased as needed until finally the above ideal objectives are achieved. This often takes several months or even a year or longer. It cannot be accomplished overnight. The teacher must be the guiding factor in this type of embouchure development.

Conclusion

In working on reeds, a cardinal rule to follow is to sand or scrape only a little wood at a time, frequently checking the reed through actual playing. Otherwise too much wood may be removed, thereby ruining the reed. Once removed, wood cannot be replaced, and it is better to do too little than too much.

Reeds which are quite moist should not be worked on with a reed knife until they are almost dry. This is especially important when thinning the tip. Scraping the tip of a wet reed usually results in chunks of the tip being pulled off in the process. At very least, the soft, pithy portion of the cane will be scraped away while the grain of the cane will hardly be thinned at all. On the other hand, working on reeds which are bone dry is not recommended either. Particularly in the case of double reeds, scraping them when they are dry will most often result in their cracking or splitting down the middle. Such a reed is then useless.

Until double reed students learn to adjust their own reeds, it is necessary that the teacher make all of the adjustments. A recommended plan is for the student to have at least four playable reeds available at all times. Two of the four reeds can be left with the teacher one week for adjustment with two reeds retained by the student for home practice. The following week the student and teacher swap reeds and repeat the cycle of reed swapping as needed thereafter. Otherwise the student has little choice but to force and strain and be continually breathless from blowing a reed which has become so hard that even a professional player could not possibly play it properly.

Finally, it is doubtful that anyone can ever learn to work on reeds, much less understand their unique peculiarities, simply by reading about them. In-depth knowledge and understanding requires study with a specialist, many hours of trial-and-error experimentation and, not the least important, patience. It is hoped, nevertheless, that this discussion at least verifies the fact that a working knowledge of reeds and the manner in which they function is essential if one is ever to teach reed instruments effectively.

5. Woodwind Mouthpieces

A woodwind mouthpiece which is severely chipped or warped will not provide good tonal response. But what about the mouthpiece which is not chipped or warped but is still unresponsive to the attack? Is there some viable way of determining the quality of a mouthpiece before purchase? Certainly the average non-clarinetist does not know what to look for, and even if he did, the mouthpiece, like the reed, must stand the test of playing before any final judgment can be made. Without going into great depth on a subject which itself could consume a book, the following general statements are offered for whatever they may be worth:

1. The mouthpiece is the woodwind player's most important piece of equipment aside from the reed, but the reed can be and usually should be *altered* to meet the needs of the player. A student should use the

best mouthpiece he can obtain. It is better to play on a poor quality instrument than with an inferior mouthpiece.

2. Mouthpieces come in a variety of facings, colors, etc., which admittedly is confusing even to reed specialists as well as non-reed performers. But the fact which many persons fail to consider carefully enough is that no two mouthpieces play the same, even if they are marked the same and made by the same manufacturer. All too often the difference between two "X facing" mouthpieces of the same make is so great that they bear little similarity to each other in performance.

3. Considering item 2 above, what recourse is available to the instrumental teacher? Having a professional check each mouthpiece before purchase is probably the best answer, although seldom possible or practical. If not this, then how does one go about securing mouthpieces of any consistency and reliability? Look to the professionals! Few symphony performers play mouthpieces which are *entirely* machine-made on a mass production basis. Reasonable consistency *still* has to be achieved by the old hand-sanding process, at least in the final stage of production. One should choose a mouthpiece of the type used by professionals, and avoid the mistaken attitude that almost any mouthpiece will do for the beginner. One gets back in equal measure what one puts in. Students and their parents should be provided with the most authoritative information available. Do not leave selection of mouthpieces to chance!

D. SUBJECTIVE FACTORS INFLUENCING TONE QUALITY AND INTONATION

The primary factor influencing tone quality and intonation is the player. This is true despite the complexity of the objective factors just discussed as well as the inherent problems associated with the design, manufacture and selection of the instruments themselves. The major source of the player's problems stems from poor listening habits. As has been mentioned repeatedly in this book, the importance of good, early instruction in ear-training cannot be overemphasized!

Stauffer points out three specific human (subjective) factors in wind instrument performance which affect tone quality and intonation: (1) embouchure formation or tension, (2) pressure of the air stream, and (3) volume of the oral cavity.[26] There can be no doubt that embouchure and proper breath support are critical to good tone quality and intonation. A detailed analysis of these subjects, however, is beyond the scope of this book, since each one could easily consume a separate volume in itself. Fortunately, a good deal has already been written about both of these topics, and the reader is strongly urged to consult the recommended references at the end of this chapter for further information.

---

[26] Stauffer, *Intonation Deficiencies*, pp. 119–20.

Vibrato, although not an integral part of the basic tone itself, is a factor which can enhance the beauty of a good tone as well as add to the musical expressiveness of a performance. It will be discussed in some detail at the end of this section.

1. Embouchure

Probably the most persistent and frustrating student problems in embouchure are those involving excessive tension of the lips and/or jaw, often accompanied by tension in the throat. These problems are not necessarily inherent in the player; they are usually the result of other faulty performance practices.

In brass playing, pinched lips, clenched jaw, and a tight throat can all be induced by premature high register playing. Young brass players often possess neither the physical strength in embouchure nor adequate technical knowledge to play in the upper range correctly, and yet they are expected to play the high notes scored in their band or orchestra parts. Teachers are therefore urged to exercise discretion in the music they choose for performances involving student brass players.

Biting of the reed accompanied by excessive throat tension among reed instrument players can be caused by using reeds which are too soft. As the player ascends into his upper range, a soft reed will sound flat in pitch and lacking in tonal center. The player soon discovers that he can improve both conditions somewhat by biting the tone up. In doing so, he raises the pitch and improves tonal focus but sacrifices optimum tonal resonance and richness. The solution should be sought instead through selecting and adjusting a reed until it meets the requirements of good pitch stability described earlier. A reed which is too hard, on the other hand, also forces the player to bite since his embouchure cannot control it for long. Such a reed should either be softened or exchanged for another one.

Many young flutists, like novice brass players, tend to produce a thin, pinched tone in their upper ranges. This is usually caused by excessive lip tension combined with lack of adequate breath support. Students need to be taught that breath pressure is what produces the tone; the embouchure merely controls it.

Which is more important, good intonation or good tone quality? In order to get certain notes in tune, one may need to sacrifice tone quality somewhat. If this is a recurring problem, the instrument, mouthpiece, or reed may be inferior, and purchase of better quality equipment may be in order. Assuming the equipment is satisfactory, however, there are two types of performance situation one needs to consider in trying to answer this question: (1) solo performance, and (2) ensemble performance.

Some will find it more pleasing in solo performance to hear the most beautiful tone possible, even at the expense of certain notes being slightly out of tune. This can perhaps be accepted as a reasonable attitude. In ensemble performance, however, poor intonation destroys good tone quality, since the presence of beats causes cancellation of some of the upper partials in the combined tones produced by all the instruments. Optimum resonance, tonal color, and blend are sacrificed and none of these three emerges as being really acceptable. In ensemble playing, therefore, good intonation and tone quality go hand in hand. If the player strives to produce the best tone possible, most intonation problems will disappear.

Let us apply this on a concrete level. In Chart 7, Woodwind Intonation, C and C-sharp in the staff are listed as "bad notes" for flute. Student flutists tend to play these notes quite sharp as a result of the faulty habit of rolling the embouchure hole out too far. This causes sharp intonation throughout the playing range as well as a strident tone. To correct this, the student should roll the embouchure hole inward and cover more of it with the lower lip. A good exercise for determining proper placement of the embouchure hole in relation to the player's lips is to play the following:

EXAMPLE 50

Listen carefully to the third note in each case and adjust until the note sounds at maximum resonance. It is at this point that optimum intonation for this note as well as adjacent notes usually becomes possible. Good intonation and tone quality are basically inseparable!

Let us see how this relates to the oboist. Third space C on the oboe is produced using the shortest length of the instrument. Such a note tends to be unstable in pitch and tone quality. (In the case of the saxophone, the note is C-sharp in the staff; on the clarinet, the throat tones and B and C above the staff; on the bassoon, E and F in the staff. C and C-sharp in the staff on the flute are also similarly affected, but to a lesser degree since one need not be concerned with the added problem of a reed which may be lacking in pitch stability.) But the problem of poor intonation and tone quality on the oboe's third space C is complicated still further by the tendency of young players to put too much reed in the mouth. This causes extreme sharpness in pitch and an un-controlled, strident tone. Taking less reed in the mouth should improve both pitch and tone quality. A good check for finding "the right spot" is similar to that recommended for flute (Example 51).

EXAMPLE 51

Listen carefully and adjust the amount of reed in the mouth so that the C is in tune. This will aid not only the intonation of the C but will also help ensure good intonation and tone control throughout the range of the instrument.

B and C above the staff tend to be sharp on many clarinets. Many students make them still sharper by biting the read. All too often stu-dent clarinetists are literally forced into this bad habit by their teachers. Students are told their pitch is flat: "Get it up, use more embouchure support!" The reason they are flat may be soft reeds, improper warmup or tuning, or even a pitch standard which is too high, but the clarinetist's only immediate response to a command of "get the flat pitch *up*, boy" is to bite the reed. The real solution must come via other channels, of course, since biting causes uneven pitch throughout the range of the instrument and prevents ideal resonance and blending of the clarinet tone with other instruments. At very best, the clarinetist has little flexi-bility in altering the pitch with lip tension, particularly in raising the pitch. In fact, the clarinet is the *least flexible* of all the woodwinds as regards pitch adjustment on individual notes.

The above problem may possibly be due to a misconception among some teachers that clarinetists should play at the "top side" of the tone in order to produce a tone of ideal quality. Players using soft reeds tend to play at the top side of the tone since any relaxation of the embouchure will not only cause the pitch to be flat but will also produce a wild, un-controlled tone, particularly in the upper clarion and *altissimo* registers. Given these conditions, the lesser of two evils is to bite the pitch up. But, again, this virtually eliminates all possibility of adjusting the pitch sharper when needed in ensemble playing. There is no more room left!

Assuming the reed is of sufficient strength, a range of pitches from concert A to C-sharp above the staff can be produced when blowing the clarinet mouthpiece alone. The player who repeatedly produces a C-sharp is biting. Those who produce C-natural are usually using proper embouchure support. Those who sound a B-natural or lower have an embouchure which is too relaxed. Therefore, for best intonation and tone quality, the clarinetist should strive to play in the "upper middle" of the tone (Example 52). This will allow some flexibility in pitch adjustment to the sharp side as well as the flat side and provide the means for optimum resonance and intonation throughout the range of the clarinet. Under these conditions, much of the sharpness of B and C above the staff will also be eliminated.

While biting the reed adversely affects pitch and tone quality on all reed instruments, the problem is especially critical on the saxophone. The saxophonist who bites the reed cannot possibly produce a valid pitch for tuning purposes; the pitch he produces will be very sharp. Pulling out the mouthpiece helps very little, since it literally forces him to bite up all of the other notes in order to play them reasonably well in tune. D in the staff and A above the staff will also sound sharper than they should. In addition, the tone quality will be very thin and nasal, this usually being the best clue to the source of the problem.

A range of pitches from first space F to third space C (concert pitch) can be produced on the alto saxophone mouthpiece alone. The player who consistently produces a second space A is using proper embouchure support. A player sounding a B-flat or above is biting, while one producing pitches below the A needs to use a firmer embouchure. Therefore, for best intonation and tone quality, the saxophonist should try to play in the "middle" of his tone. This will allow the greatest flexibility in pitch adjustment and will decrease the sharpness of the D and A. Players who continually bite the reed should push the mouthpiece further down onto the cork so that they are forced to *lip down* in order to play in tune.

When pedagogues compare clarinet and saxophone embouchures, they usually describe the saxophone embouchure as the more relaxed of the two. This is true, but the matter can and should be clarified further by pointing out that the clarinetist plays in the "upper middle" of the tone and the saxophone in the "middle," as illustrated in Example 52.

EXAMPLE 52

According to Springer, "The proximity of the barrel joint to the [clarinet] mouthpiece makes it the most critical point in the bore of the instrument [in its effect upon intonation, tone quality and projection of the sound]." Because of the instability of the wood of which the clarinet is made, the barrel, due to the effects of moisture and other climatic conditions, can become warped or expand ". . . far beyond its intended dimensions." Springer suggests that hard rod rubber is superior to wood as a material for making barrel joints, since it is not altered by moisture and can also be machined to specific dimensions more accurately.[27] As a result of personal playing experience, the author recommends the hard rubber clarinet barrel made and distributed by Springer, primarily for the following reasons:

1. It decreases the sharpness of the *altissimo* register and also darkens the tone, which tends to be excessively bright and even strident in some cases in this register.
2. It allows for greater resonance and projection of the tone throughout the range of the clarinet.

See Springer's article in *The Instrumentalist* for additional information. When ordering a Springer barrel be sure to indicate the make and serial number of the clarinet to be fitted, along with the make and model number of the mouthpiece, in order to assure a proper size barrel.

2. Breath Support

Inhalation and Exhalation

The breathing process involves two fundamental actions: inhalation and exhalation. Basic to the process of correct inhalation is the expansion of the abdominal area below the rib cage along with expansion of the corresponding area of the back. In correct inhalation the diaphragm muscle simply moves downward to allow maximal expansion of the lungs into these areas. This increases lung capacity for air and in turn allows the player to support the tone properly during exhalation.

Most discussions of inhalation are in agreement with the above: chest breathing, in which the abdomen is drawn in and the chest protrudes, is to be avoided. Concerning exhalation, however, the approaches differ. Some recommend that the muscles of the midriff should contract and be pulled inward and even upward in order to expel the air evenly and support the tone properly. Others feel this is absolutely wrong, the theory being that one should continue to "push against the belt" with emphasis on trying to retain the air as long as possible.

To further confuse the issue, some teachers refuse to discuss breathing procedure analytically, believing that this only creates additional prob-

[27] Lee Springer, "The Clarinet Barrel Joint," *The Instrumentalist* (June, 1960), 30–31.

lems for the student. Instead, they feel that the most important thing is to acquire a proper concept of tone and strive to emulate it. The muscles used to generate the air supply will then take care of themselves. The author is not in agreement with this attitude. While some students may not need instruction in how to support the tone properly in wind instrument playing, the great majority will need such instruction, and it is the instructor's responsibility to provide it. The reader is strongly urged to read the sources on breathing listed in the bibliography for detailed study of this subject. The items discussed in the next two subsections merely include supplementary information not commonly found in other writings.

Correct Posture

The matter of posture and playing position receives considerable attention in some schools, as can be observed at concerts where students sit in a military manner with all instruments smartly coming up to playing position on direct cue from the conductor. Good posture is certainly important to correct breathing; the visual aspects of good posture as conveyed to an audience are also important and should not be dismissed. On the other hand, one might question the advisability of overemphasizing this type of instruction to the extent that it becomes detrimental to good musical performance, as described below.

If the trunk of the body is tense and rigid, it is likely that the breathing apparatus and perhaps even the fingers will also be tense. Tenseness ruins technique, and anything which fosters undue tension should be avoided. On the other hand, an indifferent, careless attitude toward posture is not advocated. Both extremes are undesirable, and yet it would seem that a reasonably relaxed sitting position is also one which usually will be most pleasing to the audience as well as facilitating good performance. The question one must ask himself at this point is, "How do I feel most comfortable and relaxed when playing my own instrument?" This should serve as a guide for what the teacher should expect of his own players. If he is not sure what is correct, he should observe how the professionals behave in this area.

The same advice might be extended to other aspects of concert procedure. Is it really necessary for school musicians to tune and warm up backstage before a concert, or is it acceptable to do this in full view of the audience? Professional orchestras tune and warm up in full view of the audience. Also, should the stage curtain be closed until the concert is ready to begin, or is it acceptable to leave it open throughout? Again, the behavior of professional groups in this regard provides some rather definite answers to this question.

Is it better to stand up while practicing, or is it equally effective to practice sitting down? Should a student in a technique class be asked to stand during his lesson, or should he be seated? The author's personal experience has proved that many problems in breathing as well as poor head and hand positions can be avoided by having the student or class stand rather than sit while practicing. If a student is asked to stand in his lesson, the likelihood of his doing it at home through force of habit is greater.

Standing as opposed to sitting has the additional feature of not requiring a special arrangement of chairs—in fact, there is no need for any chairs at all. While this may seem to be a minor point, it has spared many an elementary instrumental teacher—who teaches in multi-purpose rooms in different schools—the headache of gathering chairs together for each day's classes. In extremely small practice rooms, a teacher can also move around and about his class more easily if they are standing, not to mention the fact that a class of flute players, for example, can more easily avoid collisions with each others' instruments when standing rather than sitting.

Players of larger instruments such as the tuba cannot conveniently stand up while practicing. It is also inappropriate to have a cellist or a bassoonist who uses a seat strap to stand. The latter assumption is also frequently made with reference to the French horn. The author suggests, on personal advice of several good horn teachers, that French horn students should also do some of their practicing standing up, in order to establish and maintain correct right hand position inside the bell as well as promote better breathing habits.

Specific Pedagogical Aids

"When the air is in, the stomach is out. When the air is out, the stomach is in." Although this explanation is not accurate physiologically speaking, this approach has been used effectively with young beginners in the teaching of proper breathing procedure. In addition to learning this rule, beginners should practice inhaling and exhaling, without their instruments and with their hands on their abdomens, in order to actually feel the movement of the abdominal muscles. Hissing the air between the teeth while exhaling is also recommended in order to more closely approximate the resistance to air pressure which exists when actually blowing into an instrument.

One means toward increasing one's ability to maintain a long breath span is to practice holding long tones. While this will surely work, it does not involve the most interesting type of practice. Instead, practicing scales, arpeggios, or a slow melody at a given metronomic marking is recommended toward increasing one's breath span. The student should choose a tempo which is within the realm of possibility and practice the scale or melody at this speed for one week. The next week, he should decrease the speed of the metronome by one notch; the following week, by still another notch. After several weeks, it is amazing how much longer one can sustain the air supply without the need for a new breath.

Other specific ideas regarding the pedagogy of breathing may be found on pp. 105–6 of Colwell's *The Teaching of Instrumental Music*.

3. Volume of the Oral Cavity

Many wind and voice teachers have long recognized the influence of the oral cavity upon tone quality and have considered it an integral part of their pedagogy. Others have questioned its validity stating that the whole idea is purely theoretical without practical or scientific basis. A survey by Aurand[28] shows, however, that many brass players do vary the size of the oral cavity through use of various vowel formations. This is done by having the tongue and jaw move through the vowel sounds *ee*, *oo*, *ah*, and *aw* when descending from the highest register down to the lowest tones on a brass instrument. But too little knowledge can be dangerous. While some professionals advocate this method and others may also use it in performance unconsciously, many authorities refrain from introducing it to inexperienced younger players. Student musicians usually tend to constrict the throat in the upper register anyway; why create still more problems in having them close it still more by thinking *ee* for high notes? Rather it is recommended that emphasis be placed upon proper breath support along with appropriate use of the pivot system for playing notes in the upper range. (See Reinhardt's *The Encyclopedia of the Pivot System*.) In other words, the theory of vowel formations may be appropriate for advanced players, but teaching it to younger, inexperienced performers should be done with discretion.

An *ee* vowel, used in sustaining a tone on wind instruments, tends to sharpen the pitch as well as brighten the tone. If a player's tone happens to be too dark or a little low in pitch, the *ee* vowel may possibly help solve this problem in some areas of the playing range. Experience has shown, however, that most student wind players tend to play their upper ranges too sharp and too bright in color to begin with. Thus, more opening of the throat rather than less is needed in the great majority of cases.

Saxophonists and bassoonists seem to be especially conscious of using an open throat so as to produce a big, open sound. Such emphasis may be the result of trying to counteract the frequent tendency of student performers on these instruments to play with a tight throat and tense

[28] Wayne O. Aurand, "Survey on Brass Instrument Playing" (unpublished study at University of Michigan, 1952).

embouchure. But caution should be exercised in not taking the term "open tone" too literally. Anyone who has ever heard a genuine open sound on the saxophone, particularly in its bottom register, will quickly agree that this is no more desirable than a very closed, tight sound. Moderation should be the rule. Like the brass player who strives for minimal mouthpiece pressure against the lips, the saxophonist should strive for an open sound but not one so open that it sounds "honky."

Some pedagogues describe the open throat sensation as a feeling of yawning. In any case the first requisite is that the student have an *aural* picture of the type of tone he is trying to produce. Listening to good recordings and concerts by professional artists can be helpful, but nothing can really substitute for private study with a genuine specialist and hearing him play his instrument *right next to you*. Students, particularly reed players, who sit in a concert hall and hear a fine artist at a distance, are often quite surprised when they hear the same artist play up close. What emerges as a beautiful, rich, mellow tone when heard in the balcony may sound somewhat harsh and overdone in the studio. Like an actor's makeup, it may be very effective at a distance but somewhat grotesque at close range. The importance of acquiring an authoritative concept of how one's tone should sound cannot be understated!

Acousticians have long realized that a tone which is rich in overtones will tend to sound sharp in pitch as compared to a pure tone of the same frequency.[29] In other words, a tone which is excessively bright in color tends to sound higher in pitch than it really is. Conversely, a dull, overly dark tone tends to sound relatively lower in pitch. One may conclude that both extremes should be avoided and that one should strive to produce a tone which is somewhere in between.

Intonation and tone quality are not the only considerations in ensemble performance. The matter of proper blending of tones must also be considered, and this is where tonal color exerts a prime influence. The problem is especially pertinent to wind instruments wherever considerable doubling of parts exists, particularly the clarinet section of the average high school band. When individual tones of this section tend toward excessive brightness, the combined tones will not blend well. Intonation discrepancies tend to sound greater to the listener's ear than they actually are. This may be due to the fact that our ears are more disturbed by beats caused by out-of-tune upper partials than they are by the beats which occur when fundamental tones or lower partials create the beating. Certainly this is true with respect to individual instruments themselves, e.g., an out-of-tune piccolo or E-flat clarinet seems to bother our ears much more than out-of-tune playing by lower-voiced instruments.

[29] Stauffer, *Intonation Deficiencies*, p. 127.

So what is the solution? Stressing proper embouchure and breath support, of course, are of vital importance. But also essential is proper emphasis upon the size and shape of the oral cavity. The throat needs to be sufficiently open so that the tone will be of suitable quality. When this is accomplished, intonation should improve, allowing for better ensemble blend.

There may be some who feel that darkening the tone of a clarinet section tends to rob it of much of its carrying power. This may seem true at first, but carrying power which is achieved principally through excessive tonal brilliance is undesirable because of the problems cited earlier. If additional carrying power is needed, this can be achieved through other, more valid means: (1) by increasing the resistance of the reeds so that more loudness and especially intensity encompassing a genuine *fortissimo* is possible; (2) by relaxing the bite on the reed—playing in the upper middle of the tone—and letting the reed vibrate properly so that optimum resonance is possible; and (3) by keeping the throat open, as in *ah*, up through the highest tones. This should provide adequate carrying power, better tone quality, and tonal blend as well as improved intonation, all in equal measure.

It is true that the size of the opening of a clarinetist's throat does decrease somewhat as he ascends into the highest register but, as with brass players, this change is frequently overdone. Let the rule be "as open as possible" but without flattening the pitch or creating an uncontrolled, wild tone. Generally, the vowel recommended for the clarinet throughout its range is *ah*.

4. Vibrato

Vibrato, according to Webster, is "a tremulous effect obtained by rapidly alternating the original tone with a slightly perceptible variation in the pitch."[30] The effect is perceived as a periodic wavering of the pitch which, when properly done, can enhance the tone, giving it added life and warmth. The slight variations in pitch are called pulsations and are produced in various ways on the different instruments.

Speed and Width

Not all performers agree on the speed or amplitude (width) of the vibrato. Jazz performers often use a relatively slow and wide vibrato in comparison to symphonic players. Since the beginning of this century, there has also been an increased tendency toward a slower, wider

---

[30] *Webster's New Twentieth Century Dictionary*, 2nd ed., s.v. "*Vibrato*."

vibrato even among symphonic players. The consensus of various authors, however, seems to be that the optimum number of pulsations per beat should be six, with a metronome setting somewhere between $\downarrow$ = 60 –72 . This is of course a generality; speed and size will vary somewhat in line with the unique requirements of a given musical passage or phrase as will be discussed in detail later.

Another question is: Should the vibrato revolve around the top side of the pitch, the bottom side, or equally on both? Most authorities agree that the pitch of the vibrato should begin on pitch and go under it. Playing above the pitch only, or both above and below, is not recommended since this involves pinching the tone up or biting the reed in the case of reed instruments.

The Five Types of Wind Instrument Vibrato

There are five types of vibrato used by wind instrument players: jaw, hand, slide, throat, and intensity or air column vibrato. The latter is also referred to as diaphragmatic vibrato by some.

Intensity vibrato is used primarily by flutists and double reed players. It can be taught by having the student think of saying *ha ha ha ha*. One successful approach of introducing it is to ask the player to slur an octave while holding the right hand against his abdomen. When this is done correctly, the student should feel a definite contraction of the abdominal muscles, which is much the same sensation he should feel when producing his vibrato. This helps the student find the right muscles for proper execution of this type of vibrato.

Students experimenting with vibrato on oboe and bassoon for the first time may try to use a jaw vibrato which is not satisfactory musically. The reason is that the jaw vibrato creates too much variation in pitch. Some flutists, on the other hand, contend that the desirability of intensity vibrato lies in the fact that there is *no variation* in pitch—that the vibrato consists entirely of variation in breath pressure or intensity. This assumption is incorrect. Anyone who disagrees need only observe a Stroboconn while using the intensity vibrato. While it is true that the pitch variation may be minimal, it still exists. In fact it is the actual variation in pitch that allows the ear to perceive the existence of a vibrato in the first place.

The hand vibrato is used on the trumpet and cornet, and reportedly by some baritone horn players as well. It is produced by moving the right hand forward and back, thereby alternating the pressure of the mouthpiece on the lips. Some trumpet and cornet players prefer to use jaw vibrato instead. Advocates (including the author) of the hand vibrato argue, however, that the problems of embouchure are difficult enough without the additional burden of jaw vibrato, thus the hand vibrato is preferred for this reason.

Slide vibrato is used only on the trombone and is performed with alternating back-and-forth movements of the right hand on the slide. Some trombonists prefer use of the jaw vibrato. Opponents of jaw vibrato use the same argument as cited above: placing an additional burden upon the embouchure should be avoided.

The jaw vibrato is used by saxophonists and by some brass players and clarinetists. It is produced by moving the jaw up and down as in saying *yaw, yaw*—some prefer *yah-ee, yah-ee.* In either case, the student should practice the syllables in front of a mirror to observe the movement of his jaw prior to attempting it on the mouthpiece alone. Emphasis should be on very slow, wide pulsations at first, disregarding the actual sound produced. In other words, concentrate on correct vibrato procedure first; worry about the sound later.

Some saxophonists suggest that the best sounding vibrato on their instrument is one which is a combination of jaw and intensity vibrato. The author is inclined to agree. A saxophone tone without proper breath intensity or support can be extremely dull and lifeless. Use of the breath push inherent in intensity vibrato helps ensure a tone which moves toward the next note.

If the above is true, why not use intensity vibrato on the saxophone and forget about the jaw? This is a reasonable question, but intensity vibrato alone is not always successful, possibly because the large size of the saxophone mouthpiece opening does not offer sufficient resistance to breath pressure, in contrast to the flute, oboe, and bassoon, whose resistance is considerably greater. Consider the size of the opening of oboe and bassoon reeds as compared to the various saxophones, especially the tenor and baritone. As can be readily realized, the opening between the reed and mouthpiece of the latter is considerably greater, and thus varying the breath intensity has relatively less effect upon the tone.

While use of vibrato on the clarinet is quite acceptable in jazz performance, only a very few non-jazz players use it consistently. Why is this? Tradition no doubt plays a part in the total picture. But also important is the inherent quality of a good clarinet sound which is rich in quantity and intensity of overtones including odd-numbered partials. The argument then is that the clarinet does not need a vibrato to "warm up" the sound. Others feel that use of jaw vibrato on clarinet makes the basic tone sound dull and flabby, making vibrato undesirable as well as unnecessary.

We sometimes hear mentioned the so-called throat vibrato, produced by the constrictor muscles of the throat. Some feel that good vibrato on the flute, for example, is probably a combination of throat and intensity vibrato. The author also recalls a discussion with one teacher who recommended throat vibrato, produced as in saying *khu, khu,* for the clarinet. It may well be that the throat muscles do in fact contribute to the production of what we call intensity vibrato. But until we are shown positive, scientific evidence, this idea, like many others, probably deserves to be categorized as part of that large body of theoretical information which has evolved concerning instrumental performance practice.

Teaching Vibrato

Some professional players believe that vibrato should not be taught but allowed to develop naturally as a result of having the player try to produce the best tone possible. This is a noble objective and one ideally to be desired, but experience has shown that it simply does not work for a great majority of students. The author believes that vibrato definitely can and should be taught, and the major function of this section is to explain how to teach it.

Regardless of the type of vibrato being studied, the general approach to learning it is essentially the same. First attempts should consist of trying to produce the widest vibrato possible with approximately one pulsation per second at $\quarternote = 60$. Primary emphasis should be placed on use of the correct muscles in producing the vibrato, rather than on improving the tone. The vibrato should at all times be even, and a speed of two or three pulsations per beat should not be attempted too soon; only one pulsation per beat should be practiced for several days until it can be done easily and naturally. Next, two pulsations per beat should be practiced, progressing to three, four, and eventually through seven pulsations. Again the emphasis should be on evenness and proper control.

Achieving these goals usually requires months and perhaps even as long as one full year in some cases. Vibrato should add to the beauty of the tone, not detract from it. A vibrato which is uneven or otherwise uncontrolled can be worse than no vibrato at all. Patience and diligence are required to master any type of vibrato studied.

One pitfall in practicing measured pulsations, particularly in even numbers, is the tendency to produce a vibrato which sounds mechanical. This is especially true when practicing four pulsations per beat where the player is very apt to accent the first of each four. Probably the major argument for practicing odd-numbered pulsations of five and seven is that it helps break down the feeling of measured pulsations especially inherent in groups of four and six. The eventual goal should be to make the vibrato sound free-flowing and natural. Complete control of the vibrato over the entire practical range of speed and width is essential in order for this to be possible.

The speed and width of the vibrato should vary somewhat with the dynamics and tonal intensity of the music played. In *pianissimo* passages, the speed of the vibrato generally should be slower and somewhat narrower than usual. As the dynamic level increases, particularly in playing a *crescendo*, the speed and width of the vibrato should usually increase accordingly. The reverse is true when performing a *diminuendo*. Some pedagogues also recommend that vibrato speed and width be slower and narrower in the lower register and become progressively faster and wider as one ascends into the upper range. Ultimate judgments in these areas must be based upon intelligent musical taste.

In order for a player to use vibrato so that it enhances his performance musically, he must be able to hear the results he produces. As with improving tone quality and intonation, this is best accomplished initially when the player is not hindered by having to read musical notation. Some teachers have their students practice vibrato on memorized pieces and scales, and this is highly recommended. Better yet, the author suggests the use of popular ballads and other slow, melodic pieces which can be played by ear. It is believed that this latter approach literally forces the student to draw upon the bulk of his musical knowledge and performing ability. Ideally, it will help him learn to enjoy practicing slow melodic music as well as fast technical exercises, and make his appreciate the skill and sensitivity required to play a so-called simple melody like Brahms' *Lullaby* or *Londonderry Air* and play it well.

Should vibrato be used on short notes, including staccato, or should it be used only in the performance of longer tones? This question puzzled the author for a number of years and the view held for quite some time was that vibrato on short notes was unnecessary and impractical. But some years ago, the author discussed the issue with a flutist who maintained that vibrato even on short staccato notes can serve a useful musical function. He proceeded to demonstrate this by playing a staccato passage first with vibrato and then without vibrato. The demonstration was a revelation. The passage played with vibrato was characterized by a bright, bell-like ring in each tone. In contrast, the passage played without use of vibrato was decidedly lacking in this quality.

Jazz singers and instrumentalists, however, appear to favor use of vibrato mainly on long tones. In fact, it is not uncommon to hear a jazz performer begin a long note with a straight tone gradually melting into a wide vibrato as the intensity and loudness is increased. These approaches to the use of vibrato are perfectly acceptable and musically valid for the style. When more ring and sparkle is desired, vibrato on staccato as well as other short note values is recommended. The sensitive musical ear must remain the final arbiter in each individual case.

Vibrato as a Remedial Teaching Technique

Some teachers insist that study and practice of vibrato should not be introduced until the student can produce a good tone. What does this really mean? Does it mean that vibrato should be delayed until the second or third year or even later? If so, why delay it this long? The author believes that undue delay in introducing vibrato makes no more sense than delaying the study of intonation or phrasing. In fact, study of vibrato can serve very effectively as a remedial technique in solving other performance problems.

Probably the most significant remedial application of vibrato study is where it is used to develop proper breath support, as discussed in Chapter Two under the BRIM Technique. Intensity vibrato is recommended here for all wind instruments, and its additional "positive side effects" are described in the above-mentioned section of this text.

A frequent problem with young saxophonists is that of a tight, pinched tone caused by biting the reed. Novice brass players often play with a pinched, thin tone caused by clenched teeth and or tightly pursed lips. All of these problems can be alleviated through practice of jaw vibrato which helps the players relax the jaw and open the throat. In addition, the hand vibrato can be used to help minimize excessive mouthpiece pressure against the lip among valved brass players. Trombonists with a tendency toward stiffness in the right arm can also learn to relax more through practice of the slide vibrato.

Note: Additional readings on vibrato may be found in books on individual instruments found in the selected bibliography at the end of this text.

E. THE STROBOCONN AS A TEACHING AID

Use of the Stroboconn (hereafter called strobe) as a means for improving tone quality and intonation has been mentioned repeatedly in this chapter. (See pp. 66, 71, 75, 79–80, 83, 110.) Consequently, one might be led to assume that the strobe is some sort of cure-all for problems in these areas. This is not at all its purpose. Used incorrectly, the strobe will be of little benefit, and in some cases it can even do more harm than good if its real purpose and limitations are not properly interpreted and understood. Used properly, however, it can be a most valuable aid to both teacher and student.

1. Basic Technical Information

1. "The Stroboconn is accurate to .05%. Measurement is accomplished by means of an electrically-driven, variable tuning fork made of special metal, Connivar, which is affected very little by changes in temperature."[31]
2. When the black spokes of the scanning disc stand still, this indicates that the pitch sounded is in tune. The black spokes rotate to the left when the pitch is flat—to the right when the pitch is sharp.
3. The Stroboconn is based upon a pitch standard of A-440 vibrations per second and the equally-tempered system of tuning. The unit of measurement used is the "cent" which is equal of 1/100 of a semitone. There are 100 cents in an equally-tempered half step or semitone and 1200 cents in an octave.

According to a Conn Corporation brochure, it is a well known fact that ". . . even the ear of the finest musician is not reliable as a standard of [pitch] measurement." Lack of sleep, mental fatigue, and even indigestion can affect one's ability to hear pitches accurately. In addition, subjective factors such as differences in loudness and tone quality may impair the ear's ability to ascertain specific pitch characteristics. The Stroboconn, however, provides the musician with an objective, visual representation of the pitch being produced. No reference tone is produced to distract or confuse the player.[32]

2. Pedagogical Uses of the Stroboconn

1. On the strobe, one can check pitches of harmonics as compared to an equally-tempered fundamental. This is particularly helpful to brass players concerned with the intonation of their natural harmonic series.
2. The tuning scale at the bottom half of the apparatus can be used to determine the exact amount in cents that a given pitch is "off center." While the player with his back to the strobe plays long tones chromatically throughout the range of his instrument, another person can record pitch variances for each note and graph these on an intonation chart. Such a graph is ofttimes shocking to the player, but also shows him which notes are the worst and which way they are out of tune.
3. When practicing *crescendos* and *decrescendos* on long tones, the player

---

[31] *Stroboconn Operation and Service Manual* (Elkhart, Ind.: Conn Corporation, 1964), pp. 3–5.

[32] *How You Can Use the Stroboconn in Your Work* (Elkhart, Ind.: Conn Corporation, n.d.), p. 2.

can watch the strobe and adjust his pitch as needed to keep it in tune throughout the change in dynamic level.

4. The strobe can be used as a pitch standard for initial tuning of the entire instrument; for this it is highly recommended. All too often, though, teachers use the strobe only for this purpose and tend to neglect its other potential uses. This is considered to be a great waste of money and instructional value.

5. Pitch variation of vibrato can also be observed on the strobe.

Other uses of the strobe are in the areas of piano and organ tuning, teaching of vocal music, and advanced music and sound theories including the psychology of music, physics of sound, and comparison of various other tuning systems to equal temperament. But the most important contributions of the strobe to the teaching of instrumental music, in the opinion of the author, are those which are discussed in the following three subsections of this chapter.

3. Centering the Tone on Wind Instruments

On wind instruments, every tone has a center or focal point where maximum resonance can be achieved. Players who learn to play in the tonal center will play the majority of their notes in tune. Only the genuinely bad notes will require alteration in order to be played in tune. On a top quality instrument such alteration should be minimal.

The reader is reminded that poor intonation and tone quality are often due to lack of proper emphasis by the teacher on these fundamentals in the student's early training. A player who has played with poor tone quality for several years eventually learns to tolerate mediocrity in this area without being unduly disturbed by it. Changing one's concept later is often quite difficult.

Another equally frustrating problem is one of a physical nature. Through drill and practice a player's embouchure and throat muscles eventually develop a certain feel for how a note is to be played. The player learns to play certain notes a particular way almost automatically through habit. This habit remains until the student is made to realize that something is definitely wrong, and that improvement depends upon alteration of his "feel" of individual notes, both aurally *and physically.* This is where the greatest value of the strobe comes in. All students and probably their teachers as well should spend some time with a strobe periodically playing pitches and, while watching the strobe, adjusting individual pitches until the spokes of the scanning discs stand still. The player should get the tuning note centered and in tune first, and then adjust the embouchure, breath support, or whatever is required until other notes surrounding the tuning note can be played in tune.

Players with severe difficulty in these areas should spend some time with the strobe daily until they develop *a physical feel* as well as aural picture for where the tone and pitch should be placed. Students who cannot master this challenge or who show very little improvement after several days of *sincere* trial should probably seek assistance from a specialist. It may be that the instrument is decidedly out of tune, but it is a rare student who cannot play his instrument in tune no matter how much the instrument is at fault. Mainly it takes patience, perseverance, and flexibility on the part of the player.

The author also has used the strobe successfully in this way with students who were in the process of changing their embouchure, who had played for years with a closed throat, who had pinched the tone, or had been biting the reed without realizing it. When used in this manner, the strobe becomes a fundamental teaching aid which every teacher should obtain and use on a consistent basis.

Another reason why students fail to center their tones properly is physical fatigue. According to Vincent Bach, brass players who overwork their embouchure through excessive loud, high range performance or extended rehearsals tend to compensate by using more lip pressure and tension thereby forcing all notes above center. This creates overall sharpness in pitch, and the player overcompensates in tuneup by pulling the tuning slide out further than should normally be required.[33] The same thing happens to woodwind players, especially saxophonists, who play on the top side of the tone continually. Learning to focus the tuning note properly first by dropping the jaw and opening the throat, followed by practice with the strobe on adjacent notes, should alleviate much of this problem.

4. Correcting Poor Finger and Hand Positions on String Instruments

Bacich suggests using the strobe for providing string students with visual proof of the negative effects on pitch caused by poor finger and hand positions. This is done by having the student play a first finger note with minimal finger pressure, followed by firm finger pressure while observing the deviation in pitch on the strobe. Minimal finger pressure results not only in lack of tonal resonance but also a sharpening of the

---

[33] Vincent Bach, *The Problem of Tuning Correctly* (pamphlet published by Vincent Bach Corp., Mt. Vernon, N.Y., 1959).

pitch. With firm finger pressure, the pitch becomes flatter but also more resonant. Firm finger pressure is especially important in pizzicato playing where its presence helps ensure a resonant ring to the tone.[34]

When the left hand wrist on violin and viola is allowed to cave in, this results in undesirable flattening of the pitch on all fingered tones. Having the student observe this on the strobe should help him be more aware of the negative consequences and thereby impress upon him the practical need for correcting his error. As Bacich points out, "An always consistent left hand position will allow the mind [and fingers] to measure pitch distances without confusion."[35]

The effect of bow pressure on intonation may be checked with a strobe by first playing open A with minimal bow pressure and then with heavier pressure. As bow pressure is increased, the pitch goes sharper and the color of the discs on the strobe become darker, the latter indicating increased tonal richness. Since the pitch goes sharp with an increase in bow pressure, this indicates the need for adjusting the fingers ". . . to accommodate added or lessened bow weight and speed."[36]

The effects on pitch of incorrect versus correct bow grip can also be observed on the strobe. Again, this visual proof should serve to help settle the issue of the importance of correct hand and finger position.[37]

Once a player can stop every disc on the strobe, does this mean he will play perfectly in tune in ensemble? Not necessarily. Very likely his intonation will have improved considerably although he will still be required to listen and adjust to other players. Sometimes this requires quite a bit of adjustment if the other player or players are struggling with a bad register or bad note on their instruments; therefore, *playing in tune* is not a matter of *being in tune* instinctively, but more a matter of *getting in tune* with other players—even if *they* are theoretically at fault!

Perhaps the greatest advantage to intonation of being able to stop the strobe's discs on every note is that of the player being able to play a mean pitch with relative ease. Once this is accomplished, minute adjustments above and below this central or equal-tempered pitch can then be more easily achieved. It has been said that at the highest artistic level one should be able to vary the pitch on individual notes a distance of 30 cents above and below the mean pitch. The player who is able to do this and has developed a keen ear should have little difficulty playing in tune.

The strobe cannot substitute for the development of a good ear, which is ultimately refined primarily through considerable, quality ensemble

[34] Anthony Bacich, "Outline for Orchestra Tuning Seminar," *Orchestra News* (September, 1970), 12.
[35] *Ibid.*
[36] *Ibid.*, p. 13.
[37] *Ibid.*

experience. But it can be an invaluable aid in helping develop the aural and physical performance attributes of the school musician. In this sense it is a pedagogical aid which every instrumental teacher should have at his disposal and use on a daily basis. It is therefore the author's strong conviction that every school rehearsal room should be equipped with a Stroboconn. If a severe lack of funds makes this impractical, then at least the less expensive Strobotuner should be purchased. Once either of these two devices has been acquired, the next step is to teach one's students how to use it properly. This should result in significant individual performance development as well as improved ensemble tone quality, intonation and blend.

F. CONCLUSION

Whenever a complex subject is studied in detail and analyzed thoroughly, there is a tendency to become so intensely engrossed in minuscule details that perspective of the whole tends to be lost. In other words, one is unable to see the forest because of the numerous leaves on the trees. The study of tone quality and intonation is no exception. Theoretical knowledge including Pythagorean tuning, pure intervals, harmonic content of a complex tone and related subjects are helpful toward a better understanding of the whole subject but have little practical value to musicians and teachers of music when viewed only as ends in themselves.

In an effort to help the reader of this chapter avoid these pitfalls, several general comments are included below. Items 1–9 and item 20 are taken from a paper delivered by Everett Gates at the MENC national convention, CBDNA Session, on March 21, 1960, in Atlantic City, New Jersey.

1. Learn as much as you can about tone quality and intonation in all of their ramifications.
2. Provide your rehearsal room with the best tuning forks, tuning bars, Lectro-Tuner, Strobo-Tuner, or Stroboconn you can afford.
3. Use small ensembles in teaching intonation.
4. Devote a portion of each rehearsal to intonation. This might include a study of beats, performance by small ensembles that can demonstrate good pitch control, performance of chords and the adjustment of pitch in various parts of the chord, chorales, unison scales, etc.
5. Tune to more than one note.
6. Adhere closely to A-440.
7. Listen to recordings and concerts by finely tuned ensembles.
8. Emphasize good tone quality, for good intonation and good tone quality are inseparable.

9. Buy the best instruments from a pitch standpoint that you can afford.

10. If possible, seat your students far apart in rehearsal so that they can hear themselves more easily. Until players become accustomed to this seating, ensemble precision of the group may suffer. Eventually, however, this problem should disappear, with tone quality and intonation being considerably improved. A desirable by-product of this type of seating is that each player learns to play with more confidence and to project his sound better.

11. Remind yourself and your students repeatedly that nothing makes an ensemble sound more amateur than poor intonation, while good intonation can allow even a beginning band or orchestra to sound semi-professional.

12. Take plenty of time for tuning at the beginning and during the rehearsal. After the instruments are properly warmed up, tune the first chair players first and then check individual players against the first chair players. Listen for beats and eliminate them.

13. Good intonation depends greatly upon proper understanding and application of other performance fundamentals, especially ear training and tone quality (the latter being controlled largely by embouchure, breathing or bowing habits). Be sure these fundamentals are accurately and thoroughly taught.

14. One's ability to play in tune depends greatly upon the quality and quantity of one's playing experience. Being able to play perfectly in tune with a strobe does not ensure good intonation when playing in ensemble or even with one other player.

15. Even though the strobe is not the final answer, it is a most useful pedagogical aid. Students who can play in tune with the strobe will usually be close enough to the pitch when playing in ensemble so that any pitch adjustment needed should be minimal.

16. Teachers need to be especially careful that they do not emphasize intonation to the point of making students nervous about the subject. Intonation is undeniably important, but not at the expense of making students agonize over the pitch of each tone that they play. Inducing player tension of this sort often creates more problems in intonation than it actually solves. Instead, primary emphasis should be on producing the best tone possible through correct embouchure, breath support, and size and shape of the oral cavity, and through hand position and bowing in string playing. These are the areas which most directly affect quality of tone which in turn allows for optimum intonation.

17. Establishment of priorities is as important in teaching intonation as in teaching a new piece of music. Intonation instruction should be presented in logical sequence. For example, a student needs to understand fully the phenomenon of beats before he can be expected to adjust the pitch of a bad note. The concept being introduced should also be relevant to the musical materials being studied. Why discuss the sharpness of low C-sharp on the cornet if the student is not yet performing regularly in D major?

18. The teacher should insist upon good intonation and train the players in such a way that it is possible to achieve it; he should not accept poor intonation as inevitable with school groups, even with younger players. Students will be critical of poor tone quality and intonation in direct relation to the importance their teacher assesses to it.

19. As in all other areas of teaching, the teacher must learn to be patient. Good intonation will not be achieved overnight. As a colleague of the author once stated, ". . . it takes about three years to teach good intonation [to youngsters] and another three years at least to refine it to highly superior. . . . If in the sixth year the music has to 'be played *into* tune,' then it is bad music. A good composer makes his own intonation, once the players really know what to listen for."[38]

20. Finally, LISTEN; for the sensitive musical ear is the final arbiter, regardless of all the scientific principles and equipment ever invented.

The purpose of the preceding comments has been to identify the most important items pertinent to the study and improvement of intonation. To those who might wish to have the subject narrowed down still more, the following two principles are offered as being the two most important things to remember:

1. Work toward production of a good tone, using the strobe as an aid.
2. Obtain lots of ensemble experience, especially in small ensemble.

As a final statement on the subject, a quote by Rosario Mazzeo sums it up best of all:

> I've heard quite acceptable players who really did not control their dynamic ranges well. Others who did not phrase well. Still others who played with less than perfect rhythm, whose dexterity left a good deal to be desired, or whose articulation was not refined. And finally some whose sounds were not of the best. These shortcomings were constant, yet each of the players involved had managed, by virtue of other qualities, to achieve a degree of success. Indeed some of the players in our symphonies are deficient in one or another of these areas. But show me one player who has really made the grade while consistently playing out of tune![39]

RECOMMENDED REFERENCES

Musical Acoustics

Bachus, John, *The Acoustical Foundations of Music*. New York: W. W. Norton and Company, Inc., 1969.

[38] Professor Paul Painter, University of Illinois.

[39] Rosario Mazzeo, "The Clarinet Master Class," reprinted from the *Selmer Bandwagon*, No. 59 (1970), published by the Selmer Division of the Magnavox Company.

Benade, Arthur H., *Fundamentals of Musical Acoustics*. New York: Oxford University Press, 1976.

Broadhouse, John, *Musical Acoustics: Or the Phenomena of Sound as Connected With Music*. 4th ed. London: W. Reeves, 1980.

Campbell, D. W. and Clive Greated, *Musician's Guide to Acoustics*. New York: Schirmer, 1987.

Culver, C. A., *Musical Acoustics*. 4th ed., New York: McGraw-Hill, 1956.

Rigden, J. S., *Physics and the Sound of Music*. New York: Wiley, 1977.

Tuning and Temperament

Barbour, J. Murray, *Tuning and Temperament*. East Lansing, MI: Michigan State University Press, 1953.

Bartholomew, Wilmer T., *Acoustics of Music*. Englewood Cliffs, NJ: Prentice-Hall, Inc., 1956. (Chapter 4, Harmony and Scales)

"Twenty-Five Hundred Years of Tone and Tuning," *Selmer Bandwagon*, No. 59 (1970), 1-31.

Intonation

Chenette, Stephen, "Use That Third Valve Slide," *The Instrumentalist* (October, 1967), 30.

Hindsley, Mark, "Intonation for the Band Conductor," *The Instrumentalist*, Part I (September, 1971, pp. 66-69); Part II (October, 1971, pp. 66-69 and November, 1971, pp. 61-64); Part III (January, 1972, pp. 59-62).

Kohut, Daniel L., *Musical Performance: Learning Theory and Pedagogy*. Champaign, IL: Stipes Publishing Co., 1992.

Long, R. Gerry, *The Conductor's Workshop*. 2nd ed., Dubuque, IA: Wm. C. Brown, 1977. (Chapters 1 and 2; Appendix 11)

Pottle, Ralph R., *Tuning the School Band and Orchestra*. 2nd ed., Hammond, LA: Ralph R. Pottle, 1962.

Stauffer, Donald W., *Intonation Deficiencies of Wind Instruments in Ensemble*. Washington, D.C.: The Catholic University of America Press, 1954.

Stegeman, William, "The Art of Music Intonation," *The Instrumentalist*. Part I (May, 1967, pp. 61-62); Part II (August, 1967, pp. 50-51); Part III (September, 1967, pp. 68-70); Part IV (October, 1967, pp. 50-52).

Reed Making and Adjustment

Berman, Melvin, *The Art of Oboe Reed Making*. Toronto: Canadian Scholars' Press, 1988.

Bowen, G. H., *Making and Adjusting Clarinet Reeds*. Hancock, MS: Sounds of Woodwinds, 1981.

Opperman, Kalmen, *Handbook for Making and Adjusting Single Reeds for All Clarinets and Saxophones*. New York: Chappell, 1956.

Weait, Christopher, *Bassoon Reed-Making: A Basic Technique*. 2nd ed., New York: McGinnis and Marx, 1980.

Breathing

Kohut, Daniel L., *Musical Performance: Learning Theory and Pedagogy*. Champaign, IL: Stipes Publishing Company, 1992. (Read all of Part III.)

Maxym, Stephen, "The Technique of Breathing for Wind Instrumentalists," *Woodwind* (December, 1952; January, February, March and April 1953).

Ramacharaka, Yogi, *The Hindu-Yogi Science of Breath*. Bombay: D. B. Taraporevala Sons & Co., Private Ltd., Copyright L. N. Fowler & Co., Ltd., 1960.

Smith, Douglas, "The Diaphragm: Teacher's Pedagogical Pet," *The Instrumentalist* (March 1966), 87, 88.

Chapter Four

BOWING
AND
ARTICULATION

One of the most confusing aspects of instrumental performance and pedagogy lies in the area of bowing and articulation. Part of this confusion is due to a lack of standardization in terminology. String players are obliged to learn terminology derived from English, French, and Italian, and thus a single bowing may have at least three different names. The existence of several variations based upon a single bowing style compounds the problem still further. Wind players are also plagued by a lack of standardization in terminology. Articulations such as have as many as four different labels. But the greatest problem for all instrumentalists is in the area of interpretation—realizing the composer's musical intentions as conveyed through his symbols of articulation.

We cannot hope to resolve in a single book all the problems of interpreting music of the past. An articulation symbol may be interpreted differently depending upon the composer, musical period, or even the tempo of the piece. Ultimately the solution lies in the performer's knowledge and understanding of musical style, since it is his concept which determines the manner in which a given piece or passage is played. This may mean altering or even disregarding certain articulation symbols in cases where the editor's symbol and the style of the piece appear to be inconsistent with each other. String players may also find it necessary on occasion to change certain bowings in their parts which may be needlessly awkward. In doing so, musical expression as well as bowing efficiency can often be improved.

Early composers of instrumental music did not always provide specific indications for bowing and articulation. (The same is even more true for tempo and dynamics.) Instrumentalists during this time presumably interpreted the music in somewhat the same way an experienced jazz musician of today reads a new jazz work or arrangement; his concept of style directs him toward proper interpretation including articulation. In cases where more than one interpretation seems valid, the players in a jazz section usually look to the "lead man" for establishing the interpretation for the section. The concertmaster in today's symphony orchestra often fulfills the same function for the violin section.

The problem is not confined to older music. Composers and arrangers have yet to get together with conductors, performers, and pedagogues in standardizing articulation symbols and defining their interpretation. Arrangers continue to be frustrated, for example, when transcribing keyboard music for wind or string instruments; how does one edit the music so that proper concepts of articulation are conveyed to the performer, particularly the less experienced performer? Is this to be left up to the teacher-conductor? Will he be able to give an authoritative opinion based on sound musicianship and knowledge of the composer's style, or will his instructions be based primarily upon subjective assumptions?

Some musicians contend that the only real answer lies in listening, score in hand, to a considerable amount of music in live performance and on recording. This is true, but a musician can spend a lifetime doing this and still not know all of the answers. What about the school musician, whose formal study of music is almost always too short in length and too sketchy in viable content? He needs to learn the subject in the most direct and concrete manner possible. Teachers in other fields have long realized this fact and have introduced appropriate shortcuts for more efficient learning. But music, like all art, does not lend itself entirely to mere mathematical or scientific analysis. To do this is to deny the artistic essence of music itself. On the other hand, some means of systematic analysis seems highly desirable in order to teach it to students. The following discussion, therefore, is an effort to categorize and clarify bowing and articulation so that the general practitioner can grasp their meaning and communicate them more easily to his students.

A teacher can hardly be expected to produce students who are competent in these areas unless he himself is a good musician and an adequate performer. Being able to describe a bowing or an articulation is rarely enough; also needed is the ability to demonstrate such nuances to the student. Failure to communicate the beautiful in music means that the essence of the art remains dormant, leaving nothing but the mechanical aspects of music which in themselves cannot be justified artistically or educationally.

A. STRING BOWING

To achieve uniformity of sound, uniformity of rhythm and uniformity of pictorial presentation for the audience, the orchestral string section should have uniformity of bow-motion within the section, uniformity of bow direction. Down-bows and up-bows should correlate and correspond. If this is not efficiently done, the picture presented to the audience is a hodge-podge of confusion and very often the musical result is lacking in convincing musical drive.[1]

This section will first include a review of the basic principles which influence bow direction. Specific bowing styles and terminology also will be presented as they apply to school string players. Finally, attention will be given to miscellaneous bowing problems and special bow effects.

1. Primary and Secondary Accents

In music which uses barlines, the beats in each measure are governed by primary and secondary rhythmic accents. In Example 53, the larger numbers indicate the primary (heavy) accents and the smaller numbers indicate the secondary (lighter) accents within the measure.

EXAMPLE 53

String players normally play heavily accented notes down-bow, because a greater volume of sound can be produced at the frog. Notes with lighter accents are normally played up-bow since the volume produced at the tip of the bow tends to be less.

In 4/4 meter the down-bow (heavy accent) corresponds to the primary accents on beats one and three. The up-bow (lighter accent) corresponds to the secondary accents on beats two and four. The bowing pattern in Example 54 illustrates this.

EXAMPLE 54

[1] Elizabeth A. H. Green, *Orchestral Bowings and Routines* (Ann Arbor, Michigan: Ann Arbor Publishers, 1957), p. 1.

In 3/4 meter, the first beat is the heaviest with the second and third beats being progressively lighter (Example 55).

EXAMPLE 55

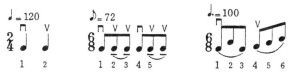

Two-four meter may be considered a derivative of 4/4. The first beat is primary and normally played down-bow; the second beat is secondary and usually played up-bow. Fast 6/8 meter may be considered a derivative of 2/4 meter and slow 6/8 a derivative of 3/4 meter (Example 56).

EXAMPLE 56

2. Bowing Styles and Terminology

The bowings indicated in Example 56 merit explanation at this point. As was mentioned earlier, discussion of this subject is not a simple undertaking. Recently, various authors have attempted to alleviate the confusion by placing bowing styles in specific groups or classifications. Green uses three classifications, namely: (1) on-the-string legato, (2) on-the-string staccato, and (3) off-the-string staccato. These will be used here as a basis for the discussion which follows.[2]

On-the-String Legato Bowings

The bowings in this category are: (1) *détaché*, (2) whole bow, (3) slur, (4) *louré*, and (5) bowed tremolo.[3]

The most basic and frequently used bowing of these five styles is the *détaché*, a legato bowing employing separate bow strokes usually performed in the middle of the bow or between the middle of the bow and the point. Generally no special symbol is used and the notes are unmarked, although occasionally the abbreviation M.B. (middle bow) is used.

[2] Green, *Orchestral Bowings*, pp. 58–59.
[3] *Ibid.*, p. 58.

What is referred to as whole bow by Green is called *grand détaché* by
Kennan. This bowing uses the entire length of the bow. If only about
one-third of the bow is used, Kennan labels it *détaché moyen*. When only
the point is used, the style becomes *petit détaché*.[4]

Galamian takes us a step further with a version called *accented or articulated détaché*, accompanied by a ". . . sudden increase in bow speed
and pressure" at the beginning of the stroke. The notes generally should
not be separated, and smooth legato connection should be maintained.[5]

(Marking symbol: ♩)

Still another variation is the *détaché lancé* (marking symbol: ♩). A
slight separation is used but without any accent. Although this is somewhat like a *martelé* stroke, the feeling of legato should be maintained.[6]

Détaché porté (♩) is performed with a slight stress on the beginning
of the note—rather like a *tenuto* effect. Although the marking is somewhat like *louré*, separate bows rather than the same bow are used for
performing a series of notes.

The *slur* (Galamian also calls it *legato*) is executed by moving the bow
". . . smoothly in one direction while the fingers change the notes on
the string or strings."[7] While the slur produces a highly connected legato
style, it is also used to help control the normal pattern of bow direction
in accordance with rhythmic accent (Example 57).

EXAMPLE 57

In *louré* bowing, "the bow *continues its motion* as in any slur, but releases pressure slightly between notes so that the notes become somewhat articulated."[8] (Marking symbol: ♩ ♩) *Louré* also has the combined
features of the *détaché* and the slur since it is "used for expressiveness

---

[4] Kent Wheeler Kennan, *The Technique of Orchestration*, 2nd ed. (Englewood
Cliffs, N.J.: Prentice-Hall, Inc., 1970), p. 55.
[5] Ivan Galamian, *Principles of Violin Playing and Teaching* (Englewood Cliffs,
N.J.: Prentice-Hall, Inc., 1962), pp. 67–68.
[6] *Ibid.*, pp. 68–69.
[7] Green, *Orchestral Bowings*, p. 58.
[8] *Ibid.*

in slurs where the notes need emotional individuality, and in slurred bowings on the *same pitch* to distinguish rhythm."[9] Its Italian counterpart is *portato*.

The *bowed tremolo* is performed with very short and fast separate bows, most often at the middle of the bow or between the middle and point. (Symbol: ♪ ♪) It is usually used "for the excitement of a fast shimmering effect in chordal accompaniments or in melodic playing."[10]

On-the-String Staccato Bowings

The two basic types of on-the-string staccato bowings are: (1) *martelé*, and (2) slurred or linked staccato.

Martelé (It., *martellato*) is produced by applying pressure on the bow at the beginning of the note, releasing the pressure after the attack, and stopping the bow on the string to release the note. The usual symbol is ♩ , but occasionally ♩ or ♩ may also be used. It can perhaps best be described as a quick, hammer-like stroke—a *marcato* bowing style. Another variation is the *sustained martelé* mentioned by Galamian where the usual *martelé* accent remains but the release is not abrupt and separated—more like a *détaché* release. The symbol for the *sustained martelé* is ♩ .[11]

The speed of all *martelé* bowings is limited since the bow must be prepared for each note. Beyond a certain point the player must use off-the-string staccato bowing in order to maintain clarity and lightness of style.

Slurred or linked staccato ♩ ♩) is similar to *louré* bowing in that the bow continues in the same direction for the duration of the slur marking. The chief differences are in the attack and release. The slurred staccato is performed much like the *martelé* but with only a slight accent at the beginning. The release is accomplished by stopping the bow on the string. Although the slurred staccato, like the *louré*, is occasionally played down-bow, it is used most often on the up-bow. Like the short slur, *louré* and slurred staccato are sometimes used to help control the normal pattern of bow direction in accordance with rhythmic accent in the measure.

---

[9] *Ibid.*
[10] *Ibid.*
[11] Galamian, *Principles of Violin Playing*, p. 73.

Off-the-String Staccato Bowings

The bowings in this category are: (1) *collé,* (2) *spiccato,* (3) *sautillé,* (4) *staccato volante,* (5) *ricochet,* (6) *ricochet tremolo,* and (7) *fouetté.*

Collé is a very short, light stroke produced at the frog with the bow leaving the string after each note. The fingers are straightened out in spring-like fashion and assume a normal curved position after the attack.[12] The effect is much like that of *pizzicato.* There is no special marking for this bowing style.

In *spiccato,* the bow is dropped on the string and rebounds on its own. The symbol used is the staccato dot, the same as for *martelé.* While *martelé* is confined to slower tempi, *spiccato* is used in fast tempi when more lightness and agility is required. Green refers to this type as *controlled spiccato.* In moderate tempi coupled with loud dynamics, the *chopped spiccato* or heavier spiccato is used. (Symbol: $ff \overset{\textstyle\bullet}{>}$)

Sautillé or uncontrolled *spiccato,* performed with separate bows flying off the string, is used in *very fast* tempi where *extreme* lightness of style is required. The symbol used is the staccato dot.

Staccato volante or flying staccato is akin to the slurred staccato in its marking: ♪ ♪ ♪ ♪ . Used in fast tempi, it is limited to the up-bow stroke with the bow dropped on the string and rebounding after each note without changing direction.

Ricochet (also called *jeté* and *saltando*) is marked in the same manner as slurred *staccato* and *staccato volante* except its use is limited to *down-bow only.*

Green mentions the *ricochet tremolo* which is used in fast tremolos of long duration where the single *spiccato* is less practical. It is played middle of the bow with "two down-bow bounces followed by two up-bow bounces"[13] (Example 58).

EXAMPLE 58

Prestо

Galamian mentions still another off-the-string bowing called *fouetté* or

---

[12] Samuel Applebaum, *Building Better Strings and Orchestras* (Rockville Center, N.Y.: Belwin, Inc., 1960), p. 62.
[13] Green, *Orchestral Bowings,* p. 59.

whipped bow. (Symbol: ⨍) "It is derived from the accented *détaché*, but here the accent is produced by quickly (and barely) lifting the bow off the string and striking it down with suddenness and energy."[14]

3. Miscellaneous Bowing Problems

Normally, the first beat of a measure is played down-bow and an anacrusis is played up-bow. Green points out an exception to this general rule which she calls the *Law of Compensation*. "The *Law of Compensation* states that if the bowing naturally readjusts itself in the space of two measures, the player need not change it in any way"[15] (Example 59).

EXAMPLE 59

As seen in Example 59, this law is particularly applicable to music written in 3/4 meter. It should be applied to other time signatures as well when the style and tempo of the music require it.

For physical as well as musical reasons, wind players separate musical phrases with a brief silence when taking a new breath. School string players, with no physical need for breathing, sometimes tend to play continuously without ever lifting the bow. The result is musical monotony and poor phrasing between the winds and strings. String players, like wind players, need to be taught when to "breathe" and, if necessary, to mark the parts with a comma (,) so that all players will phrase together.

According to Green, "The dotted-eighth-with-sixteenth figure is generally played on *one* bow, the bow stopping momentarily between the notes."[16] (Example 60.)

EXAMPLE 60

---

[14] Galamian, *Principles of Violin Playing*, p. 69.
[15] Green, *Orchestral Bowings*, p. 12.
[16] *Ibid.*, p. 27.

The bowing in Example 61, at the tempo indicated, is similar to Example 60. Green refers to both of these as "linked bowing," which is essentially a slurred staccato style used to avoid rhythmic distortion and to provide ease in bowing technique.[17] Both Example 60 and 61 are performed by stopping the bow momentarily before and after the linked second note.

EXAMPLE 61

Another exception to usual bowing technique is seen in Example 62. Notice that when the upbeat is slurred over the barline, the entire slur is played down-bow.[18]

EXAMPLE 62

A final consideration is the relationship of slurs and separate bows to dynamic levels of tone. When a loud dynamic is desired, separate bows will achieve this goal most easily and effectively. Separate bows are also recommended when the style is *marcato*. In *legato* passages at a moderate tempo and a soft dynamic, the slur is usually preferred. Also important is the fact that ". . . crescendos are somewhat easier on an up-bow;" conversely, the down-bow achieves a diminuendo more easily, particularly when the diminuendo is tapered to a whisper with complete silence at the end.[19]

4. Special Effects

Although the following terms do not specify bowing style or articulation, they are included here to differentiate them from the actual bowing styles just discussed.

Col legno means that the wood rather than the hair of the bow should

---

[17] *Ibid.*, p. 29.
[18] *Ibid.*, p. 12.
[19] Kennan, *Technique of Orchestration*, p. 53.

be used in playing on the string. It is a dry, brittle effect used for special, repeated rhythmic effects.

Sul ponticello means to play near the bridge. The sound is very bright and tinny, giving a rather shuddering effect.

Sul tasto or *sur la touche* means to bow the string over the fingerboard, resulting in a tone which is more mellow, dark, and soft than a normal tone. Use of this effect is found most often in scores by French composers, according to Kennan.[20]

B. WIND INSTRUMENT ARTICULATION

Orchestras will produce better sounding music when all concerned—composers, conductors, and performers—agree on the articulations to be used in passages played by the wind instruments. To convey this information in writing, we must have symbols that mean the same to all persons concerned. These do not exist at the present time, but we must work toward that goal.[21]

While several authors have addressed themselves to the task of categorizing and explaining string bowing, comprehensive discussions of wind articulation and notation are nonexistent. This does not mean that standardization of wind articulation is any less important. On the contrary, performers in wind bands and chamber ensembles need just as much if not more concrete direction in this regard. While orchestral wind players can imitate the articulations of the string section to some degree, players in a band or wind ensemble must assume a more independent role; they need to know how to coordinate the tongue and the breath so that accurate, artistic articulation is possible.

The lack of standardization of wind articulation symbols and their exact meanings has resulted in a number of mis-markings in editions of orchestral wind parts and wind music in general. For example, it is incorrect to assume that wind articulations should always directly correspond to bowing indications in the string parts. Musical passages which can be played smoothly with separate bows (*détaché*) by the string section, for example, may need to be marked slurred for the winds in order to achieve a more uniform, musical effect.

Transplanting *louré* and slurred *staccato* markings into the wind parts can also complicate matters. One should remember that these bow markings serve the string player in two ways: (1) they affect musical style; (2) they also indicate bow direction. Since wind players are not

---

[20] *Ibid.*, p. 62.
[21] Merle J. Isaac, *Practical Orchestration: A Method of Arranging for School Orchestras* (Robbins Music Corporation, 1963). Used by permission.

concerned with bow direction, the slurs in *louré* and slurred *staccato* markings may be superfluous, and use of another marking can often convey proper wind articulation more effectively.

Wind instrument teachers who have neglected to read the preceding section on string bowing are urged to go back and read it before going ahead to the next section. Since today's wind instrument performance and teaching is still largely dominated by orchestral wind players, an understanding of the musical effects created in orchestral playing is highly important. At very least, such understanding should allow for easier comprehension of interpretation as it pertains to wind articulation.

1. Tone Production

The tongue, the lips, and the breathing mechanism are the wind player's bow, and much of the technique of clean articulation and phrasing is directly dependent upon the player's ability to coordinate the individual muscles which control them. A major cause of faulty attacks is inadequate breath support when the tongue is released. Also, players who relax the breath after each note in a sustained, legato passage fail to achieve musical continuity in phrasing. The student must therefore learn to synchronize his tongue and breathing mechanism so that articulations from the smoothest slur to the shortest *staccatissimo* are possible.

Unlike the string teacher, who can observe problems in bowing visually, the wind teacher cannot observe the size and shape of the wind player's oral cavity or the movements of his tongue. Frequently he has to diagnose performance problems primarily on the basis of what he thinks a player may or may not be doing *inside* the oral cavity. Sometimes his only choice may be to teach a particular type of tonguing through imitation of sound alone. It is therefore important that the teacher have a comprehensive understanding of this subject in order to teach it intelligently.

Tongue Position

A theory generally accepted among brass players is that the tongue is placed at the base of the upper teeth or near the gum line for normal tonguing. Occasionally the tongue may be placed between the teeth on the lower brasses in order to facilitate production of the instruments' lowest tones, but such usage is rare and should not be employed indiscriminately. As the player moves in the direction of legato attacks, the tongue tends to move further back and touch the roof of the mouth in order to cushion the release of the air. (See Hunt's *Guide to Teaching Brass Instruments* for illustrations of brass tonguing positions.)

The flutist's tongue operates much like that of the brass player. According to Timm, "The tip of the tongue [in flute performance] may work anywhere from the roof of the mouth to between the lips." Tonguing between the lips should be confined to "exceedingly sudden attacks," however, and is "especially effective in the low register."[22] Hauenstein, on the other hand, states that the flutist's tongue *should not* be placed on the teeth, but that the top of the tongue should *touch the gum above the upper teeth.* Use of the tongue between the teeth is rare and, when used, should be limited to one attack at a time.[23]

The reed player touches his tongue against the reed rather than the upper teeth. A standard formula which has evolved with regard to clarinet playing is to have the tip of the tongue against the tip of the reed. While this is a simple and concrete explanation, the validity of this concept is questionable. First of all, such tongue action can often produce a rather heavy attack. It can also limit tonguing efficiency at faster speeds. Instead, the following method is recommended for clarinet players: place the tongue about one-quarter of an inch below the reed tip, using the top side of the tongue slightly beyond its tip. This approach helps avoid excessive tongue pressure since the tongue is placed lower down on the reed. It also helps minimize extraneous tongue movement, thereby making it easier to tongue more rapidly.

On the saxophone the player's tongue normally touches the reed tip since the mouthpiece enters the mouth horizontally rather than obliquely as with the clarinet. The tendency toward closing the reed against the mouthpiece on the saxophone is not as prevalent as on the clarinet, presumably because the tip opening is significantly larger. But the area of the tongue touching the reed is the same as on clarinet: the top side of the tongue beyond the tip touches the reed, not the actual tip of the tongue.

Single reed players who wish to determine specifically how they tongue can do so by applying food coloring to the tongue, tonguing the reed, and then checking to see where the coloring rubbed off on the reed. The reverse procedure may be used to determine which part of the tongue actually touches the reed. Until such time when research via X-ray or some other process can define woodwind tongue action and position more scientifically, this test should serve to illuminate the situation insofar as it applies to individual reed instrument performers. (For additional information concerning woodwind tongue position, see Westphal's *Guide to Teaching Woodwinds* and Edlefsen's *Symbolization and Articulation of Oboe Tones.*)

---

[22] Everett Timm, *The Woodwinds: Performance and Instructional Techniques* (Boston: Allyn and Bacon, 1964), p. 39.

[23] Nelson Hauenstein, *The Flute: Tonguing and Articulation* (pamphlet distributed by W. T. Armstrong Co., Elkhart, Ind., n.d.).

Double reed players, particularly oboists, tend to close the reed tip opening when tonguing against the center of the lower blade. This results in a hard, accented attack. To avoid this, some oboists and bassoonists employ the following procedure: the reed is turned *slightly* to the right and the instrument also moved *slightly* to the right. This places the reed in a position so that the tongue touches the right hand corner of the lower blade. This keeps the reed from vibrating until the tongue is withdrawn but does not close the tip opening. As with single reed instruments, it is not the tip of the tongue which touches the reed but an area just beyond the tongue tip. In this case, however, the reed tip (lower right hand corner) is the contact point and not an area further down the reed as is the case on the clarinet.

The generalizations in this discussion are made in reference to the student with average tongue length. A player with an unusually short or long tongue, however, may need to alter the placement of his tongue against the reed, the upper teeth or roof of the mouth. Any deviation of this sort should be made, of course, only after careful consideration of all related factors which might make such deviation desirable and prudent.

Anchor Tonguing

Anchor tonguing involves placing (anchoring) the tip of the tongue against the lower teeth with the area behind the tip of the tongue moving up and forward to touch the reed. The tip of the tongue remains anchored against the lower teeth and does not pull away during the attack. While this type of tonguing is generally not advocated, some single reed players use it and presumably prefer it. If one inherits an advanced student who has learned to use this method successfully, then the student should probably be allowed to continue using it; otherwise the more traditional type of tonguing is recommended, especially for those who are in the formative stages of tonguing development.

Mention should be made regarding a modified style of anchor tonguing for oboe discussed by Westphal[24] and Sprenkle. Sprenkle recommends that the tip of the tongue be allowed to rest "gently against the top of the lower lip" which positions the tongue between "the 'V' formed by the reed and the lower lip."[25] The top of the tongue tip moves up and down to contact the reed rather than back and forth like that of a snake. (The latter statement applies to normal tonguing for all of the wind instruments, excluding heavy accents on brass instruments and the flute which will be discussed in detail in the next chapter.)

[24] Frederick Westphal, *Guide to Teaching Woodwinds* (Dubuque, Iowa: Wm. C. Brown, 1962), p. 132.
[25] Robert Sprenkle and David Ledet, *The Art of Oboe Playing* (Evanston, Ill.: Summy-Birchard, 1961), pp. 8, 14.

The Attack Syllables

The attack involves the tongue releasing the air to start the tone on a wind instrument. A number of teachers avoid using this term since they feel it implies a connotation of pronounced accent at the beginning of a tone. While this may be true, the term is used here for purposes of clarity since it is a standard word understood by most performers and teachers.

In playing a series of unmarked detached notes, the syllable normally used is one which begins with the consonant "t." As for the complete syllable, there are several variations of vowel sounds used: *tawh, too, tah,* and *tee.* Brass players may use all of these vowels at various times depending upon the range in which they were playing. Woodwind players sometimes prefer one over the others. For example, some clarinetists choose to use only the *tawh;* some flutists prefer to use *tee,* reportedly because this syllable more closely approximates the feeling of a correct flute embouchure. In any case, when one of the "t" syllables is used in playing a series of unmarked detached notes, the musical effect is akin to a slightly accented *détaché* bowing. This also means that breath pressure should not be relaxed until the end of the phrase or until a written rest appears in the music.

If the style is marked *legato,* a "d" syllable as in *doo* or *dah* is used (some teachers prefer *loo* or even *noo*). In slow *pianissimo* passages, legato syllables may also be in order. Musically, the result should correspond to the smooth *détaché* in string bowing. Physically, the tongue of a brass player or flutist moves back toward the roof of the mouth depending upon the lightness of articulation desired. Reed players must be especially careful to avoid excessive tongue pressure against the reed in legato playing. The more pressure that is used, the more pointed and accented the attack will be.

Double and Triple Tonguing

This type of tonguing is used primarily by flutists and brass players in performing a variety of detached duplets, triplets and quadruplets at a rapid tempo—a tempo at which regular single tonguing would be quite difficult if not impossible. Basically these tonguings alternate a "k" syllable with the regular "t" syllable. In double tonguing the pattern is *tu ku tu ku* etc. In triple tonguing two variations may be used: *tu tu ku* or *tu ku tu.* Brass players who use the vowel concept as it relates to different playing ranges may prefer to use *tu ku* in the lower range, *ta ka* in the middle range, and *tee kee* in the upper range.

In order to produce a more legato effect, *da ga* and *da da ga* are sometimes used. Flutists especially seem to prefer the "g" syllable over the "k" syllable. Even in non-legato passages, flutists often prefer the "g" syllable as in *ta ga* or *ta da ga* since they claim these syllables are easier to use and create a lighter tonguing effect.

The use of double and triple tonguing by reed players is not very common and the reasons why this is true should be fairly obvious. While one could cite certain reed players by name who have developed this type of tonguing to a high level, it is only fair to point out that these players are the exception, not the rule. Even those who accept its use in reed instrument performance admit that perfecting the technique is difficult and tedious. Experience has shown that proper development of the single tongue including proper execution of the tongue release will fulfill the needs of most reed players at the public school level; therefore, double and triple tonguing are advocated primarily for flutists and brass players, not reed players.

Since double and triple tonguing are primarily related to rapid tongue technique, no further discussion of these tonguings will be included here. Numerous writings including detailed explanations on this topic are already available, and the reader is urged to consult these sources for additional information.

2. The Basic Articulations

There are four types of basic articulations: (1) the slur, (2) the *tenuto*, (3) detached notes, and (4) slow staccato. All other wind articulations are considered as derivatives of these and will be discussed in the following subsection.

The Slur

Since young students frequently confuse the meaning of a slur and a tie, it is recommended that the two be introduced and explained concurrently. A *slur* is a curved line connecting two or more notes of *different pitch*, the first note of which is tongued and the others connected smoothly without use of the tongue. A *tie* is a curved line connecting two notes of the *same pitch;* the first note is tongued, the second note is held through without tonguing. The tie has rhythmic significance, while the slur has to do with articulation. Breath pressure should remain constant throughout an entire slur or tie.

Students are often confused when they encounter what appears to be a tie and a slur combined (Example 63).

In order to sound the second note in Example 63, a legato "d" attack should be used, otherwise the first two notes will sound tied together. The G and the A should be connected in the usual manner without use of the tongue.

EXAMPLE 63

Syllables: tah   dah ————

An instrument with a unique problem in slurring is the trombone. If a trombone player tongues only the first note of a slur and tries to slur the others without tonguing, he will produce, in most cases, a smear or *glissando*. To avoid this, a soft legato tongue ("d" syllable) should be used on each note of the slur, combined with rapid, efficient movement of the slide.

There are instances where the *glissando* problem on trombone will not be present. One of these is where the notes used appear in the natural harmonic series of the instrument, all played with the same slide position. This type is referred to as the natural slur. The other instance is where the trombone slide moves in contrary motion to the direction of the melodic line. This is called a contrary motion slur. In the contrary motion slur as in the natural slur, the *glissando* is not present. The trombonist can therefore connect the notes without legato tonguing, the same as other wind players. But when the slide and melodic line move in similar directions, the *glissando* effect is inevitable requiring the use of a legato tongue (Example 64).

EXAMPLE 64

Natural Slur

Contrary Motion Slur

Similar Motion Slur

Slide position: 1 1 1 1   1 3 ♭4   1 2 4 6
Syllables: tah ————   tah ————   tah dah dah dah

The natural slur in Example 64 contains the third, fourth, and fifth partials of the harmonic series based upon pedal B-flat in first position. The player need only adjust his breath support and lip tension in order to produce the pitches desired. In the contrary motion slur, the player must play the third note D in flat fourth position rather than first position in order to keep the slide moving in an opposite direction to the melody. Use of first position D in this example would create similar slide-melodic motion requiring a *dah* tonguing to prevent a *glissando*. The similar motion slur requires use of *dah* tonguing throughout, since the slide and melody both move in similar (in this case downward) motion.

To the non-trombonist, slurring on the trombone may seem quite confusing. In performance, particularly sightreading, how does the player determine quickly which of the three slurs should be used? Player experience and competence usually determine ability in selectivity. Just like the woodwind player who responds almost automatically to the use of alternate fingerings in certain passages, the experienced trombonist will know which type of slur is best suited to the specific passage being played.

Most slurred passages for trombone will require at least some use of legato tongue. If this is true, why not use legato tongue all the time and thereby eliminate confusion, particularly with young players? Some teachers feel that this is in fact the most practical solution. Others believe that the natural and contrary motion slurs should not be neglected since they produce a more genuine slur, thus creating a more beautiful interval in music where very smooth connection of tones is desired. Regardless of one's point of view, this much is certain: the legato tongue slur must be performed with accuracy and finesse or else it will never approximate acceptable legato style.

In developing a good legato tongue on trombone, the player should first practice legato tonguing on a single pitch like first position F in the staff. Next, the F should be alternated with E in second position, a half step lower. The slide should be moved quickly between notes with emphasis on relaxed wrist movement of the right hand. This should be followed by F to E-flat in third position, F to D in fourth position, etc.

The same procedure can be used for other first position notes of the harmonic series such as the B-flat above and the low B-flat in the staff. Example 65 illustrates a legato tongue exercise based upon F in the staff. Notice that the tempo marking is slow and the note values are relatively large. This is so the player can learn to coordinate rapid slide action with the tongue and still give attention to intonation as well. Later, as progress allows, the speed should be gradually increased.

EXAMPLE 65

Being able to produce a good slur is one of the most important facets of artistic trombone technique. There is no real shortcut to mastery of this fundamental; it requires patient practice and perseverance. Those who are willing to work toward its accurate execution, however, will be amply rewarded in the beauty of style and phrasing which it provides.

The Tenuto

Tenuto (marking: ♩) means to play the note full value and often implies legato style as well to the wind player. Consequently, one would assume that one of the "d" syllables should be used for starting the tone, but not everyone agrees on this point. Timm states that the regular "t" syllable should be used.[26] Isaac points out that ". . . the tone is to be tongued neither lightly nor forcibly, but just in the ordinary manner."[27] If these viewpoints are accepted, then how does one distinguish between *tenuto* articulation and the performance of normal, detached notes? (Detached notes without staccato dots are normally played full value.) If one agrees that *tenuto* also implies legato style ("d" syllable), then how does the normal *tenuto* differ from the slurred *tenuto* marking? (♩ ♩) Considering that the *tenuto* symbol is also sometimes used to indicate agogic accent (a slight lengthening of the tone), the ambiguity of this symbol is further amplified.

We can be relatively certain of only one aspect of the definition of the word *tenuto:* a note so marked should be sustained full value. The *Harvard Dictionary of Music* supports this definition and so do most pedagogues. The author leaves it to the reader to use his own judgment in resolving the question from a given stylistic standpoint.

Detached Notes

Notes in wind instrument parts which are unmarked with reference to articulation should be tongued. (This is akin to string bowing where the absence of bow markings implies *détaché* or separate bows.) The tonguing syllable normally used is the "t" syllable. Slow, melodic passages often imply legato style, and so the "d" syllable should be used. Faster dance-like or martial styles require more pointed attacks ("t" syllable) accompanied by appropriate spacing or separation between successive notes. Any deviation from this normal pattern will usually be indicated by the composer or arranger through use of symbols, e.g., accent, staccato, or *tenuto* marks, or via written terms, e.g., *sempre legato, marcato, staccato,* etc. This is not always done, but composers and arrangers are reminded that young players in particular need this information, especially when rehearsal time is at a premium. In cases where the composer or arranger fails to give adequate direction, the conductor-teacher is advised to supply the missing information by editing each part personally *prior* to the first rehearsal. This will help avoid boring the players with time-consuming instruction during rehearsal and will free extra time for polishing the group's performance in other areas.

---

[26] Timm, *The Woodwinds*, p. 8.
[27] Isaac, *Practical Orchestration*, p. 113.

Slow Staccato

How do we define the word *staccato?* Ask this of a pianist or string player and the definition given may be considerably different from that given by a wind player. But even if it were possible for all three players to reach some consensus on the subject, the matter of interpretation, as related to the traditions of various musical periods, would require additional compromise of any general definition previously adopted.

We are told that Baroque staccato notes should generally be longer than in music written by nineteenth-century composers. In contemporary music, wind players are often expected to produce very short, dry staccato effects. Supposedly the only real answer lies in listening to and analyzing authoritative recorded or live performances of representative composers from all musical periods and basing one's conclusion upon what is heard. But how does one introduce a student, particularly a beginner, to staccato without misleading him or being unnecessarily vague in one's explanation?

Generally speaking, staccato means short in duration and light in style. More specifically it means to play the note at approximately half its value. Based on this definition, quarter notes and eighth notes should be played as indicated in Example 66.

EXAMPLE 66

Written

Played

The analogy illustrated in Example 66 is a traditional one found in several standard beginning method books. Accompanying this is usually the suggestion that the rests be created by stopping the breath. In order to execute a good staccato in this manner, the player must learn to coordinate the tongue, fingers, and breathing mechanism effectively; otherwise the tone may be distorted by lack of sufficient air pressure behind the tongue at the moment of the attack.

For the beginner, the half-value staccato generalization has proved to be useful, but only as a simplified introduction. Obviously this generalization will not hold true for longer note values and staccato notes in slow tempi. Such notes will usually need to be played longer than half value. In slow tempi staccato eighths should also be played longer unless staccatissimo (♪♪) is indicated. Note values and tempo as well as style, therefore, have a direct influence on the length of staccato notes and must not be ignored.

Care should be taken that young players do not acquire the careless habit of playing regular detached notes in staccato fashion, i.e., "huffing and puffing" for each note. Unless the notes are marked staccato, regular detached notes usually should be played in one breath without any breath separation. The only separation which should occur is when the tongue is used to enunciate a new note, and generally this interruption of the tone should be minimal. The tongue is used simply as a valve to release kinetic air pressure which remains constant until reaching a written rest or the end of a phrase.

The chart below is an attempt to group all of the basic articulations together so that the differences and similarities of each can be more easily understood. It is also hoped that the pictorial diagrams of each articulation will be helpful in illustrating the abstractions of articulation in a more concrete setting.

Chart 10

BASIC ARTICULATIONS

Label	Marking Symbol	Pictorial Diagram	Interpretation
The Slur			Tongue the first note and connect all others smoothly by change of fingering and maintaining constant flow of breath.
The Tenuto		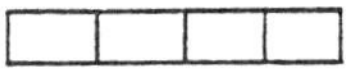	Sustain notes full value; implies use of legato tongue although this point is controversial.
1) Detached notes	(♩ = 60)		"d" syllable used with same separation between notes.
2) Detached notes	*sempre legato* (♩ = 132) 2/4 *sempre marcia*		"t" syllable used with definite separation between notes. For more definition, such a series of notes may be played with a slight dynamic accent.
Slow Staccato	(♩ = 96 ) (♩ = 72 )	 	Definite silence between each note, the exact amount determined by tempo, note value and musical style; each note slightly tapered due to breath release.

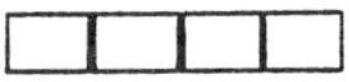

3. Combined Forms of Basic Articulations

EXAMPLE 67

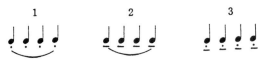

Considerable confusion exists in reference to labeling of the articulations in Example 67. One author calls the first one *portato*, another calls it *legato staccato*, a third one *semi-staccato*, and a fourth one *half-staccato*. The first label, *portato*, has also been used to identify the third articulation which uses both the *staccato* and *tenuto* symbols. (Galamian calls the second articulation *portato* in reference to string bowing.)

Diversity of opinion in regard to the articulations in Example 67 is not confined to editing and labeling problems alone. Performers, teachers, authors, and conductors also disagree regarding their musical interpretation. In reference to the first articulation, Whybrew attempts to clarify the issue as follows:

> . . . This marking [ ] is commonly used to indicate legato tonguing for the winds, a technique more similar to the interrupted legato of the strings. Legato tongue for the winds would be more accurately indicated by the use of dashes with a curved line ( ).[28]

Timm also points out that the marking is sometimes used incorrectly in the edition of wind parts. In his view, this articulation should be legato tongued with ". . . more of a lightening between notes than an actual cessation of each tone." (He labels this marking *portato*.)[29]

To present the problem in still another way, Timm labels ( ) as *tenuto legato*, stating that it should be played in the same manner as ( ). ". . . except that each note is caressed slightly.[30] Cuirczak labels this articulation simply "stress marks under slurs."[31] Issac states that legato tongue ". . . is indicated with a slur and *either* dots or dashes" and that both ". . . are played in much the same way."[32] Teal does not include the articulation ( ) in his discussion.[33]

---

28 William Whybrew, "A Basic Course in Arranging for School Orchestra" (unpublished doctoral thesis, Eastman School of Music, 1953), p. 42.

29 Timm, *The Woodwinds*, p. 8.

30 *Ibid.*

31 Peter L. Cuirczak, "The Symbols of Style," *The Instrumentalist* (December, 1964), 52.

32 Isaac, *Practical Orchestration*, p. 114.

33 Larry Teal, *The Art of Saxophone Playing* (Evanston, Ill.: Summy-Birchard, 1963).

It seems unnecessary to belabor the point any further: the lack of standardization in labeling and interpretation of wind articulations is obvious and needs to be resolved. Even though nothing can be done to alleviate the diverse editing practices of music written in the past, the intention here is to establish a guide for articulation edition which can benefit today's composer and arranger whose notes are yet to be written. Isaac points out that "Musicians would do well to clarify markings such as these, because finer distinctions in meaning would produce better interpretations."[34] The question is what shall serve as the prime basis for decisions in these matters? One answer is to utilize the precedent given us by string players. As stated earlier, orchestral wind players frequently emulate the style of the string section, and we still tend to look to our wind artists in the major orchestras as our primary sources of guidance and inspiration.

There are some who argue that the "typical" band style and orchestral style are not necessarily synonymous. This may be true to a degree, but one might also seriously question whether such diversity of opinion can truly be justified in a genuine musical context. Insofar as articulation and musical expression are concerned, there should be practically no difference if one accepts the idea that the composer or the musical period should exert the greatest influence, rather than the conductor or the medium of performance. Regardless of one's point of view, we all surely agree that the basic problem of standardization of wind articulations merits our critical attention and sincere efforts toward solution. It is hoped that the following chart may at least serve as partial fulfillment of this objective.

Chart 11

COMBINED FORMS OF BASIC ARTICULATIONS

Label	*Marking Symbol*	*Pictorial Diagram*	*Interpretation*
Tenuto Staccato			Simply a long staccato executed through use of the breath release.
Slurred Staccato			Legato tongue (d syllable) is used; each tone is diminished in volume but not to the point of *conscious* separation between notes.
Slurred Tenuto		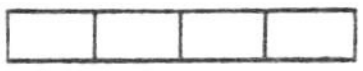	Indicates legato tonguing but, in contrast to slurred staccato, there is no diminuendo after the start of each note.

[34] Isaac, *Practical Orchestration*, p. 114.

The labeling terminology used in Chart 11 is based entirely upon the terminology used to identify the *basic articulations*. This seems to be the most logical approach, since anyone familiar with the basic articulation symbols and labels should find little difficulty in deducing the name of a combined articulation. Although string bowing labels could also have been used for all three combined articulations, it was felt that no significant purpose would be served in using such an approach. Bowing technique involves bow direction as well as musical interpretation. Specification of bow direction, as mentioned earlier, is irrelevant to the wind player.

For purposes of comparison, however, the interpretation of slurred staccato in wind performance tends to be similar to the slurred or linked staccato used in string playing. The wind player who thinks of imitating the string player's slurred staccato on the up-bow will have a fairly clear picture of how his own slurred staccato should sound. Slurred *tenuto* should sound similar to *louré* bowing and the *tenuto* staccato may be said to have its bowing counterpart in the *détaché lancé*. (See the previous section on string bowing for a review of these bowing styles.)

Some editors give the wrong cue in editing Baroque music by using the staccato dot alone. Such music might be more appropriately marked *tenuto staccato* (ㅗ ㅗ ㅗ ㅗ) where definite separation between notes is used but without the notes sounding unduly short or chopped. If regular staccato notes are to be played half value, then *tenuto staccato* notes should probably be played approximately three-fourths of the notes' normal length.

In addition to the articulations discussed thus far, various accent symbols and staccatissimo are also available for enlarging the wind player's musical vocabulary. *Staccatissimo*, the wind player's counterpart to the off-the-string staccato bowing, will be discussed in the following sections of this chapter. Accent symbols and related topics will be discussed in Chapter Five, Phrasing and Interpretation.

C. THE TONGUE RELEASE

Do your wind players have problems with precision in ensemble performance? Is their tonguing generally sluggish with the tone lacking in resonance? Are their tones tapered in volume and pitch in the attack as well as the release? Are they able to produce a short "pinpoint" staccato with a resonant tone when the character and style of the music demands it? Does their execution of fast, articulated passages in the older transcriptions sound clean, or is there frequently a lack of precision, lack of resonance and clarity? Are they able to produce a "dry staccato" effect which is sometimes required in contemporary band, orchestra and chamber music literature? Are they able to imitate properly the *pizzicato* of string instruments when playing in unison with them? And what about their ability to duplicate the lightness of style achieved by string players in the various off-the-string bowings? If your players are plagued with performance problems of this nature, then the following discussion should be of value.

If the duration of a staccato note should be approximately one half of the note's written value, this means that a series of staccato sixteenth notes (as in Example 68) should sound like thirty-second notes, each followed by a thirty-second rest. It also means that each staccato note in the series should have silence *before* as well as *after* it. (Students who think of short staccato in this way are often able to get a clearer picture of the musical effect they should strive to produce.) In a sense it is as if

each staccato note were enclosed in quotes ("♪"); each one tends to be

an entity unto itself as well as part of a broader scheme of melodic grouping and/or musical phrase.

EXAMPLE 68

Tempo, note value length, and stylistic considerations will require some modification of the half-value generalization, but let us use Example 68 as a starting point.

In order for staccato notes to sound light in character, they should sound as if produced with minimal effort. This is hardly possible, however, if a player depends entirely upon the breath release to produce a genuine staccato at faster speeds. The result is that he produces tones which are tapered in volume and pitch at both ends, with problems in rhythmic precision as well. Or else he simply does not produce genuine staccato notes at all, playing them as one would play a series of regular detached notes in one continuous breath. Such an approach simply does not work for the clarinetist in the "Scherzo" from Mendelssohn's *Midsummer Night's Dream* or for the bassoonist in Dukas' *Sorcerer's Apprentice*. These works require a light, agile as well as short staccato in order to sound clean and precise.

Consider also the matter of proper interpretation as well as execution

of staccatissimo or "pinpoint" staccato (symbol: ♩). According to Issac,

in staccatissimo ". . . each tone is produced by a forceful attack of the tongue, and is shortened to about one-fourth of its written value. These tones are likely to be played *forte*."[35] Performers who try to produce

---

[35] Isaac, *Practical Orchestration*, p. 112.

staccatissimo with the breath release alone find difficulty in doing so for the same reasons cited earlier. Consequently the need for a more efficient method in stopping as well as starting the tone becomes increasingly more acute when one is asked to play fast staccato and staccatissimo articulations.

Considering the reverberation factor of most auditoriums, the need for a staccato note to have silence both before and after it becomes still more evident. Once a tone is reflected back and forth many times in a large concert hall, normal staccato begins to sound like legato and regular legato tends to sound slurred. Even in the most ideal acoustical situations, these problems must be considered. But if we consider the usual acoustical inadequacies of rooms where most school groups must rehearse and perform, then the problem takes on still greater significance. The school gymnasium or "multi-purpose room" may be the only choice for rehearsal and/or presentation of public school concerts, and this is a fact that must be lived with. At the same time this makes it imperative that school music conductors be especially conscious and critical of clarity and clean execution of articulation in the training of their groups.

Considering all of these factors, how does one go about achieving good, clean fast staccato and staccatissimo articulation with school groups? If the breath release alone tends to be impractical in faster tempi, what method of execution shall we use? These are difficult questions to answer since considerable disagreement still exists among players of different wind instruments as to how the problem should be resolved. It is the author's belief, however, that the tongue release, properly understood and accurately performed, will fill the need in most situations. We accept the risk that there may be some who patently disagree with use of the tongue release at any tempo in any situation. Nevertheless, it is hoped that all will read the following discussion with an open mind and withhold final judgment until they have given the suggestions therein fair trial.

Investigation of published writings reveals that single reed performers were probably the first to advocate use of the tongue release and openly admit to using it themselves in certain types of staccato playing. Robert Willaman was among the first to discuss it in any detail in his book, *The Clarinet and Clarinet Playing*, published in 1949. Since that time Bonade and others have addressed themselves to the subject, and one finds increasingly fewer writings each year which condemn its use on single reed instruments.

Double reed players of the past and particularly authors of books on double reed performance and technique have been more hesitant in discussing this topic. Today, however, this conservatism also seems to be on the wane, and now we find the tongue release for double reeds becoming more widely accepted and discussed in a positive frame of reference.

With regard to brass instruments and the flute, discussion of the tongue release as an acceptable performance technique is still in somewhat of a pioneering stage of development. Recently, however, two writings (to be discussed later) have appeared which provide the teacher and player with more specific information in this area.

In the discussion immediately following, the single reeds, double reeds, brass instruments, and the flute will each be treated separately. This is followed by a commentary on the breath release and tongue release in combination and the use of the tongue release as it applies to mixed articulation (alternating slurred and staccato patterns). The tongue release also has relevance to jazz articulation which in turn has a direct influence upon jazz phrasing and style. This topic will be followed by a discussion of miscellaneous considerations relative to starting and stopping the tone which concludes this chapter.

1. The Clarinet and Saxophone

Since the tongue release will seem unnatural to most students in their first attempts, the entire procedure outlined below should be approached in "slow motion" using only the mouthpiece at first. Each step should be carefully analyzed to ensure that it is being done correctly before going ahead. Moving from one step to another haphazardly will only produce negative results and frustration. The outline below pertains to single reeds only. Take your time—weeks if necessary—and try to be patient!

Producing the "Hiss Sound"

Have the student place his tongue *lightly* against the reed just below the reed tip. While the tongue remains in this position, dampening the reed's freedom to vibrate, have the student blow *gently* through the mouthpiece opening. A free flow of air should be heard hissing through the mouthpiece; no tone should be heard at this point.

Failure to produce the "hiss sound" may be due to one or a combination of the following problems:

1. Tongue pressure is too heavy and is closing the reed against the mouthpiece. Use lighter pressure with the tongue further down on the reed.
2. The reed is too soft and is collapsing against the mouthpiece. Try a harder reed.
3. The instrument is being held at too high an angle with the tongue

blocking the mouthpiece tip opening. Pull the instrument downward so that the first ligature screw on the mouthpiece *almost* touches the chin (clarinet only).

4. Biting of the jaw is closing the reed against the mouthpiece. Relax, think of blowing downward, think *aw*.
5. Closed throat in an *ee* position is restricting the free flow of air. Think *ah* or *aw* to open the throat.

The problems above are among those which frequently plague intermediate to advanced clarinet and saxophone students. The longer one has studied, the more difficult it is to break bad habits such as these. Introducing the "hiss sound" early in the student's training helps avoid these problems from the start and prepares the student for proper execution of short, fast staccato at a later time.

Only after the "hiss sound" can be done successfully should any of the following steps be attempted. Naturally, if the teacher does not explain the procedure any further, there will be no danger of the student going ahead prematurely.

Starting the Tone

With the tongue against the reed and air flowing through the mouthpiece as described above, ask the student to withdraw the tongue from the reed as in saying the syllable *tah*. The tone should respond immediately. If not, then first try more air pressure. The reed tip may also be too heavy making a good attack a near impossibility. Be sure to use the syllable *tah* rather than *tee* since the latter tends to close the throat while the former serves to open the throat to its desired size. Nothing should move during the attack except the tongue; the embouchure and jaw should remain motionless. If exterior movement is visible, this usually means that tongue action is too heavy. *Think* of using the tip of the tongue and withdraw it rapidly.

Stopping the Tone with the Tongue

Start the flow of air with the tongue against the reed and then withdraw the tongue from the reed as in whispering *tah*. While the reed is in vibration and the tone is sounding, *gently* bring the tongue back to the reed as in whispering *aht*. The tongue should stop the vibration of the reed but not the flow of air. Breath pressure should remain constant, with the sound of air being heard as it travels through the mouthpiece tip opening. If the tongue stops the flow of air as well as reed vibration, good staccato may never be accomplished, the result being instead a chopped, abrupt, unmusical effect. The natural thing for a student to do is either stop the flow of air by relaxing his breath support or else completely prevent the flow of air by closing off the mouthpiece tip opening with the tongue. Both of these practices should be avoided at this point.

One can determine whether or not breath support is being relaxed by observing the exterior of the player's neck. The area directly beneath the jaws expands appreciably when blowing through a reed instrument. Once breath pressure is relaxed, this area contracts back to its normal size. Sometimes it helps if the student is asked to think of doing a breath crescendo as the tongue returns to the reed; this will help counteract the tendency to relax breath support and will help keep a steady stream of air moving through the mouthpiece. If the student still has great difficulty, review the preceding steps and have him practice them daily until he is able to do them with reasonable success.

As soon as the student can execute the above correctly with the mouthpiece and reed alone, the same procedure should be applied using the entire instrument. The first note used should be one with minimal resistance to breath pressure such as open G on the clarinet or open C-sharp on the saxophone. Following this, a practice routine as illustrated in Example 69 has proved to be successful. Take a deep breath and prepare to play a series of whole notes followed by whole rests. Start each tone with *tah* on the count of one, continue the tone for four beats, bring the tongue back to the reed with *aht* at the end of the fourth beat, keep the breath pressure constant with the tongue remaining against the reed so that it cannot vibrate, and maintain four beats of tonal silence. Repeat this process several times without relaxing breath support until a new breath is needed. Be sure that the hiss of air is heard during each rest.

EXAMPLE 69

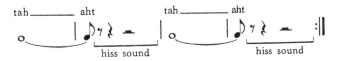

Next have the student practice half note-half rest, quarter note-quarter rest, eighth note-eighth rest, and finally the sixteenth note-sixteenth rest pattern.

When playing fast eighth notes and sixteenths up to tempo, the separate *tah* and *aht* syllables will, of course, be combined into one syllable, *taht*. Syllables like *tut* should be avoided since they tend to produce a staccato which is too short and lacking in resonance. Keeping the *ah* in the *taht* helps keep the staccato notes resonant and also of sufficient length.

Using whole and half notes at first, also have the student practice ascending and descending scales as illustrated in Example 70.

EXAMPLE 70

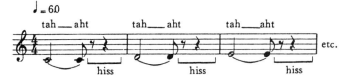

The pattern in Example 70 should also be done later with quarter notes and shorter note values.

Even though the musically sensitive student may find slow motion staccato practice uninteresting, he must learn to concentrate on this technical problem even at the expense of producing poor musical results for the time being. A similar problem frequently accompanies a major change in embouchure. For example, a student who is asked to pull the chin down after having learned to play with chin muscles in an upward direction will usually find that his tone quality is quite flabby and his pitch noticeably flat at first. Again he must discipline himself to concentrate first on the technical problem and patiently allow nature, aided by consistent practice, to bring about the desired musical results *gradually.*

When practicing in the upper register, the student may become annoyed if his tone sounds flat and poor in quality when he relaxes the jaw sufficiently to allow proper flow of air through the instrument. He may also find it necessary to open the throat more than usual and relax the jaw somewhat in order to maintain constant air flow. All of this serves to point up other errors in his playing. Contrary to the student's opinion, poor intonation and tone quality are probably not the fault of the new playing technique he is using. Instead, an inferior mouthpiece, soft reeds, or a number of other variables may have forced him to bite with the jaw in order to bring up the pitch in the upper register and also to arrive at a tone with more "center." A reed of sufficient resistance along with a good mouthpiece should not require abnormal biting to maintain good intonation and tone quality. A firm embouchure with proper balance of both upper and lower lip muscles in conjunction with an open throat will keep the tone open and dark in quality. With the lip muscles as the principal support surrounding the reed, the player will find more freedom in adjusting a flat tone and achieving better response in *pianissimo,* along with greater facility for smooth slur connections between wide ascending intervals.

As the speed of tongue release staccato is increased, a point will be reached where maintaining the "hiss sound" during the rests is no longer possible. In fact when one reaches the point where the tonguing syllables are combined into one as in *taht,* further attempts to produce the hiss sound as an effect for its own sake become unnecessary. Assuming that the slow motion practice was sufficient in quantity and quality, the resultant staccato played up to tempo should be accurate and musically acceptable. If it is not and the tone sounds excessively chopped and lacking in resonance, then additional slow motion practice is probably needed. The reader is advised that patience is a necessary virtue in this respect. A considerable amount of practice may be required of some students before genuine success is possible. Take plenty of time with each step and proceed cautiously lest errors in execution become in-grained habits which will be difficult to change later.

Remember that it takes more breath support to play a series of staccato notes than it does to play a series of normal detached or even legato notes. This concept may not be entirely accurate, but the player who *thinks* this way is more apt to produce positive results. All too often we hear staccato passages performed by students where the notes seem to "stick inside the horn," i.e., response is poor, the articulation is muddy, the tone is lifeless, and the phrase just doesn't go anywhere. If one thinks "breath crescendo" and intensity drive toward the principal or final note, then the staccato is more apt to bounce and sparkle as it should when performed correctly. Ultimately one must depend upon the ear. It is still the player's greatest aid in evaluating artistic performance.

2. Oboe and Bassoon

Some double reed players contend that the breath release in fast stac-cato is more adaptable for double reeds than it is for the clarinet and saxophone. Their argument is based upon the small size of the tip open-ing of double reeds and the resultant need for a smaller quantity of air. And yet the author has observed among these players the same problems in performance that were described earlier, i.e., poor response and pre-cision, tones tapered in volume and pitch at both ends, and articulation generally lacking in clarity and tonal resonance. With some slight modi-fications, the tongue release prescribed for single reeds can also be applied to double reeds.

When the tongue is placed against the center of the lower blade of cane on an oboe or bassoon reed, the pressure of the tongue may either close the tip or to some degree restrict the proper flow of air through it (because of the small opening of the tip and the thinness of the cane in this area). But if the reed is turned downward *slightly* to the right and the instrument is also shifted slightly to the right of the player, the tongue will touch the lower right hand corner of the reed. This tongue position stops the reed's vibration but also allows a free flow of air through the tip opening. It also helps counteract a tendency to close the reed if the player bites the reed on tones above the staff. Air pressure always remains constant, of course, and the throat should be open as in *ah*.

A word of caution: After the reed has been turned downward and the instrument shifted to the right, the reed itself must enter the mouth through the center of the player's lips. The head must not shift to the right along with the instrument or else the original purpose will have been defeated. The reverse procedure, with the reed turned slightly to the left and the instrument shifted toward that direction, is also acceptable. Usually, however, the right hand method seems to feel more natural to most players.

A reminder about the modified anchor tongue position for oboe suggested by Sprenkle and discussed in Section B of this chapter is in order at this point. This tongue position is especially important in fast, short staccato playing on the oboe since it helps avoid harsh, heavy tongue action in the attack and release of individual tones. It also tends to minimize tongue movements, thereby increasing the player's ability to articulate at the faster rates of speed. Aside from the foregoing modifications, the procedure for study and practice of the tongue release for double reeds is essentially the same as that described earlier for single reed instruments.

3. Brass Instruments

While a number of authors discuss fast staccato and staccatissimo styles relative to brass performance, their explanations are not always clear. In many cases there seems to be an inconsistency between their explanation of how these notes should sound as compared to how they should be executed. For instance, an author may specify that the notes should be very short and should be performed using the syllable *tu tu tu tu* where the release of one note is also the beginning of the next note. Accompanying this is the usual reminder that the syllable *tut* should be avoided! This implies that "short notes" is interpreted to mean *fast* notes in terms of speed, not short notes in terms of relative note value length. One tends to be left with the impression that brass players do not concern themselves with creating silences *before* and *after* short staccato and staccatissimo tones.

This brings us back to the problem of how different instrumentalists apparently possess different concepts of what the word staccato really means. Some brass authors state that staccato does not necessarily mean short in duration—it only signifies a separation betwen notes. While Baroque staccato fits such a description to a degree, the definition of staccato as given in *The Harvard Brief Dictionary of Music* is not in agreement with this notion. According to this source, staccato is "the shortened performance of a note (or group of notes) so that it sounds only for a moment, the major part of its written value being replaced by a rest."[36]

Despite this problem, Schmid provides us with specific answers to staccato performance in brass playing as follows:

> A note can be terminated in two ways, by stopping the air flow or by touching the roof of the mouth with the tongue (closing the gate). The air-flow method should be used for slow tempo and long note values. The fast repetition of staccato notes requires the use of the tongue, because any change in the air stream would be awkward and undesirable. Two points of caution are necessary at this point. Do not constrict the throat to control the air flow. This constriction is easily detected by listening for grunting or other throat sounds. The second point is to avoid using the flat part of the tongue to stop a note. This fault is characterized by a *too-it* sound. If only the tip of the tongue is used, this sound can be avoided.[37]

Schmid further explains that staccatissimo ". . . is characterized by the stopping of a note almost immediately after it is begun." The tongue release is used here with a *toot* syllable. He again cautions against using the flat (middle) part of the tongue in stopping the tone. The *tip* of the tongue should also touch the roof of the mouth instead of touching the teeth.

Perhaps this explanation serves to remind us of the old axiom that too little knowledge can be a dangerous thing. Used incorrectly and in the wrong context, the tongue release in brass playing will be anything but musical and aurally satisfying. When performed correctly it should allow the brass player to extend his ability toward reproducing many of the articulated effects which we so admire in artistic string and woodwind performance.

In final analysis, the problem is one of understanding musical concepts, both aurally and intellectually. The player needs to know the sound or style he is after. Once he knows this, patience and self-discipline become the major factors which determine the degree of his success in performance. If he is also a teacher of school musicians, he needs to be

---

[36] Willi Apel and Ralph T. Daniel, *The Harvard Brief Dictionary of Music* (Cambridge, Mass.: Harvard University Press, 1960), S.V. "Staccato."

[37] William Schmid, "Brass Articulation," *The Instrumentalist* (August, 1967), p. 85.

able to tell his students *how* to produce the particular sound desired. But the concept must come first—one aural picture is often worth a thousand words. Then the ear must decide. If the ear says it is wrong and intelligent experimentation fails to produce desirable results, then we revert to analytical teaching. Such an approach becomes not only desirable but essential when all other resources of pedagogy have failed to produce positive results.

Despite the fact that Schmid's theory happens to satisfy the needs of our argument for the tongue release, we would be remiss to ignore completely the writings of various brass experts even though their solutions to the problem are contrary to our own. The following paragraphs include quotations from the writings of recognized brass performers and teachers who do not appear to advocate the tongue release under any circumstances.

With specific reference to stopping the tone on French horn, Schuller explains that the larynx can be used to end a note. "This is achieved by closing this valve . . . to the point where the air stream being allowed to pass is not sufficient to vibrate the lips and the horn."[38] He also points out that the larynx is a valve-like organ which can shut off the air completely or encompass any graduation up to a complete unrestrained opening. Later, he specifically advocates use of the larynx to stop the tone in staccato playing. He also points out that among the common faults in staccato playing is the instance where ". . . the tongue, rather than the larynx, is used to stop the note."[39]

Kleinhammer says much the same thing, although he explains it a bit differently. He advocates use of the throat or "cough muscle" for stopping the tone in certain types of staccato and staccatissimo performance.[40] He also mentions that many of the percussive sounds produced by brass players in the performance of staccato are caused by misuse of the embouchure. The aperture should not close after each staccato note; instead, the lips should remain open in their normal playing position. Failure to maintain proper aperture size results in each new tone starting slightly above center—the lips first vibrate at a higher pitch until they open sufficiently to center the tone properly. Finally, Kleinhammer properly reminds us that a good short tone should sound like the "middle-cut chunk out of a good long tone."[41]

Farkas clearly advocates the breath release and describes the function

---

[38] Gunther Schuller, *Horn Technique* (London: Oxford University Press, 1962), p. 29.

[39] *Ibid.*, p. 49.

[40] Edward Kleinhammer, *The Art of Trombone Playing* (Evanston, Ill.: Summy-Birchard, 1963), p. 66.

[41] *Ibid.*, p. 64.

of the breath and tongue in playing staccatissimo passages on the horn as follows:

> Never stop the air column abruptly by using the tongue, as in forming the articulation "toot." Simply stop all air pressure immediately, at the moment the note is to stop. Perhaps the most accurate description of the articulation would be the syllable "tooh" or "tuh."[42]

4. The Flute

What has been said regarding use of the tongue release in brass playing is equally true with respect to the flute. Authors are apparently still hesitant to break with older, traditional concepts for fear of arousing considerable controversy, and thus we still find most discussions of this topic to be too general to be of much concrete value. If raising the issue here serves to stimulate other, more competent persons to set the record straight, then the author will feel that his efforts have not been in vain.

According to Timm, ". . . using the diaphragm is impractical when notes come in rapid succession." He explains that the tone may be stopped by the tongue ". . . as it prepares to release the next note."[43] This leaves us with the impression that a double action of the tongue (stopping one tone completely and starting a new tone independently) is not recommended.

Westphal, however, is more specific with respect to the matter of silence between staccato notes:

> . . . in staccato articulation [on the flute] the tongue returns to its place on the teeth or gums to stop the flow of air, but the air pressure against the tongue remains the same during the period of silence as during the production of tone. Staccato articulation is the only type in which the tongue is used to stop the tone.[44]

If we accept Westphal's explanation for flute along with that of Schmid for brass instruments, then the tongue release is a valid and necessary technique applicable to fast staccato and staccatissimo performance on *all* of the wind instruments. The reader is reminded, however, that the tongue release should not be used indiscriminately. It is to be used primarily when the breath release alone can no longer produce satisfactory results. Beyond this point the player must listen carefully to see that his execution of this technique is done correctly, that the staccato is not

---

42 Farkas, *The Art of French Horn Playing*, p. 51.
43 Timm, *The Woodwinds*, p. 39.
44 Westphal, *Guide to Teaching Woodwinds*, p. 90.

only short but also musical and not chopped or "pecky." Let the sensitive musical ear decide! If the staccato sounds too long, try to make it shorter. If the release is too abrupt, soften the action of the tongue. Practice in slow motion until the desired effect is achieved. Listen for the hiss sound on reed instruments. Strive to use only the tip rather than the flat portion of the tongue on brass instruments; then gradually increase the speed until the staccato can be executed correctly up to tempo. Here again, patience and perseverance will likely be the prime factors which spell success or failure. The teacher can do much to influence his students in these areas.

5. Use of Breath and Tongue Release in Combination

Up to this point our discussion has centered upon staccato performance at the slower and faster rates of speed. In between these extremes lies a rather broad area of so-called medium speeds. For lack of a better term, staccato in this area will be referred to as medium speed staccato.

As might be expected, there are times when a combination of the breath release and tongue release needs to be used in order to perform staccato notes properly. The degree to which the breath and tongue are used will vary depending upon the musical style, note values, and the tempo. The player who has mastered the tongue release as well as the breath release should, however, be prepared to deal effectively with staccato performance at any tempo. His own ear and that of his teacher will help determine what is acceptable musically and what is not. Performance skill is here again dependent on the learning and teaching of valid musical concepts.

In an effort to provide a more concrete description of staccato performance, Chart 12 is offered for the reader's examination. Particular attention should be given to the pictorial diagrams which illustrate the length of the notes and the shaping of the release.

6. Mixed Articulation

Mixed articulation refers to alternating slurred and staccato note patterns (e.g. ♩♩♩♩ ♩♩♩♩ or any permutations of the same). The major question here has to do with the length of the last slurred note in each group: should it be shortened or should it be played full value? This is another area where the experts do not all agree. While some performers favor shortening the last note of a slur, a number of flutists and brass

Chart 12

VARIOUS TYPES OF STACCATO ARTICULATIONS

Label	Marking Symbol	Pictorial Diagram	Interpretation
Slow Staccato			Played approximately half-value using the breath release alone.
Medium Speed Staccato			Sounds the same as slow staccato but a combination of breath and tongue release is often used to perform it correctly.
Fast Staccato			Played approximately half-value using the tongue release.
Staccatissimo (Secco or dry Staccato)			Played as short as possible without destroying resonance of the tone; performed using the tongue release.

players in particular believe it should be played full value. Among string players, too, one can find advocates of both concepts.

If we accept the idea that a staccato note generally should have silence before as well as after it, then the last note of a slur in mixed articulation must be shortened in order to create silence *before* the first staccato note. In slower tempi this is best done through relaxation of breath pressure (breath release). In fast tempi, on reed instruments at least, this is accomplished by bringing the tongue back to the reed as in *aht*.

Some persons argue that silence or spacing should not necessarily be the objective here. Instead the goal should be one of diminishing the volume by phrasing down the last note of the slur ( ). Some also advocate this approach for successive slurred groups as well ( ). Performing in this manner at slower tempi is easy enough, and there are certain musical styles in which such interpretation is both desirable and appropriate. But it is unwise to assume that all such articulations should be interpreted in this manner. Use of such diminuendo effects, for example, may be appropriate in a slow movement by Mozart but not necessarily so in one by Brahms.

What about use of diminuendo with slurred groups at rapid speeds? Here we find much the same problem as in trying to perform with the breath release a rapid series of separate staccato notes. Even in the slurred group sequence (), the breath diminuendo at rapid speeds becomes awkward and tends to lack musical continuity.

If one must satisfy a need for making the slurred note softer than the tongued note, this can perhaps be justified by the following explanation: The first note of each slurred group already sounds slightly accented in wind playing due to use of the tongue ("t" syllable). Since the second note is slurred and is therefore without the tongue accent, this note will inherently sound softer in comparison to the first or tongued note. The need for additional dynamic shading therefore seems unnecessary. The impracticality of using breath diminuendo at rapid speeds further impedes the plausibility of additional dynamic shading. By keeping the breath pressure constant and allowing the tongue to do the work, the result will be better precision, greater resonance of tone and cleaner articulation. Example 71 illustrates the specific tonguing syllables to be used. Also note that a check mark after a note means the note should be shortened. A plus sign indicates that the note should be played full value.

EXAMPLE 71

tah aht taht taht tah   ah aht tahttaht tah ahttaht tahttaht tah   ah   tah

Notice that the last note of each slurred group in Example 71 is marked with a check except for the last sixteenth which is marked with a plus sign. Why? The answer is that shortening the last sixteenth would be in poor taste musically. This becomes obvious if one tries performing the passage both ways. This particular example, then, provides us with an exception to a general rule: If the note following the slur—in this case a whole note— is at least twice the rhythmic value of the preceding note, the last note of the slur should not be shortened but should be played full value.

In passages containing a series of consecutive slurred groups, the tongue should not be used to shorten the last note of the slur (Example 72).

EXAMPLE 72

tah ah   tah ah   tah ah tah ah tah_____   tah_____   tah

Example 72 is not another exception to the above rule since there is no mixed articulation here. If, however, we have a pattern such as that seen in Example 73, then the third note of the second rhythmic group would be shortened since it precedes a staccato note.

EXAMPLE 73

tah_____ tah____aht taht tah

Understanding mixed articulation and being able to execute it properly are clearly two different matters. Standard method books are filled with study material in this area, but the real secret is in *how* one approaches study of the subject. The first attempts with actual mixed articulation should include singing the tonguing syllables in slow motion. Next, the pattern should be performed using only the mouthpiece. Then the entire instrument is added and the passage played slowly on a single pitch. Finally, the written pitches are added and gradually worked up to tempo. In other words, one should avoid trying to solve problems of tonguing, fingering, and note reading all at once. Isolate the problem to its smallest denominator at first. Later, one new problem can be added at a time, at a slow enough tempo so that clean articulation can remain the focal point of attention.

Practice of the type described above is tedious but also highly beneficial. The young, immature student may have some doubts on this question, but his teacher should not. The competent teacher who himself has a background of concentrated study and practice on his major instrument will be in a position to influence his students through personal demonstration. His own confidence in his teaching methods will also do much to convince the students.

7. Application to the Jazz Idiom

Regardless of whether or not it is done consciously or unconsciously, jazz musicians do use the tongue release, particularly in what is sometimes called the *legato staccato* effect. The first major departure of jazz playing as compared to so-called legitimate playing is in the interpretation of rhythmic notation. The next mode of departure is in the attack syllable used. In jazz, the *dah* syllable is used much more often than the syllable *tah*. The latter is used primarily to produce sharp, accented attacks.

Ensemble jazz style, like other styles, requires an interpretation with both clarity and intensity. Clarity is gained through shortening certain notes, and intensity drive is achieved through maintaining adequate breath support throughout the phrase. Try to picture aurally a jazz musician using *tah* to start each detached tone and the breath release to produce the staccato in a phrase such as that seen in Example 74. Use of the breath release results in a complete lack of intensity within the phrase as well as poor rhythmic precision. If *tah* is replaced with *dah* and *aht* is added, the interpretation of this jazz phrase is much improved.

EXAMPLE 74

The staccato and legato markings included in Example 74 will not always be written in the jazz score. These are included here merely to clarify the interpretation. The experienced jazz professional will usually do these things through intuition, based upon considerable playing experience. (For a comprehensive discussion of this particular topic, see Hall's *Teacher's Guide to the High School Stage Band*.)

8. Miscellaneous Considerations in Starting and Stopping the Tone

Performance of "After Beat" Patterns

In the performance of rhythmic patterns as in Example 75, one often sees students relaxing not only breath support but also the embouchure during each rest. This means that the embouchure and breath support must be readjusted for each new attack. The result is a picture of physical awkwardness and wasted motion along with a tempo which seems to drag incessantly. Actually the most negative feature is the lack of continuity in phrasing—nothing really moves ahead. The line is chopped up and one gets a "downhill" feeling concerning the direction of the notes. Most of this can be eliminated by keeping the breath pressure constant and using the tongue release. Properly applied, this method will produce the best musical results with minimal effort (Example 75).

EXAMPLE 75

High Note Pianissimo Attacks

Many wind players, particularly first chair orchestra players, have been known to "freeze" when confronted with a high note marked *pianissimo* in a solo situation. These players find themselves exposed with no one to hide behind and must enter with a soft, legato attack while the ears of the whole world seemingly are listening in. With inexperienced brass players this often means tensing up and splitting the note. Inexperienced reed players tend to bite the reed and choke off the sound. Novice clarinetists are forever fearful of squeaking in such situations.

Professional players will agree that the problem sometimes is a psychological one due to lack of confidence, the only real cure being lots of playing experience. But if one's performance experience is to be fruitful, it should include repetition of positive results. Repeated failure will hardly increase one's confidence. The following suggestions are intended to help the player achieve positive results in these performance situations.

Excessive muscular tension in the breathing mechanism, throat, and embouchure must be avoided. The player who inhales too soon and has to restrain his air pressure, waiting for the start of his entry, will surely be tense and will produce a faulty attack. To avoid such tension, the player should learn to inhale and exhale in uninterrupted sequence; that is, he should inhale one beat (or even a half beat if the music is slow) prior to his entry so that he can begin the release (exhalation) of the air immediately after completion of the inhalation process. In this way the tension caused by premature preparation of breath support can be avoided.

The brass player needs to be mentally prepared for the specific pitch he intends to produce—he must hear the pitch with the eye. If breath support is lacking, the lips will not begin instant vibration and the attack will be late. If the throat is tense and the lips pinched, the attack will also be late. Practice of repeated attacks on the entry note, with proper control of the inhalation-exhalation sequence in order to avoid tension, will, in final analysis, usually prove to be the best prescription for alleviation of most of the problem.

Much of what has been discussed in the previous two paragraphs has equal relevance to reed instrument performance. Reed players who have mastered the hiss sound, however, possess an additional resource for preventing a faulty entry on a *pianissimo* high note. Much undesirable tension of the breathing mechanism, throat, and embouchure as well as lack of proper breath support can be prevented by placing the tongue against the reed and allowing the air to pass through the tip opening just before the start of the tone. When the time arrives for the tone to start, the player need only¹ withdraw his tongue gently and allow the reed to vibrate. The result should be a soft legato attack, starting on time with a full-bodied resonant tone.

If the above fails to produce positive results, then the problem will most likely be found in the instrument, mouthpiece or reed. A flute pad which does not close perfectly, for example, will impede the player's ability to achieve good response in *pianissimo*. The player should avoid squeezing the pads shut by using excessive finger tension, as this only creates additional performance problems. An instrument which leaks needs to be properly repaired.

D. CONCLUSION

The purpose of this chapter was to shed some light on the basic principles of bowing and articulation which have evolved through tradition and practice, and to illuminate some of the problems faced by the pedagogue in trying to communicate these principles to his students, particularly those of public school age. Orchestral string players know that the master composers did not always indicate specific bowings in the score. Wind articulation, like dynamic markings, was not always clearly specified but left up to the player instead. Performers in these periods reportedly played the work in the most logical manner consistent with the performance practice of that period.

The view may be taken that music with minimal editing regarding style and articulation is actually preferable since it allows the performer to assume a more creative role in performance of the music. In other words, music in which all articulations are marked precisely leaves the player with little freedom for subjective interpretation, and this is viewed by some as a detriment to spontaneous musical expression. This view may have some merit in regard to solo performance and some aspects of chamber music performance. In the context of large ensemble performance, and especially in the case of those organizations which have little time for rehearsal, such a point of view seems difficult to justify.

Schweitzer tells us that investigation of Bach's scores will reveal some instances where the notes appear to be wrong, but the articulations seem always to be quite clearly specified. Unfortunately not every composer has been this concerned in this regard. The author extends a plea to all editors, composers, and arrangers to give careful attention to edition of articulation, dynamics, and other symbols of style in all published materials, including those produced primarily for public school use.

RECOMMENDED REFERENCES

Bowing

Green, Elizabeth, A. H., *Orchestral Bowing and Routines*. Ann Arbor, MI: Campus Publishers, 1957.

Lorrin, Mark, *Dictionary of Bowing and Tonal Techniques for Strings*. Denver: Charles Hansen Educational Music and Books, 1968.

Rabin, Marvin and Priscilla Smith, *Guide to Orchestral Bowings Through Musical Styles*. Madison: University of Wisconsin Press, Extension Arts, 1984.

Articulation

Colnot, Cliff L., "Understanding Jazz-Rock Articulations," *The Instrumentalist* (March, 1975) pp. 103–106.

Keller, Hermann, *Phrasing and Articulation*, trans. Leigh Gerdine. New York: W. W. Norton & Company, Inc., 1965. (Chapters 4–6, 8–12)

McBeth, Francis, *Effective Performance of Band Music*. San Antonio, TX: Southern Music Co., 1972.

Chapter Five

PHRASING
AND
INTERPRETATION

Our system of notation has been developed to the extent that a composer can record his musical ideas with much greater precision and thoroughness than can an author or poet who deals with written language. Pitch, intensity, duration, and, to some degree, articulation are the basic elements of information found in musical notation. To these are added the speed of the tones (tempo), tone quality, and musical expression, but all of these aspects are largely under the control of the performer or conductor whose role is that of interpreter.

Metronomically correct playing, with precise observance of dynamics and articulation along with good tone and intonation, is sometimes passed off as artistic performance, but because of its sheer mechanical nature it can never be considered more than a superficial treatment of the music itself.[1] Intelligent interpretation requires artistic sensitivity and profound musical understanding. The interpreter's responsibility is therefore a most important one, since it is he who must analyze the composer's blueprint and breathe life into his musical ideas.

Every interpreter is faced with several difficult problems. First, should he use his own ideas in interpreting a given piece of music or must he remain loyal or even entirely subservient to the composer's score? Toscanini reportedly favored the latter attitude. Verdi likewise believed that the interpreter should ". . . perform simply and exactly what he [the composer] has written."[2]

[1] Attributed to William Kincaid.
[2] Fredrick Dorian, *History of Music in Performance* (New York: W. W. Norton & Company, Inc., 1942), p. 8.

Accepting Verdi's view and trying to apply it religiously is not always an easy task. Composers of the Classical, Baroque, and earlier musical periods provided very little information on how their works were to be performed stylistically. The metronome was an invention of Beethoven's time and the use of dynamic markings reportedly had its beginnings in the Mannheim era. Extant writings by composers and literary discussions dating from these periods are also insufficient in quantity and depth to provide us with all of the necessary information needed to recreate the music authentically. The best we can do is turn to legends of the past and rely on the guidance of musical scholars, good conductors and other experts in the field.

In the performance of jazz, however, subjective interpretation usually plays a significant role in the stylistic outcome of a composition. In jazz improvisation specifically, the composer or arranger generally supplies only the melody line along with a suggested harmonic outline. The jazz performer then supplies his own style and interpretation to the piece. In order to do this intelligently, he needs to have developed a feel for jazz style, especially rhythms, and to possess appropriate technical command of his instrument. Otherwise the interpretation will probably sound "square" and his execution awkward and clumsy.

According to Richard Wagner, the interpreter's first responsibility is to establish the correct tempo. This is easy enough if the metronome marking is provided. If it is not, then the interpreter must rely upon his own knowledge of the composer's style and upon guidelines established by acknowledged authorities in order to help eliminate some of the guesswork. Next, he must decide on the dynamics, the phrasing to be used, and how to interpret any articulations and accents which may (or may not) be written in the score. In other words, his job is to decipher the musical essence of the work, the unwritten language which must be blended into the total musical fabric.

This chapter will deal primarily with melodic phrasing and rhythmic interpretation. Jazz style and interpretation, conspicuously absent from most texts, will also be discussed. The subject of ornamentation, particularly as it applies to eighteenth-century music, is not included although it is considered important; the reader is urged to read the sources listed in the bibliography for specific information on this topic.

Musicianship, quite obviously, cannot be acquired by reading a book. Even so, an attempt will be made in this chapter to establish some general guidelines as well as to identify some of the more common problems in interpretation encountered by student musicians and suggest how to treat them pedagogically. Success in these areas will depend largely upon the teacher's own background, including his knowledge and sensitivity to the expressive qualities of music.

Some clarification in terminology seems appropriate prior to delving into the body of this chapter. The term "phrase" and "phrasing" are sometimes used interchangeably by musicians, implying that they mean much the same thing. This is incorrect. A phrase is analogous to a line of poetic verse or a sentence in prose. To put it another way, a phrase may be considered to be a musical thought or musical sentence. Phrasing, on the other hand, involves dividing a musical thought (phrase) into melodic groups or subdivisions. Phrasing, in a sense, means to punctuate musically.

Occasionally the term "articulation" is used as if it were synonymous with the word "phrasing." This is also a mistake. Articulation has to do with the degree of separation and/or connection of individual notes; it is basically a mechanical process, while phrasing deals directly with musical expression. Generally we think of only one type of phrasing as being acceptable, while there may be two or more acceptable articulations which could be used in a given passage.

Similarly, the words "interpretation" and "musical expression" are often used interchangeably but do not mean exactly the same thing. Interpretation in music is the *process* of analyzing the elements of a musical composition in order to make an intelligent judgment on how to perform them artistically. Musical expression is the *performance outcome* of this analysis. If the interpretation is inaccurate, good musical expression will be lacking. Good interpretation executed in good taste results in what might be called a musically intelligent performance.

A. MELODIC GROUPING

In notating divisions and subdivisions of the beat, beams are used to organize the notes into separate rhythmic groups. These allow the player to determine quickly where the downbeats occur, the number of notes within each beat, and the distribution of these notes within the beat. While this type of grouping has definite practical value from a rhythmic standpoint, it does not provide any viable information concerning the melodic function of these notes within a musical phrase.

Single, isolated rhythmic groups are musically static in themselves; therefore, an extra note moving to the next beat is needed in order to define the phrasing. In other words, "it takes four notes to define a triplet, five notes to define a quadruplet."[3] In Example 76, brackets are used to outline the melodic groups while the beams outline the rhythmic groups. Arrows pointing to the left indicate that the last note of each melodic group should be phrased down by diminishing its tonal intensity slightly.

---

[3] Attributed to William Kincaid.

Arrows to the right indicate that the notes so marked should travel or move toward the next downbeat.

EXAMPLE 76

The first note in Example 76 might just as well have been eliminated since it is musically static; it is the end of a melodic group which does not exist. Bach often eliminated this type of note and put a rest in its place, as the scores of his fugal works in particular will reveal.

When teaching melodic grouping to students, it is recommended that the phrasing be practiced first at a slow tempo and even exaggerated to the point of obvious rhythmic distortion. Later, once the feeling for melodic grouping has been firmly established, the speed should be increased until rhythmic distortion is eliminated and the melodic grouping of notes is felt rather than heard. In other words, the player should merely "think" the groupings rather than make a point of emphasizing them. Practice with a metronome at this time is highly recommended as a means for helping eliminate rhythmic distortion.

Melodic grouping can and generally should be used in scale and broken arpeggio passages. Passages like that in Example 77 clearly indicate a need for melodic grouping because of the melodic sequence or structure of the notes. Note that each melodic group begins after a change of direction in the melody.

EXAMPLE 77

The *tenuto* symbols under the first note of each melodic group in Example 77 are included for the following reason: there is a tendency, particularly in passages such as the second one, to play the first note too late and consequently too short. Instead, the player should consciously try to get to the first note of each melodic group a bit early and play it full value in order to avoid unevenness in his playing. If a sincere effort is not made to do this, problems similar to those shown in Example 78 often result.

EXAMPLE 78

Another solution to this problem is to think 2-3-4-1 2-3-4-1, etc, instead of 1-2-3-4 1-2-3-4. This also helps break down the inherent feeling for rhythmic accent on the count of one. With eighth note triplets the recommended counting is 2-3-1 2-3-1, etc.; with sextuplets, the counting would be 6-1-2-3-4-5 6-1-2-3-4-5.[4]

The use of brackets for identifying melodic groupings is one of very few visual aids we have for teaching musical phrasing. It not only leads toward more musical phrasing; it also helps students avoid rushing the tempo and allows them to develop better evenness in fingering. Naturally this approach does not substitute for the expert guidance of a teacher, but it can be helpful to both teacher and student alike as a supplementary aid.

B. MUSICAL LINE

Related to melodic grouping is the broader concept of musical line which involves the continuity and direction or movement within a complete musical phrase. It includes location of the peak note or climax and the function of individual notes and melodic groupings which come before and after the climax. Also important is the matter of identifying the point at which each phrase begins and ends, which in turn determines where one takes a breath in wind instrument performance. These items comprise the content of the following discussion.

Crescendo and *diminuendo* are sometimes thought of as the primary clue to the perception of musical line. Related to this is the terminology of "rainbowing the phrase" where in a four measure phrase a crescendo is made during the first two measures and a diminuendo on the last two. This explanation is useful as a starting point, but students must also realize that an increase in loudness and an increase in intensity are not necessarily the same. Also, a phrase may be more or less than four measures and may begin before or after a bar line.

The first requisite for achieving good continuity and direction within a phrase is to make the tone move, especially on long sustained tones. The player should give the tones direction by changing the intensity, loudness, tone quality, and also the speed and/or width of the vibrato when appropriate, using vibrato so that it becomes a direction indicator.

[4] Attributed to William Kincaid.

He should also concentrate on singing "through the notes," over and through the bar lines as needed so that continuity of the line is maintained. Breath pressure must be kept constant, leaving no gaps between articulations unless they are specifically indicated.[5]

Some performers use a number continuum of one to ten as a means for analyzing the relative intensity of each note up to and away from the peak note of the phrase. But whatever system is used, no two pieces of music should ever sound exactly the same musically. Each work will possess its own unique combination of musical components requiring that it be performed in line with its own special requirements.

Finally, remember that music should never be static. It is a friction between line (melody) and rhythm. Rather than striving for one hundred percent accuracy with the metronome, think of the freedom of the line against the discipline of rhythm.[6]

Concerning the matter of breathing between phrases, Keller states that ". . . 'to phrase' means equally 'to breathe'; 'to phrase well' means 'to breathe intelligently.' "[7] In vocal music, identifying the beginning and end of a phrase is greatly simplified in that musical phrases tend to correspond to the phrasing of the text. Since instrumental music does not provide such a clue, the player and conductor must learn to decipher phrases primarily through analysis of the harmonic and melodic structure of the work.

A common notational aid used to indicate when and where to breathe is the comma symbol (,). Keller reminds us that "the whole corpus of instrumental music remained entirely without indication of phrasing until the beginning of the eighteenth century. . . . The first composer to use the (,) symbol was Couperin."[8] Some composers and arrangers use this symbol rather frequently in their scores; others do not. Whenever the phrasing is obvious, there is no point in including it. When it is not, the author extends a plea to composers, arrangers and publishers to include this symbol, especially in music designed for younger players.

Another method used by some composers for indicating where one phrase ends and another begins is one where the beam is broken, as seen in the second measure of Example 79.

EXAMPLE 79

[5] *Ibid.*
[6] *Ibid.*
[7] Reprinted from *Phrasing and Articulation*, p. 14, by Hermann Keller. Translated by Leigh Gerdine. By permission of W. W. Norton & Company, Inc. (Copyright © 1965 by W. W. Norton & Sons, Inc.)
[8] *Ibid.*, p. 17.

Keller discusses several irregularities in the construction of phrases: phrase-end concealment, phrase linkage, phrase elision, and phrase overlapping. For detailed discussion of these, see pages 21–27 of his book.

Some transcriptions for band may require that several measures be played without a break in tone. In such a case, two players at a stand need to work out a system so that each one breathes in a different place. This helps maintain continuity of sound without creating obvious breaks in between and is commonly referred to as "staggered breathing." In order to ensure such continuity, player number one might indicate his breathing place with a small circle (o) and player number two use a plus symbol (+). Probably no one should breathe at the end of any measure, especially the fourth measure.

C. LARGE INTERVALS

The largest interval within a phrase normally should be considered unique and be given special musical consideration. This is especially true in the case of wide ascending intervals in slow melodic passages. The usual error made by students is to play the second note of a wide interval too loud without due regard for its musical significance. Instead, the first note should usually be played a little longer and with slightly more intensity; the second note played somewhat softer so that it does not stick out. This is called "stretching the interval" so that it will be somewhat prominent, but the amount of stretching done should be very subtle. Stretching an interval also means playing it with the smoothest legato possible. The lower note should "melt" into the upper note.

EXAMPLE 80

The octave leap of D to D on the third beat in Example 80 is clearly an interval which should be "stretched." Note the use of a straight line between these two notes, a symbol which may be used by the teacher to remind the student of the interval's melodic significance.

Trying to avoid an explosive sound on the top note of a wide ascending interval presents special problems for wind players, brass players and flutists in particular. The player must eventually learn to counteract this tendency by supporting more on the lower note and relaxing somewhat on the high note. Perhaps even more important is to think of playing the top note just a little before actually making the note change.

Taking a big breath before or in the middle of a wide intervallic skip generally should be avoided. The musical reason for this is obvious, but student musicians who are thoroughly engrossed in other performance problems often forget, and therefore need occasional if not frequent reminders in this area.

D. ACCENTS

"Rhythm, in music, is the organization of duration in ordered movement."[9] It consists of four basic elements: meter, tempo, pattern and accent. The meaning and function of the first three elements is generally well known and understood. Proper understanding and accurate execution of the accent is not as common. To accent a note means to make it prominent through some means of stress or emphasis so that it can be clearly distinguished from the notes which surround it. There are seven types of accents, namely, dynamic, agogic, metric, harmonic, pitch, pattern, and embellishment. Each of these will be discussed here in the above order.

1. The Seven Types of Accents

Dynamic accent is the type best understood by most players and the one used most often. It is designated with wedge-shaped symbols (> ∧) and performed by increasing tonal loudness so that the accented note sounds one dynamic level louder than the notes surrounding it. The vertical wedge (*marcato* accent) normally means to play the note with somewhat more emphasis or force than if the horizonal wedge (regular accent) were used. Not all composers of the past scored their music with these clear-cut distinctions in mind, and these symbols are sometimes used interchangeably. The author suggests that normally some distinction between the two should be made. The *marcato* accent (∧) should be the heavier of the two and should be employed in passages where a definitely sharp, pointed type of accent is desired.

There-is another category of dynamic accents which includes *fortepiano*, *sforzando*, and *rinforzando*. Some believe that these along with the regular and *marcato* accents all mean much the same thing, implying they all are played the same way. Since the author does not accept

[9] Paul Creston, "The Importance of Being Rhythmic," *The Instrumentalist* (June, 1960), 31.

this point of view, the chart below is included so that the reader may be able to distinguish the differences more easily.

Chart 13

SPECIAL ACCENTS

Term	Abbreviation	Diagram
Forte Piano	fp	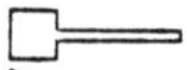
Sforzando	sfz	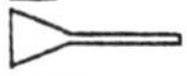
Rinforzando	rfz	

Agogic accent is actually an extended form of *tenuto* where the note so indicated (with a *tenuto* symbol) should be played slightly longer than normal in length. In other words, emphasis is achieved through extended duration rather than by an increase in loudness.

Metric accent is based upon the inherent primary and secondary accents in a measure, as described in Chapter Four in the section on string bowing. Players tend to execute this type of accent automatically as a result of following a conductor's beat pattern. Care should be exercised, however, that metric accent is performed very subtly and not overdone; otherwise, the performance will sound very mechanical.

Harmonic accent is used when a dissonance occurs on either a primary or secondary beat in the measure, especially on a secondary beat. When an accidental foreign to the tonality appears, it also deserves special emphasis as a rule. The emphasis can be accomplished through either increasing the loudness or the length of the note or chord. In some cases, both types of emphasis are used but the dynamic form is more common.

Pattern accent, as the term implies, exists in a repeated figure of characteristic contour. Since music should never be static except on certain isolated chords (usually at the end of a piece), the rhythm as well as melody and harmony should have a feeling of moving ahead toward completion of a musical idea. Pattern accent is often most obvious when applied correctly by an artist snare drummer.

Syncopation accent is another form which is done almost unconsciously by fine players, especially when properly indicated by the conductor. In addition to increasing the loudness, it may also be appropriate to shorten the previous note and delay the syncopated note somewhat as indicated in Example 81.

EXAMPLE 81

Embellishments such as the *appoggiatura*, mordent, and trill often require emphasis of some type in order to serve their musical purpose effectively. In the case of the *appoggiatura*, this will usually be in the form of a dynamic accent. Trills, on the other hand, are often played by lengthening the first or principal note somewhat before actually going into the trill itself. Knowledge of the literature and style are necessary requisites to arriving at satisfactory answers in this area.

2. Performing the Various Types of Accents

Accents in brass instrument playing are controlled by: (1) the amount of air pressure behind the tongue, and (2) the speed with which the tongue is pulled away. Performance of regular accents depends primarily upon increased air pressure. In starting the tone, the tongue should be used in the usual manner ("t" syllable). The increase of breath pressure used for the accented note generally should be maintained throughout the tone's duration unless a diminuendo is indicated. There is a tendency among student musicians, however, to use excessive forward tongue pressure (*thu*) in producing accents, this manifesting itself in an explosive effect at the beginning of the tone. This should normally be avoided unless a sforzando (*sfz*) or similar effect is definitely desired.

In *forte-piano* and *sforzando* reed players use increased tongue pressure against the reed which causes the beginning of the tone to be significantly louder and more defined. Brass players use a more pointed attack, as in *thah* rather than *tah*, or *thu* rather than *tu*. Rinforzando is executed through momentarily increased breath pressure shortly after the beginning of the tone.

When several accented notes appear in series, some space or silence should exist between each note. This helps ensure a feeling of accented style whereas a series of accented notes performed with no space in between tends to be heard simply as a group of regular notes played at a louder dynamic.

Young students sometimes become confused when comparing a series of accented notes to a series of staccato notes. "Both are played with silences between them; they sound the same," students will state. In simplest terms a possible explanation might be "Yes, except that staccato notes are usually light in character while accented notes are louder. Remember that accented notes are usually played one dynamic level louder than the notes surrounding them."

In an effort to review and compare accent marks with other notation symbols, Chart 14 is included for the reader's perusal.

Chart 14

COMPARATIVE ARTICULATIONS INCLUDING DYNAMIC ACCENTS

Label	Marking Symbol	Pictorial Diagram	Interpretation
Tenuto	♩ ♩ ♩ ♩	▭▭▭▭	Sustain full value.
Regular Accent	♩ ♩ ♩ ♩ (> > > >)	▢ ▢ ▢ ▢	Played one dynamic level louder; successive notes should be slightly separated.
Marcato Accent	♩ ♩ ♩ ♩ (∧ ∧ ∧ ∧)	▢ ▢ ▢ ▢	Heavier accents with more separation than successive regular accents.
Staccato	♩ ♩ ♩ ♩ (· · · ·)	▢ ▢ ▢ ▢	Played approximately half-value and softer than all of the above.

Another student performance problem is that of playing individual accented notes too soon, accompanied by a tendency to rush the tempo. This also tends to be a problem in playing staccato notes and, to some degree, in trying to play softly as well. Students surely would not make these errors if they were aware of them, and some sort of measuring device to help them be aware of steady tempo is in order. The metronome is strongly recommended for this purpose.

E. RHYTHMIC INTERPRETATION

1. Mental Division and Subdivision of the Beat

A persistent problem with advanced students as well as beginners is their failure to think through carefully the divisions and subdivisions of the beat. This results in careless interpretation of rhythmic figures and is often a major reason for lack of good precision in ensemble performance.

Beginners not taught from the outset to divide the beat both mentally and physically will have a tendency to rush the tempo. They must learn to realize that it is not enough to concentrate on the downbeats alone. What happens *during* the beat and how it is interpreted is of equally great importance. Proper concepts in this area can be instilled in early instruction through counting appropriate syllables aloud while clapping the notes.

A divergence of opinion exists as to whether or not is is necessary to count divisions and subdivisions aloud on every beat. Examples of these opposing views are illustrated in Example 82.

EXAMPLE 82

In Method 1, syllables are used only where divisions and subdivisions occur with number counts used on each downbeat. Most mature musicians and some advanced students will find this type of counting adequate. Less experienced players are apt to produce unsatisfactory results unless they use a counting system similar to that indicated in Method 2. Note in this instance that all divisions of the beat are counted; subdivisions are counted on long tones which precede the subdivision, as well as the subdivision itself. This is so that the player can mentally prepare himself for the subdivision *before* actually playing it.

2. The Dotted Quarter-Eighth Note Figure

As was explained in Chapter Two, failure to divide the beat properly when playing the dotted quarter-eighth note figure can result in the following problem with beginning students: When counted 1 2+ rather than 1+ 2+, this figure is often played . Advanced students, on the other hand, are sometimes guilty of another error related to division and subdivision of the beat. The error is especially obvious when performing a pattern as in Example 83.

EXAMPLE 83

The tendency in the above is to play the eighths too late and therefore too short. This creates a feeling of heavy accent on the dotted quarters with relatively little emphasis on the eighths. When this occurs we say that the eighths tend to sound rhythmic rather than melodic. In other words, the listener becomes unduly aware of the rhythmic aspects of the music at the expense of the melodic line, and thus the musical intent of the composer is distorted. Legato "melodic eighths" should have as much emphasis as the longer notes and, if anything, should be stretched (lengthened) rather than shortened. To solve the problem, first be sure to subdivide (1+2+3+4+). Hold on to the eighths a little longer than you think you should, "pour plenty of tone into them" and consciously think of making them an integral part of the melodic line. Avoid playing them as if they were unimportant notes; do not treat them like *appoggiaturas*.

3. The Dotted Eighth-Sixteenth Note Figure

A question of interpretation exists concerning the length and style of the sixteenth in a dotted eighth-sixteenth note figure. Some believe that the sixteenth should always be played precisely as notated (excluding jazz interpretation of course), while others feel that a shorter, "energetic" sixteenth is preferable in certain musical situations. In the author's experience, the latter view is valid when applied to military marches, particularly European marches, whose tempi are at $\quarternote = 120$ or slower.

Use of the "energetic" sixteenth is also appropriate in the music of certain Romantic composers. Here again, the need for teachers possessing a high degree of musical sensitivity and knowledge of music literature along with stylistic characteristics of the various musical periods and composers is self-evident.

2. Notes Following a Tie

In a passage such as the one in Example 84, many players tend to hesitate after the tied note, causing the note following the tie to be played late. When this happens, the phrase simply does not go anywhere, and the result is a group of meaningless notes in a sort of musical limbo. The problem is particularly troublesome in slow, sustained melodic passages where the student is apt to take a breath after the tied note thus increasing the tendency toward being late for the next note.

EXAMPLE 84

As a solution to the above, the student should prepare himself for the triplet and quadruplet by subdividing the long tones (quarter notes in this case), and should aim toward the first note after the tie. He must think of getting there a bit ahead of time, "sing" on the note following the tie, and then move toward the next long tone.

Some teachers use a *tenuto* symbol to indicate that the player should think of anticipating the note following the tie. Others use an arrow or both symbols to aid the student further in overcoming his problem in rhythmic interpretation.

5. Notes Following a Rest

An even greater problem than the foregoing occurs when a rest comes on the downbeat with notes immediately following to be played on the division or subdivision of the beat (Example 85). Musically, such patterns require a feeling of anticipation or leading toward the principle note which follows. The slightest hesitation robs the pattern of its melodic direction or intensity. The result is a lack not only of rhythmic precision but also of convincing musical drive. Note that the *tenuto* symbol and arrow are again used here as pedagogical aids.

EXAMPLE 85

6. Problems Due to Technical Difficulties

Some problems in rhythmic interpretation are due to technical difficulties in coordinating the fingers and the tongue or bow. Although these problems do not involve musical interpretation directly, they distort the continuity of phrasing and line so that good musical expression is impossible.

One of the most common problems is found in the performance of "inside articulations" as illustrated in Example 86. The tendency is to play the second note too late and too short. To counteract this, some instructors merely mark in a *tenuto* symbol under the second note or use an arrow to remind the player that he should move ahead to the second note. The probability of error increases greatly when the second note is approached by leap, as seen in the second beat of Example 86.

EXAMPLE 86

7. Interpretation of Military Marches

March style in itself implies separation or spacing between tones except when slurs are used. A general rule is to play divisions of the beat (♩ ♩ in simple time, ♩ ♩ ♩ in compound time, and ♩ ♩ in *alla breve*) in staccato style. The ▯▯ frequently is played ♩ ♪ ♩ or even ♩ ♪ ♩ , and in 6/8, ♩. ♩♩ is often played ♩ ♪ ♩♩ . A series of accented one-beat notes such as ♩ ♩ | ♩ ♩ or ♩. ♩. | ♩. ♩. should be played with a definite space between each note, or the march will sound dull and uninspired. In 6/8 marches ♩ ♪♩ ♪ usually is played ♩ ♪ ♩ ♩ ♪ ♩ .

Correct tempo is important to good style and interpretation in march playing the same as in all other music. Sousa marches played significantly faster than the military march tempo of ♩ = 120 are seldom successful. German marches are sometimes played still slower.

Finally, students need to be taught that music is, in a sense, a plastic art. The beat is the subtle outline within which musical ideas are pulled and stretched into a living, humanistic language. We say that tempo ceases to be strict in a *ritardando* or *accelerando* or even in free *rubato;* here we stop the metronome. But in an otherwise regular tempo we try to play with the metronome. If a slight *tenuto* is used on one note for stylistic or expressive reasons, the notes which follow are usually played with a slight *accelerando.* In this way a steady beat is maintained despite the pull and push of the notes in between. This type of elasticity within a controlled setting is necessary if an entire orchestral violin section, for example, is to play expressively and still be able to stay with the conductor's beat.

F. JAZZ STYLE AND INTERPRETATION

The relatively recent increase in the number of jazz bands in public school music programs in this country has been phenomenal and there is no reason to believe we have begun to reach a saturation point. That the inclusion of jazz music at one time received such negative response from professional music educators may seem strange to us now since it has been legitimatized, by the MENC as well as by individual leaders in the field. Even so, it seems particularly odd that for many years many American musicians denied the youth of this country the opportunity to study in the classroom the first original contribution which modern America has given to the world of music.

It is not our purpose here to engage in a lengthy philosophical discussion. The fact remains that jazz has become a bona fide part of many music programs and instrumental teachers need to learn how to teach it. Biased attitudes, including the idea that anyone with a bad tone and poor technique can play jazz, are finally becoming things of the past. Musicians and teachers are beginning to realize that the high standards attributed to so-called "serious music" apply equally to the intelligent performance of jazz. The primary differences actually involve phrasing and interpretation.

One of the most important differences between jazz and traditional interpretation has to do with rhythm, especially the performance of consecutive eighth notes. In non-jazz music, consecutive eighth notes are played equal in length; the beat is divided into two equal parts. This is also done in some types of jazz. As a rule, however, jazz musicians think of a beat division of three—a triplet feeling resulting in uneven eighths. The note on the downbeat gets 2/3 of the beat and the other note gets 1/3 (Example 87).

EXAMPLE 87

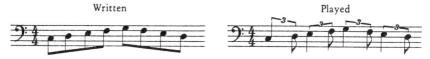

In addition to altering the rhythm, jazz performers often give a slight breath push to the off-beat eighths resulting in a slight accent. Care must be taken that this is not overdone to the point of being "corny." Tempo governs this to a large degree. In faster tempi, the accent is more obvious; at very slow tempi, very little or no accent is used, the emphasis here being on equal loudness for all notes.

Another basic difference is in the performance of syncopated figures (Example 88).

EXAMPLE 88

EXAMPLE 88 continued

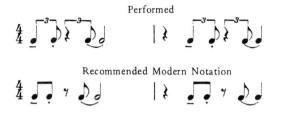

G. CONCLUSION

This chapter, in fact the entire text, is based upon the premise that the prime objective of instrumental instruction in the public schools is to help students become more sensitive to the expressive qualities of music. This means that significant emphasis in teaching and learning should be placed upon the study and practice of phrasing and interpretation. It also means that such instruction should be introduced early with reasonable results expected on a consistent basis.

Some public school teachers may be tempted to view the preceding as being unrealistic and rather secondary to the most basic problems of public school teaching. "How can I afford to be concerned with phrasing and interpretation when the student is still having difficulties with rhythm?" they may ask. "Why should I worry about dynamics when the student cannot finger the notes properly?" Playing correct rhythms and notes is surely important, but these are only two of the *means* toward the end objective of making music. If we allow ourselves to be satisfied once the student has surmounted his rhythmic and fingering hurdles, then we fail the student by not taking him the rest of the way. He may be a fourth-grade horn player playing a three-note solo after only three months of study, but is it really inevitable that he should play his solo like a machine? It need not be. All it takes is a simple demonstration of how the solo should be played in order to sound musical: possibly a slight *crescendo* in moving to the second note and perhaps a slight phrasing down after starting a third note. The musician-teacher will probably expect this instinctively from his students. The teacher who is not sensitive to the expressive aspects of musical performance will probably settle for much less, and so will his students.

Applying the above concept requires that students be taught that home practice is meaningless unless they keep one prime objective in mind: every note that is played should be musical. Even a single, isolated tone should have a good attack, good quality and intensity so that it moves ahead and finally ends with a "musical" release. One must *think* beautiful tone, phrasing, and line; every note is important and has musical significance. Even scales should be played musically, as will be discussed in a later chapter.

RECOMMENDED REFERENCES

General References

Barra, Donald, *The Dynamic Performance: A Performer's Guide to Musical Expression and Interpretation.* Englewood Cliffs, NJ: Prentice-Hall, 1983.

Dart, Thurston, *The Interpretation of Music.* London: Hutchinson's University Library, 1954.

Keller, Hermann, *Phrasing and Articulation,* trans. by Leigh Gerdine. New York: W. W. Norton & Company, Inc., 1965. (Chapters 1-3, 7)

Thurmond, James Morgan, *Note Grouping.* Camp Hill, PA: JMT Publications, 1982.

Ornamentation

Apel, Willi, Harvard Dictionary of Music (2nd ed., revised & enlarged). Cambridge: The Belknap Press of Harvard University Press, 1969.

Dolmetsch, Rudolph, *The Interpretation of the Music of the XVII and XVIII Centuries.* London: Novello, 1946.

Tartini, Giuseppe, *Treatise on the Ornaments of Music,* trans. by Sol Babitz, New York: Carl Fischer, Inc., 1956.

Jazz Interpretation

Baker, David N., *Jazz Pedagogy.* Chicago: Maher Publications, 1979.

Gridley, Mark, *Jazz Styles: History and Analysis.* 4th ed., Englewood Cliffs, NJ: 1991.

Guiffre, Jimmy, *Jazz Phrasing and Interpretation.* New York: Associated Music Publishers, 1969.

Henry, Robert, *The Jazz Ensemble.* Englewood Cliffs, NJ: Prentice-Hall, Inc., 1981.

Nanry, Charles, *The Jazz Text.* Van Nostrand Reinhold Co., 1979.

Chapter Six

ACQUIRING PERFORMANCE TECHNIQUE

Experience in judging school music contests and observing class lessons and rehearsals has shown that many students play much better technically than they do musically. Is this because fingering, tonguing, or bowing skills are easier to master, or is it because the student instinctively finds greater interest and challenge in working on technique as opposed to phrasing, interpretation, tone quality, and intonation? The answer to both of these is no; the real reason lies with the teacher. He more than anyone else influences the student's performing attitudes. The student needs to be told which performance qualities are most important. He needs to be reminded when an imbalance between technical and musical skills exists. Most importantly, the teacher needs to provide a learning environment in which students can, from the very beginning, learn to listen and properly evaluate their own performance results. This is best accomplished by starting with the imitative or playing-by-ear approach described in Chapters One and Two.

Students and teachers who emphasize sheer technical skill at the expense of tone, intonation, phrasing, and interpretation commit a serious error in doing so. But to emphasize the latter to the point of neglecting finger dexterity, for example, is an equally great mistake. The superior performer cannot afford to be deficient in either area. He needs command of his instrument in all areas.

Students sometimes possess a distorted view of what is meant by "good technique." Some seem to think that all one needs to be able to do is "rip through" a difficult passage and get most of the notes, but this is hardly the answer. Good technique involves the ability to play passages with flawless accuracy at all reasonable speeds. The player who can play a given passage reasonably well at only one tempo does not possess command of his instrument. He needs to develop relaxed control of his fingers, hands, tongue, embouchure, *and*, especially, self-confidence that he will not make frequent mistakes.

Acquiring good technique is not easy. Talent is of little help; hard work is the real answer. One can even be a so-called poor musician and still become technically proficient on an instrument. What is needed most is patience, perseverance, knowledge, and proper application of correct practice procedures. Correct practice procedure is the primary concern of this chapter.

A. HOW TO PRACTICE

> The pattern for efficient musical learning is (a) an aural concept of what is to be achieved, (b) provisional tries, (c) reflection on what is right and what is wrong, and (d) a decision on changes to be made in the next tries.[1]

The traditional prescription for developing instrumental technique has been to drill the fundamentals: scales, arpeggios, lip slurs, and related items along with covering a sequence of studies specified by the teacher. Teachers of the old school sometimes placed great emphasis on this approach to the total neglect of using any actual musical literature; voice and piano students in particular were expected to work on technique for several years before being allowed to give a public recital of "real music." In cases where the pedagogy used was effective and the student possessed very strong interest accompanied by a resigned willingness to limit his study in this narrow manner, the results were often successful. Those students with only average interest and perseverance undoubtedly never continued long enough to reach the concert stage.

At the other extreme is the type of teacher whose pedagogical approach is based solely upon singing or playing of tunes to the total exclusion of systematic training in performance fundamentals. In fact, current practice in some school instrumental programs indicates a retreat from the teaching of fundamentals, or at best involves ill-conceived pedagogy. Even when traditional study materials are used, students are often sent home with the instruction merely to practice the same page for next week or simply advised to practice the "hard spots" over and over.

---

[1] Charles Leonhard and Robert W. House, *Foundations and Principles of Music Education* (New York: McGraw-Hill Book Company, 1959), p. 134. Used by permission of McGraw-Hill Book Company.

Such instruction without accompanying guidelines of specifically *what* and *how* inevitably results in considerable waste of human energy.

There is no doubt that certain technical problems need to be isolated and studied with microscopic thoroughness. The idea of going through a complete book of studies in consecutive order until the last page has been covered, however, is open to serious question. Such an approach implies use of study material as an end unto itself. This may satisfy the misguided needs of the "practice room" musician, but blind mechanical practice has little relevance to the performing musical artist. The latter must be prepared to deal with the technical problems of real music to be played for an audience of real people. His success or lack of it will be measured by his ability in evaluating properly the *musical* results achieved in the practice room; identifying the underlying reasons for failing to achieve these results; woodshedding the "hard spots" along with study of appropriate technical studies or exercises as needed; and finally going back to the real music and re-evaluating the overall musical results.

B. THE IMPORTANCE OF SLOW PRACTICE

Good technique includes the ability to play with great speed. Students often assume that in order to play fast, one should also practice fast. The paradox here is that the most important requisite in being able to play fast is the need for a considerable amount of slow practice. Yes, we all know this is true, but actually disciplining ourselves to do it is another matter. Somehow the whole idea seems irrational. It is like the idea of the brass student practicing pedal tones in order to improve his high register. At first thought the idea does not make much sense; but both are highly important if one is to get the most in return for the time and effort expended. Both are also a means toward developing the type of control which is necessary in order to achieve consistency in performance.

Despite this, very few students practice difficult passages or challenging technical etudes slowly enough for a sufficient period of time; most students devote too much time to fast practice alone. There is also the mistaken impression among some that if one simply puts in enough time playing the thing over and over, success is bound to come. In either case the results are usually quite discouraging. Neither approach brings about control of technique or accurate rhythmic precision. The teacher scolds the student for not practicing enough, and the student decides he really wasn't cut out to be a violinist in the first place. But the future need not look so dismal. Adequate slow practice with a metronome on a consistent day-to-day basis can do much to alleviate earlier difficulties. As one's ability to play the music increases, the tempo should be increased accordingly until finally, playing up to tempo with accuracy becomes a reality.

What are the hazards of practicing everything up to tempo? First of all, tension ruins technique! Continual practice above and beyond the point of control creates tension not only in the fingers but in other parts of the body as well, including the breathing mechanism, the throat, the embouchure, and the player's hands and arms. The student who practices slowly is better able to concentrate on relaxing his body sufficiently and thereby to resist muscular tension. As the speed is increased he strives to maintain continued relaxation in his playing. He learns to slow down the metronome and do additional drill at a slower tempo whenever he feels tension creeping in. This first step is where most students fail. Many are impatient since repetitive slow drill can be terribly boring. But nature cannot be prodded ahead by wishful thinking. Technique development takes time and considerable self-discipline. To those with the necessary fortitude, the dividends are well worth the effort.

Secondly, students who tend to practice everything too fast are usually unaware of how inefficient they are in the use of their fingers. When the distance of finger movement to and away from the fingerboard, valves, keys, or tone holes is excessive, this inevitably causes awkward, uneven fingering. The rule is to move the fingers just enough so they can perform their function properly and no more. The fingers should remain close to the keys, valves, or fingerboard and operate with minimal movement, like tiny, precision machinery. Slow practice allows the student to concentrate on this item while fast practice diverts his attention to just trying to keep up.

Finally, the finger tension caused by excessive practice at fast speeds sometimes fosters the use of heavy finger action—"popping" the fingers against the fingerboard or tone holes. Some teachers recommend this type of fingering in rapid passages, but this author does not recommend it since it often causes unwarranted tension in the fingers. The goal should be to eliminate all sources of tension so that fingering feels effortless. Soft fingering is recommended instead.

Not the least in importance regarding finger dexterity are the matters of correct breathing and posture. Many a student whose approach to breathing has created excessive tension, particularly in the exhalation process, has had this tension carry over into the fingers. Since posture can affect the breathing process, the source of a finger tension problem can sometimes be traced to a cramped position of the abdomen or the throat.

Lest the author's intentions be misinterpreted, let it be known that learning to play with fast technique also involves fast practice as well as slow practice. A certain amount of practice should be devoted to pushing oneself a little beyond the point of absolute control. A swimmer can hardly be expected to win a race if he practices slow motion all the time! But fast practice should always be preceded by sufficient slow practice to eliminate muscular tension.

C. DEVELOPING A STEADY BEAT

The ability to play with a steady beat is of great importance to every musician. Acquiring this ability takes considerable time as a rule, but it can be mastered if proper concentration and procedures are used. Probably the most efficient and effective procedures available are those which utilize the metronome.

The metronome is one of the oldest mechanical teaching aids available to musicians. Today's technology has provided us with electric metronomes equipped with flashing lights, combination metronome-tuner devices and the Trinome, which produces three different sounds (bell, tick, and tock) for outlining divisions and subdivisions of the beat as well as the basic unit. All too often music teachers simply give lip service to these devices without seriously considering them as an integral part of their instructional programs. In this section, special attention will be given to the metronome as a means toward solving specific rhythm problems. A listing and description of other available audio-visual aids can be found in the Appendix of this text.

A common problem with beginning players is that of rushing the tempo. Once basic rhythms, fingerings, and pitches have been learned, the only challenge many of them see is speed—how fast they can play a given exercise or piece of music. But rushing the tempo is not limited to very young players. Advanced players also tend to rush tempos, particularly in staccato and/or pianissimo passages. Failure to solve it in the lesson will mean increased frustration in band or orchestra rehearsal when the director tries to maintain a steady tempo with his group.

Asking the student to think subdivision (1+2+3+4+, or 1e+a 2e+a where more complex subdivisions are involved) frequently helps hold the tempo down. Tapping the foot, being certain that the upbeat gets as much emphasis and duration as the downbeat, can also help. The teacher counting aloud or clapping the unit beat and the subdivision if needed is also recommended. If rushing still continues to be a severe problem, probably the only real answer is to purchase a metronome for use in home practice.

What if the student cannot play with the metronome? Some will emphatically insist they cannot do it, that it hinders rather than helps them. Teachers who are not thoroughly sold on the idea may be tempted to agree with the students. But just as in using foot tapping, time counting and other pedagogical aids, getting results takes patience and perseverance on the part of the teacher and students alike. It requires drill, repetition, and most importantly, confidence that the method will actually work.

Some marching bands spend considerable time and effort drilling "8 to 5" (8 steps to each 5 yards) so that each individual marcher can place the left foot on the yard line on the count of one with flawless consistency. Once this becomes second nature he need not concentrate on it so much any more; ranks will be straight without the need for continually looking to the right or left. The same principle applies to feeling a steady beat. Once it becomes second nature, there is no longer a need to concentrate on it so much, and the student can then give greater attention to other elements of performance. Precision problems will also tend to disappear. When a tempo is established which all the players *feel* "in unison," the conductor can also devote more of his attention to things other than the more naive aspects of time beating.

Percussion players as a section usually exert the greatest influence on tempo aside from the conductor. In a marching band or jazz band they literally "rule the roost" in this area. Anything less than reasonable perfection regarding steady tempo, therefore, should not be tolerated. This is why the author, in his own teaching, finally decided to require all of his beginning percussionists to buy a metronome as part of their basic equipment, along with sticks and a practice pad. While this may at first seem too much to ask of the parent economically, the initial investment made by parents of beginning wind and string players is no less financially and eventually becomes much greater when the instrument is finally paid for. Experience also showed that this policy tended to discourage the surplus of percussion hopefuls who chose percussion because they felt that learning to beat a drum was easy technically and financially.

Let us assume that a student has difficulty in keeping a steady beat on a given exercise or musical passage. He tries using a metronome but is unsuccessful in staying with it. What should he do? First, decrease the speed of the metronome until he can actually play along with it. It may even be necessary to put the metronome near its lowest setting in order to accomplish this goal. In passages involving rapid sixteenths or related subdivisions, it may advisable to let each tick of the metronome represent an eighth note rather than a quarter or dotted quarter unit. As soon as the student is ready, the tempo should be increased until he reaches the point where he is able to play up to tempo with good rhythmic accuracy. This will probably not happen after one lesson. Conquering the fundamentals of playing can sometimes be a difficult challenge and this

area is no exception. Drill and practice in the proper manner usually results in some improvement, however, and this is the ultimate goal of all
the energies expended in the practice room.

If problems still persist, the only recourse may be to have the student
practice scales in slow quarter or half notes with the metronome. You
have to start somewhere. If your band or orchestra is ever to play with
good precision and if you as a conductor are ever going to control the
tempo, then acute sensitivity to a steady beat on the part of all the players is essential. Are you satisfied with the precision of your group? Do
your players follow your tempo? Does the percussion section continually
drag the beat while the cornets rush? Practicing with a metronome will
not solve all of these problems, but it is a starting point. In any case the
real burden rests on the shoulders of the teacher. Avoid blaming the
students. You show them how; you teach them!

D. PRACTICING SCALES AND RELATED EXERCISES

Almost everyone who has ever studied an instrument seriously has at
some time or other been asked to practice scales. In addition, pianists,
string players, and woodwind players usually spend considerable time
practicing arpeggios, broken chords, scales in thirds, and other related
exercises. Brass players, on the other hand, are usually expected to
practice long tones and lip slurs while the snare drummer concentrates
on rudiments.

Students are sometimes asked to practice scales without knowing why
they should be practiced. It may be that the teacher himself is not fully
aware of why he assigned them in the first place except that one of his
teachers did it, everyone he knows does it, and therefore it must be a
good thing. There has to be a better reason than this. Practicing scales
like eating vegetables and brushing teeth can become terribly routine
and not much fun. But if one understands why these things are good, one
is more likely to do them regularly with at least a token degree of sin-
cerity. Practice is time-consuming and can also be fatiguing. To practice
hour upon hour without a clear sense of purpose and understanding of
why one does certain things is foolish.

The central purpose of practicing scales and related exercises is to
develop one's technique along with training the ear. Also important are
the matters of finger dexterity, learning to play certain combinations
of notes which are indigenous to specific keys, and being able to discern
differences between major, minor, whole tone, semi-tone, augmented
and diminished intervals and chords. Unless the student becomes aurally
sensitive to tonality, knowledge of key signatures alone will be of little

help in keeping him off the C-naturals, for example, when playing in D major. Being able to play in the right key is largely an aural process, not just a physical process based upon finger manipulation.

As one tries to increase speed in performance, it is important to be able to coordinate the fingers, use proper alternate fingerings, and develop the ability of the tongue or bow to move at a rapid rate. Scale practice can serve as the means for achieving these objectives. Scales can also serve as an effective vehicle for warmup. But much of the potential value of scale practice can be lost unless the scales are memorized. Only then can the player give full attention to listening for tonality, accurate intonation, and tone quality. Only then can he evaluate all of the other elements which make up a polished performance. In fact, once scales are memorized, the potential for using them as vehicles for learning new musical concepts is virtually limitless.

Although major and minor scales contain eight notes per octave, there is no reason why all eight notes need to be practiced all at once. Instead, practicing up and down the lower tetrachord several times followed by similar drill on the upper tetrachord is highly recommended. The student who has difficulty, for example, with the upper tetrachord of a harmonic minor scale is wasting time by practicing the entire scale repeatedly. He should spend the bulk of his practice time on the upper tetrachord.

Scale practice can be made more interesting through effective use of variety and challenge. Variety can be created through use of different rhythm patterns, articulations, and bowings. Challenge can also be created in ensemble rehearsal by sudden changes in tempo, style, dynamics, use of *rubato*, accents, fermatas, and cut-offs.

E. DEVELOPING EVENNESS OF FINGERING

When students find difficulty in playing rapid passages evenly, altering the rhythm to include dotted note values is frequently helpful. This is particularly true where numerous cross-fingerings exist, as in the third octave of the flute. The problems of efficient finger coordination are difficult enough; add to this the problems of tongue or bow as well as finger coordination in staccato performance, and the difficulty increases considerably. Slow practice of ♩♫♫♫ is helpful, but ♩.♫♩.♩ and the reverse ♫♩.♫♩. is also recommended.

Other rhythmic variants are shown in Example 89. The purpose of all these is to develop control which leads to flawless consistency, the ultimate goal of every performer.

EXAMPLE 89

RECOMMENDED REFERENCES

Galamian, Ivan, *Principles of Violin Playing and Teaching*. Englewood Cliffs, NJ: Prentice-Hall, Inc., 1962. (Chapter 1)

Farkas, Phillip, *The Art of French Horn Playing*. Evanston, IL: Summy-Birchard, 1956. (pp. 30–48)

Gibson, Daryl J., *A Textbook for Trumpet*. Minneapolis, MN: Schmitt, Hall and McCreary Co., 1962. (pp. 31–45)

Chapter Seven

TEACHING
CLASS
LESSONS

One of the most important developments in instrumental music teaching during this century was the advent of the class instruction approach. Previously, instrumental instruction was limited almost entirely to private lessons. Class instruction made it possible, however, for a single teacher to teach a much larger number of students at proportionately less cost per student.

The first instrumental class lessons offered in this country on a wide scale were taught by Albert G. Mitchell, a violinist and music supervisor in Boston, who was one of the first to try the "new idea" in this country after having observed it in England during the winter of 1910–11. Wind and percussion teachers later adopted the idea, which led to a spectacular growth of bands in the public schools by the 1930s.

Nevertheless, one still hears occasionally that the reason why the band or orchestra in a particular school system is so good is because all, or at least most, of the students take private lessons. The implication is that private study is still the only *real answer* to building a superior performing organization, and that those groups without the benefit of private study do not really stand a chance. There can be no doubt that private study is highly beneficial, but this does not mean that students cannot learn to play reasonably well without private study. There is ample evidence that in many highly successful instrumental programs practically none of the students studied privately.

When private lessons are not possible, the next best alternative is to offer class lessons. Since this is the primary type of instruction used in most public schools, instrumental teachers need to be prepared to teach class lessons effectively. Teaching classes of like instruments is in itself challenging, but teachers are often expected to teach heterogeneous instrument classes as well. While the latter is probably the most difficult and least desirable way to teach, reasonable success is possible so long as the teacher knows all his instruments well and is capable of dealing with class situations.

Despite the alleged superiority of private lessons, there are some aspects of performance which can often be taught more effectively in class situations, specific examples being intonation, rhythmic precision, balance, and blend. But probably the most positive feature of class lessons is the fact that many students, especially younger ones, actually prefer to study in a class with their peers rather than alone with a private instructor. Friendly competition between members of a class can also foster greater desire toward home practice. Realization of these attributes is not automatic, however, Much depends upon the structure and content of the lesson and the personality of the teacher. The teacher and his methods are the primary limiting factors in most teaching and learning situations.

The ability to teach heterogeneous instruments is especially important if one is to be very effective in directing full band or orchestra rehearsals. The question is what should be taught in the large group rehearsal, and what should be reserved for the class lesson. Each situation has its own function and needs to be viewed differently. Common sense and practical experience will provide the answers in most cases, but a brief review of some of the more common problems related to these topics is in order.

The obvious things which need to be taught in class lessons are those things which cannot be efficiently taught in the large group rehearsal or sectional. This should not include rote drill of difficult band or orchestra parts, although class lessons are sometimes erroneously used for this purpose. Emphasis instead should be placed upon developing individual instrumental techniques such as embouchure, fingering, etc. The student who learns how to use this knowledge to improve his individual performance will become a greater asset to the large and small ensemble groups in which he participates. Frequent use of class lesson time for other purposes is difficult to justify.

Several items need to be considered in setting up a class lesson schedule: the size of the class, the type of grouping, and the structure, content, and length of the class lesson. All of these considerations are dependent upon overall scheduling within a particular school and upon other related factors which will be discussed in detail in the following sections. Attention will also be given to special problems in teaching the slow beginner and advanced classes.

A. GROUPING OF STUDENTS

In starting classes of beginners, classes of like instruments are definitely preferable to heterogeneous classes. Like instrument classes beyond the beginning level are also desirable, although this may not always be possible because of scheduling limitations. Even when scheduling is not a problem, rather distinct differences in student ability and achievement soon emerge after several weeks of study. The better students tend to become bored and the slow students become frustrated because of their inability to keep up with the rest of the class.

Possible solutions to the above dilemma are to prepare supplementary remedial exercises for the slower students, to give the better students additional assignments from other study material, or even to recommend private study where possible. Another possibility is to dismiss the majority of the class five or ten minutes early so that the teacher can give special assistance either to the fast or the slow students. None of these solutions is really satisfactory, however. The preferred alternative is to group students according to reading ability rather than by instrument.

Any attempt to group and regroup students according to reading ability usually results in scheduling problems if the class teaching schedule is set up so that students attend their lesson at the same time each week. If a rotating schedule is used, the teacher can easily shift students from one class to another without needing to consult other faculty and the administration. Since such flexibility is highly desirable, a rotating class schedule is preferred over the former type of scheduling.

Grouping by reading ability usually results in heterogeneous classes of instruments. Ideally, arrangements can be made so that the classes contain only instruments of the same family, i.e., woodwinds, brasses, strings, percussion. If there is no other choice but to mix instruments of different families, then mixing of woodwinds, brasses, and percussion is possible. Mixing strings with winds or percussion should generally be avoided for obvious reasons, among which is the lack of instructional materials for such diverse combinations.

If one must teach classes of students of varying achievement levels, how does one adjust his teaching objectives to meet the situation? Teachers of classroom subjects are faced with this problem daily. The usual prescription is to aim at the "middle" of the class. The slow students should not be coddled at the expense of the others, although admittedly this is often difficult to avoid. The better students should be provided with reasonable challenge. One of the primary incentives of instrumental study is the challenge it can provide; take this away from the better students and many will soon lose interest. In an effort to please everyone, it is possible in the end to please no one. Failure is then inevitable.

Class size and the length of the lesson period directly affect the quantitative and qualitative outcomes of any instrumental lesson. Experience has shown that six to eight students in a like instrument class and four to six in a heterogeneous class are maximal numbers if one hopes to maintain sufficient progress to keep the students interested. A forty-five-minute to one hour period for junior and senior high students is recommended. Although some authorities feel that an equal amount is also desirable at the elementary school level, not all youngsters of this age are able to concentrate for this long a period. Often no more than thirty minutes of lesson time is available, but successful teaching and learning is still possible as long as the teacher paces the lesson properly.

The type of method book used depends upon the type of grouping which exists and the system of scheduling employed. With classes of like instruments meeting the same time each week, materials designed for private teaching can often be used. Where a rotating schedule along with ability grouping is used, resulting in heterogeneous grouping of instruments, the same full band or string method series should be used for all classes. This allows the teacher to shift students from one class to another at will without the need for having students buy a new book for each class change.

B. STRUCTURE AND CONTENT OF THE LESSON

Every good performing musician knows that it takes much more than so-called talent to become a fine player. A student can also have the finest instrument made and take lessons from the best teacher available, and still not learn to play. Learning to play an instrument involves a high level of coordination and skill. These must be properly developed through extensive drill and repetition in home practice. There is no other way!

Methods to be used in getting students to practice faithfully will not be discussed here. This area will be left up to each teacher to resolve in his own personal way. What is of concern here is that the teacher be reminded of his responsibility for showing students the *correct way* to practice, with proper musical as well as technical goals in mind. Since correct practice habits need to be established right from the start, this makes the responsibility vested in the teacher of beginners especially great.

A primary function of any lesson, therefore, is for the teacher to show the student *what* to practice and *how* to go about it in the most productive manner. One means of achieving these objectives is to structure the lesson so that it follows much the same pattern as a good home practice session. This means devoting attention in proper sequence to tune-up, warm-up, and playing by ear, as well as playing through the assigned lesson book material. If the former items are important enough to be practiced at home, they also deserve to be heard in the lesson. One way to ensure that students in a history class, for example, actually read an assignment is to tell them they will be tested on it. Much the same principle applies to what instrumental students practice at home. If they are merely told that proper warm-up is important and should be practiced, the tendency is to forget about it unless they are expected to do it at the next lesson and succeeding ones as well. This also provides the teacher a means of continually checking to see that these things are being done correctly.

Each lesson should begin with tuning the instrument, using a strobe Lectro-tuner, the teacher, or the group of players as a criterion. This should be followed by a brief warm-up on a scale, lip slurs or other special warm-up material designed for the class. Warm-up exercises should be played slowly so that the students as well as the teacher can listen for intonation, tone quality, blend, balance, attacks, and releases. Adjustments should be made as needed to set the proper atmosphere for the lesson. Do some "teacher plays–students imitate" ear training followed by one or two tunes the class can play together by ear.

Next go to the class method book and spot check specific exercises. Since most class lessons will only be thirty- to forty-five minutes long at most, there is seldom enough time to hear the entire assignment. Actually, this is usually unnecessary. The important thing is to pace the lesson period so that there is sufficient time left at the end to properly introduce a new assignment, including a clear explanation of any new techniques or notational symbols. Demonstration by the teacher should be included followed by a first trial by the class, where appropriate, to be sure they understand the "hows and whys" of the new assignment. This will help avoid incorrect practice at home. Instructions such as "Practice the next page" should definitely be avoided.

Beginning teachers and teachers in training sometimes express real concern that the class lesson does not let each student be heard alone. This need not be the case. In less than a minute the teacher can hear each student play individually by going around the room having the first student play the first two measures of a given piece or exercise, the next player the next two measures, etc., without stopping in between until every member of the class has had his turn. Not only does this put each player "on the spot" before the rest of the class; it also helps him learn to listen to the mistakes of other players so that he becomes more critical of his own playing. Some teachers also use this approach as a means for determining who sits in what chair for the next lesson. This promotes competition among class members which in turn gets them to practice harder at home.

Another concern of some teachers in training is how to give personalized attention to individual players in a class lesson situation. The answer is to work with individual students while the entire class is playing. There is no need to stop the whole class to correct a hand position, embouchure, or other problem possessed by only one student; the teacher can walk over to the student, adjust his hand position until it is correct, and move on to correct other student errors as needed. Not only does this approach save lesson time, but it is often more effective pedagogically than stopping the class and explaining the problem verbally.

As a further aid toward saving lesson time, it is recommended that the teacher provide a pencil for each music stand, since students usually forget to bring their own despite persistent reminders. In addition to marking counts and footbeats, students can also write reminders to themselves at the top of the page, such as "work for a bigger tone," "start each tone with tongue," etc. They can also mark their own assignments and circle exercise numbers to be repeated for the next lesson. All of these can save considerable time in the lesson and allow more time for actual teaching.

C. TEACHING INTONATION

The first rule and last rule of good intonation is *listen.* While this is sound advice, it is not enough. The teacher must make his students *conscious* of intonation; he must also help them learn *what* to listen for as well as *how* to improve poor intonation on their own. Beyond this his function should become one of a prompter or guide. Principal responsibility for good intonation should rest with the student. If the student fails to accept this responsibility seriously, it is to be hoped that the teacher's pitch sensitivity is such that he cannot easily tolerate consistently poor intonation and will *insist* that improvement be made!

As was explained in Chapter Three, Section B, changes in dynamics have a direct effect upon intonation which must not be overlooked when tuning wind instruments. All pitches sounded for tuning purposes should therefore be at a *mezzoforte* dynamic level with no lipping. Failure to adhere to this principle will invalidate the bulk of one's efforts to tune up properly.

1. Pedagogy for Beginning Players

Intonation is not a topic to be postponed until the intermediate or advanced stages of study, or applied exclusively in a remedial sense. As in all phases of ear training, intonation development should begin as early as possible, just as a young plant must be cultivated properly from the beginning lest its growth be permanently stunted.

The following is a systematic approach intended for helping the beginner to become, first of all, conscious of intonation, and secondly, aware of how to solve his own intonation problems.

1. *Start teaching intonation when the student produces his first tones.* The teacher should tune the student's instrument initially so that it is reasonably close to A-440. The student should be instructed to adjust tuning slides, barrel joints, etc. to approximately the same position when practicing at home. Marking a spot in ink on the mouthpipe cork of the saxophone is an example of a specific, concrete aid in this area. Tuning rings for the clarinet may also be in order.

   Quality instruments are usually built to play with best intonation at A-440, 72° Fahrenheit, when the tuning slide or joints are pulled out somewhat. Some leeway on the sharp side as well as the flat side is necessary in order to adjust to changing temperature conditions, atmospheric conditions and out-of-tune pianos. Most brass instruments, flutes, clarinets and saxophones will, therefore, be sharp when pushed all the way in. In addition, the inherent intonation deficiencies of the individual instruments will be increased—sharp notes will be sharper, flat notes will be still flatter in relation to adjacent notes. But, perhaps worst of all, playing an instrument which is consistently sharp or out of tune with itself often results in a mistuning of the player's *ear*. Many a student has experienced a genuine revelation when told for the first time that a note or notes he thought he had been playing in tune all those years were in fact out of tune, as evidenced by the whirling discs of the strobe when his pitch was sounded. "How can this be?" the student asks. "It sounds in tune to me." But further analysis shows that beats also occur when he plays the note in octaves with another player. Finally he is convinced that the note is indeed out of tune, and wonders why this condition existed for so long. It is, therefore, of considerable importance that the student be taught to play *and hear* pitches reasonably well in tune right from the start.

2. *As soon as the student can produce a relatively steady tone, teach him to listen for beats.* "Two notes out of tune create a 'rough' sound. Two tones in tune should sound like one instrument; they should sound 'smooth.'" (These are descriptions made by beginning instrumental students.) One of the best methods for illustrating the effect of two

tones sounding in tune is to use two trombone players with one keeping his playing slide stationary while the other one slowly slides up to the correct pitch. This allows the class to hear a wide spectrum from very out of tune to perfectly "smooth" (in tune).

Studio teachers frequently use duets as a means for teaching intonation and listening for beats. Here the student learns to listen to his teacher's pitch and adjust to it. The teacher and student check especially poor intervals, playing them in sustained fashion until beats are eliminated.

The unison, of course, is not the only available interval for matching pitches or eliminating beats. Octaves, fifths, fourths, and thirds are equally good and in some cases preferable to the unison. Students (and teachers) who find difficulty deciding who is sharp or flat on a unison, for example, may find the problem greatly reduced when playing an octave or fifth as a check for intonation. The goal is still the same— elimination of beats—the only real difference being that the *direction* of individual pitch discrepancies may be more easily determined through the latter method. Therefore, if a scale is used for warm-up in the lesson, playing it in octaves may be more effective than playing it in unison. Another application of this idea is for the private teacher to play, where practical, an octave above or below the student when he plays etudes or exercises from his method book. The resulting sound tends to be more interesting as well as more pedagogically useful.

3. *As soon as it is practical to do so, teach the student how to tune his own instrument.* He must learn to pull out to lower the pitch and push in to raise the pitch. Some wind instrument beginners will find greatest success through use of the technique, employed by string players, of starting flat and tuning upward.

For those who need additional drill in tuning up, the "back to back" idea has proved helpful. Two students sit with their chairs back to back. Player No. 1 tries to adjust to player No. 2, whose tuning slide, barrel, or string is set to a specific position unknown to player No. 1, and vice versa.

Young students frequently are confused as to whether they should pull out or push in to raise the pitch. The following analogy has proved helpful with very young students: The piccolo is a small, short instrument, high in pitch. The tuba is a large, long instrument, low in pitch. Therefore, if you want to raise your pitch, shorten (push in) your instrument like the piccolo; to lower the pitch, lengthen (pull out) your instrument like the tuba.

4. *As the student's playing range extends to an octave or more, teach him:*
    a. Which notes are out of tune on his instrument.
    b. Which way these notes are out of tune.
    c. How to adjust intonation on individual tones.

For a detailed discussion of these items, please refer to Section D, Chapter Three, of this book.

2. Tuning the Woodwinds

When tuning adjustments on woodwind instruments are made near the reed or mouthpiece, the note fingered nearest the mouthpiece or reed usually provides the best tuning check. The clarinetist should use open G to determine proper adjustment of the barrel joint. In checking the middle section of the clarinet, low C is recommended. If the low C is sharp, the player should also check the G above the staff, a twelfth higher. If both notes are sharp, the clarinet should be pulled out at the middle joint. If one note is sharp and the other flat, pulling out at the middle joint will not solve the problem. All other conditions being equal, clarinetists should rarely need to pull at the middle joint. More frequently, however, some pull at the bell is necessary; the amount of pull is determined by checking the pitch of the bell tones, B and C in the staff.

It is conceivable that the oboist, like the clarinetist, could adjust the middle joint and the bell to secure optimum overall intonation on his instrument. As a general practice, however, this is not done and apparently is not necessary. Pulling out the tenor joint and the long joint of the bassoon is sometimes necessary, but the player who does this frequently may be using a reed which is either too hard or too short. His bocal may also be of improper length or of poor quality.

Flutists normally confine their basic tuning adjustment to the headjoint only. When poor intonation between octaves is a persistent problem, adjustment of the cork inside the headjoint may be required. The combination tuning-cleaning rod which comes with the instrument is designed to help with this process. The cork should be adjusted so that the mark on the tuning rod falls across the center of the embouchure hole. If this does not solve the intonation problem, the flutist should check the flute's octaves against the strobe, or consult a specialist teacher.

Alignment of the headjoint with the body section of the flute affects tone quality as well as intonation. If the headjoint is rolled out too far, the tone becomes thin and the pitch sharp; when rolled in too far, the tone sags and the pitch goes flat. Generally speaking, proper alignment is achieved when the center of the embouchure hole is in line with the center of the first key on the instrument. It has been observed, however, that some professional flutists tend to turn the headjoint inward slightly (toward the player's lips) from the central position. Tone quality, resonance and consistency of intonation throughout the range are all affected by this alignment. Intelligent experimentation with these factors in mind is often needed to find the proper alignment for each instrument.

Some flutes are made with one or more notches on the headjoint and body to facilitate proper alignment. The player can then align his instrument the same way each time he prepares to play. Flutes which do not possess such notches may be notched by the teacher once the ideal alignment is determined. This can be done by *lightly* scratching a line on both joints with a scoring tool, just enough so the player can see it. In this way one is assured that the alignment will be the same for each playing period. This in turn provides a feeling of security for the player who can expect consistency in the way the embouchure hole fits or feels on his lower lip.

The primary factor which determines the prevailing pitch on both the oboe and bassoon is the reed itself. When the pitch is noticeably flat or sharp, the player should either alter the *length* or *strength* of his reed. The longer the reed is, or the softer it is in the center or "heart" section, the flatter it is; the shorter or harder it is, the higher it is.

If an oboe is extremely flat in pitch and no other immediate recourse is available, a small portion of the cork end of the reed staple can be sawed off to raise the pitch. This is an emergency measure and should be understood as such. Eventually the source of the problem, the reed cane itself, should be altered as described above.

If an oboe is consistently sharp, the pitch can be lowered by pulling out the reed. The player must realize, however, that pulling out in this area creates an air trap between the bottom of the reed and the body of the instrument. This causes poor response of the low notes in particular, manifesting itself in a "gurgle" or splitting of the octave.

Creation of an air trap between joints also causes problems in response on the clarinet. Tuning rings are recommended to eliminate the air trap and to prevent the barrel accidentally slipping back in place. In cases where students were negligent in keeping the barrel properly pulled out, some teachers have reportedly glued the proper size tuning ring inside the barrel to prevent its being easily removed.

The air trap problem can also be a frustrating one on the saxophone. The existence of the problem is usually due to carelessness or ignorance on the part of the player. When finished playing, the saxophone mouthpiece should be removed and stored separately in the case. If the mouthpiece is left on the neck pipe, the cork will shrink. This creates an air trap at the end of the neck pipe when the mouthpiece is pulled out to lower the overall pitch. This in turn causes poor response on the low tones.

Most bassoonists will have at least two bocals in their case, a number 1 and a number 2. The number 1 is the shorter in length; the number 2 bocal is the longer and also the one used most often. If the player needs to raise his pitch, he may change to the number 1 bocal. If the pitch is still consistently flat, he may acquire a number 0 bocal and if necessary, ream out the butt of the reed so it will fit further onto the bocal. As with the oboe, such extreme adjustments are emergency measures. As soon as possible, the player should deal with the real source of the problem—the reed, which either lacks sufficient heart or is of improper length or needs scraping.

The tone chamber or bore size of the clarinet and saxophone mouthpieces can have a significant effect on the overall pitch and tone quality of these instruments. If the instrument is consistently sharp, requiring excessive pulling out to get down to pitch, this may be due to the mouthpiece rather than the instrument. In such a case a change to a mouthpiece with a larger tone chamber is probably in order.

3. Tuning the Brasses

G on the second line is recommended as the initial tuning note for cornet or trumpet. Since it is in the heart of the range, the beginning player is less likely to pinch it sharp as he often does when first trying to play C in the third space. Later, when the player's range and control increases to third space C and above, he should begin on second line G and play upward diatonically to the C as recommended by Hindsley. Approaching the note from below helps avoid playing above the center of the tone and thereby provides a more valid pitch for tuning. The same concept is applicable to other brasses and woodwinds as well. (See Hindsley Tuning Guides in the Appendix of Pottle's *Tuning the School Band and Orchestra.*)

According to Righter, "When the main tuning slide is pulled [on a valved-brass instrument], the relationship of all fingered tones to the open tone pitch is destroyed, and there must be a retuning of the valve slides to bring about an agreement."[1] Hindsley advocates much the same principle, but his method for achieving the goal is somewhat different.[2] (See both sources for a detailed discussion of procedure in each case.)

According to Farkas, the following procedure for adjustment of French horn valve slides is recommended: Pull the first valve slide "twice as far as the second slide and the third valve slide three times as far as the second." Farkas further suggests that the player who is being tuned sound his pitch before the tuning note is sounded. This procedure will

[1] Charles Boardman Righter, *Teaching Instrumental Music* (New York: Carl Fischer, Inc., 1959), pp. 63–64.
[2] Ralph R. Pottle, *Tuning the School Band and Orchestra*, 2nd ed. (Hammond, La.: Ralph R. Pottle, 1962), p. 66.

help prevent the ear and lip adjusting immediately to a pre-determined pitch standard. The goal at this point is to tune the instrument, not the player.[3]

An area of considerable confusion among student musicians and teachers is how to determine which slides on the double horn are main tuning slides and which ones are water slides. The truth is that there is no set rule as to the exact placement of these slides. Even different model horns built by the same manufacturer may differ somewhat. (Consult *How to Tune a Double French Horn*, published by the Conn Corporation, for further information.)

The basic fingerings for the B-flat horn and F horn are the same from G-sharp in the staff to C in the third space. Players of the double horn, therefore, can check these notes against each other to determine if the two sides of the horn are in tune with each other.

Of special importance to proper French horn tuning is the position of the right hand in the bell. All too often public school players do not put enough hand in the bell. This results in a tone which is very open in quality and sharp in pitch. To compensate, the player—often at the director's recommendation—will pull the main tuning slide out too far without making corresponding adjustments to the valve slides. Problems in overall intonation are thus increased rather than improved. (See Farkas' *Art of French Horn Playing* or Colwell's *The Teaching of Instrumental Music*, both of which contain excellent illustrations of proper right hand position.)

Another factor affecting French horn intonation is that of muting. Muting can be accomplished either with the hand (stopped horn indicated most frequently by a plus sign) or use of a cardboard, metal, or wood mute inserted in the bell. With regard to the latter, care must be taken that the mute chosen fits a given horn or else serious intonation problems may result. Also, some mutes are of the transposing variety, while others are non-transposing.[4] (See pp. 79–80 of Farkas' book.)

Hand-stopping causes the horn to sound one half step *higher*, therefore, the player must transpose *down* a half step. In order for this rule to hold true, the hand-stopping process must be done correctly (see Farkas, pp. 80–81).

In summation, the first step in tuning a valved brass instrument is to get the open tones in tune to A-440. Regardless of what procedure is used in adjusting the valve slides, the end result will be a compromise. Perfect intonation on one valve can be achieved only at the expense of good intonation on the various valve combinations. The goal is to tune

[3] Farkas, *Art of French Horn Playing*, pp. 17–18.
[4] Farkas, *The Art of French Horn Playing*, pp. 79–80.

the instrument so that it is possible for all combinations to be played in tune by the player.

Lipping down a sharp note is much easier than lipping up a flat note on a brass instrument. The same is true on clarinet. (Flute, double reeds, and saxophone have much greater flexibility in these areas, which can be an asset or a liability depending upon the competence of the individual player.) Flat notes should therefore be eliminated where feasible in favor of sharp notes.

Basic tuning on the trombone is a relatively simple matter, since there is only one tuning slide and no valve slides to contend with. F in the staff, which is in the heart of the range, is recommended as the most valid tuning check for young players. Tuning the baritone horn and tuba involves a procedure similar to that of the cornet or trumpet. (See Hindsley Tuning Guides.)

4. Tuning the Strings

The open strings should be tuned in fifths by bowing two strings together rather than by plucking the strings one at a time. The former method helps ensure perfect fifths since the teacher (or player) can check for beats and eliminate them. In addition, the tuning process should involve starting flat and tuning upward. Not only is it easier to hear the correct pitch when tuning in this manner, but it also helps avoid breaking strings.

Special care should be taken in the tuning of the lowest strings of the violin, viola, and especially the cello. The tendency is to tune the lowest string sharper than it should be. Tuning by harmonics is recommended for string bass since the very low frequency of the open strings makes it difficult to hear the pitch for tuning purposes. (Additional, detailed procedures for tuning the string bass and the other string instruments are outlined in the appendix of Pottle's book.)

In working with string beginners, there are special intonation considerations which should be included here. One of these is the matter of quality of strings used. If a youngster has a violin equipped with all steel strings, tuning them and keeping them in tune is virtually impossible even when fine tuners exist for each string. The only real solution is to use wire-wound gut strings for the A, D, and G, and to be certain that the steel E string is of good quality. Student violins should also be equipped with a fine tuner on at least the E and A strings, and possibly even the D and G if the instrument is very small in size.[5]

[5] A black plastic tail-piece with four built-in fine tuners called THOMASTIK is available through Ernest Deffner, 461 8th Ave., NYC.

An area of considerable debate among some novice teachers is the matter of who tunes the young string player's instrument: should the teacher tune the instrument, or should the youngster be taught how to do it right from the start? It is critical that young string players should be made aware of good tuning and intonation right from the beginning. Much can be accomplished by having the students listen and indicate to the teacher when a string has been brought in tune. Beyond this, the student should be shown how and encouraged to tune his own instrument to the extent that he is capable of doing so.

All of this may sound very easy but the answer is not that simple. First of all, young players frequently do not possess sufficient physical strength or manual dexterity to tune their instruments properly. Part of this problem can be alleviated if the instruments come equipped with Caspari pegs. But despite a young player's most sincere efforts, some adjustments in tuning by the teacher will usually be necessary.

D. DRILLING DIFFICULT PASSAGES

Most intermediate students will be able to play the majority of their assigned lesson material correctly except for certain difficult passages which always seem to stump them. The source of the difficulty may be fingering or articulation. If so, then the remedies to be applied are ones which were discussed earlier in this text. But assuming the problem is of a melodic or rhythmic nature, the following procedures are suggested:

1. With rhythm problems, the student should practice the entire passage first on a single pitch. Once the rhythm problem is solved, he should go back and play the passage as written, slowly at first and then up to tempo.
2. If the problem is a melodic one, he should practice the passage slowly in equal note values, afterward combining the written rhythm with the written pitches and gradually working the passage up to tempo. Actually the theoretical basis for the above pedagogy is really very simple: Take one thing at a time, drill until it is mastered, and then move on to the next.

The above points up two items of significant importance to all teachers. First, the student who has learned to "get around" on his instrument via the rote approach *before* attempting to read musical notation will have much less trouble conquering the hurdle of music reading when it is introduced later. Secondly, one should search for instructional materials with ample drill material for the average student so that he does not become discouraged. If one must use a book which does progress quite rapidly, then supplementary drill materials, either published or original with the teacher, will probably be necessary. Also, *alla breve* and fast 6/8 exercises which appear early in the book would best be practiced in "slow motion" entirely rather than be forced upon the students at a tempo of which they may not be capable.

E. TEACHING THE SLOW BEGINNER

Among the most frustrating of situations is to have a beginning instrumental class with one student who just cannot get going. This may be a beginning cornet player who cannot play above low C, or a tuba beginner whose playing range is confined to the upper portion of the bass clef. Some flute beginners may also go for an entire week without being able to produce an acceptable tone. Clarinet players may produce only squeaks during the first lesson or even no tone at all.

What is the answer? First of all, the teacher must learn to relax and avoid frustrating the student still further by being overly anxious and impatient. Above all, he must resist the temptation to give up on the youngster too soon. Some of his better players six months later may be among those who had the greatest difficulty at first.

Next, the teaching procedure should be analyzed. Perhaps too much is being expected too soon and the student just cannot produce. Was enough time spent on playing the mouthpiece alone, the lip buzz, and other preliminaries? How about the strength of the reed—too soft? Is the instrument in good repair? If in doubt, the only real way to be certain is for the teacher to try playing the student's instrument himself.

If problems persist with brass players, for example, who are unable to get up or down to the desired note, one can use a technique employed by voice teachers: Take the student *where he is* and work from there. Let *his pitch* be "homebase" and work down or up diatonically until the desired starting pitch is achieved. For example, if G on the second line is the desired pitch for trumpet and one player in the class can play no higher than C below the staff, write out the following exercise for him.

EXAMPLE 90

Home base

Have him sing the exercise first so he knows *how* it should sound. Then have him practice it at home in stepwise motion as written. In most cases he will overcome the problem in one week or less.

A descending diatonic passage may be written in similar fashion for tuba or trombone when a beginner easily produces tones of the upper range but cannot get down to the next lowest partial of the harmonic series. Often the source of the problem is psychological rather than physical. Working up or down diatonically to the desired pitch makes the note in question seem much easier for such students.

Brass beginners who cannot produce a tone when playing the entire instrument should spend additional practice time with the mouthpiece alone. Flutists who cannot produce a normal sound on the headjoint should practice "whistle tones." Clarinetists should try more or less mouthpiece in the mouth, or possibly change reeds or even mouthpieces.

The question remains of what to do with a slow beginner when the class attempts to play together. The answer is to provide supplementary exercises for him to practice at home and to place primary emphasis in class on helping the other class members. If the student in question continually plays the wrong notes, which he probably will, ignore it for the time being. You can be assured that he is aware of his problem, is embarrassed about it, and wants to overcome it. Avoid making life more miserable for him than it already is. If problems persist for three weeks or more, consider transfering the student to another class with students facing similar problems. If the problem still continues, suggest that he change instruments.

F. TEACHING ADVANCED CLASSES

Pedagogy should not be an end in itself; it should be a means to an end. The primary purpose of pedagogy should be to provide a remedy for a student's performance ailment. But before a remedy or prescription is administered, proper diagnosis by the teacher is essential. It is this first step—proper diagnosis—which usually is the most difficult and should be made with extreme caution.

Without question, the first few lessons taught to a beginner are among the most important lessons he will ever receive. Correct embouchure, hand position, etc., must be introduced properly, with the student being reminded repeatedly to correct any bad habits which appear. But, assuming the teacher is well grounded in the proper fundamentals of the instrument being taught, this should not be the source of any great difficulties. Mistakes are made more frequently by teachers when they inherit advanced students who received their start from another teacher.

When hearing an advanced class at their first lesson, attention should be confined to listening and evaluating the students' performance, with minimal immediate diagnosis and prescription administered in regard to suspected performance problems. Changing a student's embouchure on first impulse, for example, is not recommended! Remember that the embouchure is only a means to an end. Musical results should be evaluated in terms of tone quality, range, and other factors first. If these are deficient and faulty embouchure is definitely diagnosed as the reason, then a change in embouchure is probably in order.

There are some aspects of instrumental technique which are absolute. A flat, pointed chin in clarinet playing is essential and illustrates the question in point. Resist the temptation to force a highly personalized technique on advanced students, however, if what they are doing is producing satisfactory results.

Another error sometimes made in teaching advanced students is to allow pedagogical aids such as those dealing with rhythm and ear training to get in the way of student progress. If drill in rhythmic clapping and marking footbeats is not needed, if the class experiences no significant problem in rhythm, then do not waste their time and yours through extensive drill on this fundamental. Instead, apply emphasis elsewhere where it really is needed.

Another temptation, when hearing the first lesson of an advanced class, is to analyze *all* of the students' problems and send them home to practice tone, fingering, rhythm, tonguing, etc., etc., ad infinitum. Such an approach invariably leads to frustration on the part of all concerned. The students go home without any specific, concrete goals to work toward. Since their teacher found so many things wrong (let us hope he found at least one item worthy of praise!) they feel they must indeed be failures. A student may decide that he never really liked the saxophone very much anyway—why not just forget the whole thing? To avoid this type of situation the following approach is recommended:

1. When an advanced class comes for their first lesson, let them play a recital of sorts for you. Audition them so you can learn as much as possible about their playing.
2. Find at least one quality in their performance which merits your sincere praise. The younger the students, the more they thrive on praise and positive attitude on the part of the teacher. It is very important that their first impression of you be one of patience, understanding, and kindness. These are not signs of weakness in a teacher!
3. During the lesson write down the things which seemed to give them the most trouble. Toward the latter half of the lesson, choose one or two specific points which you consider to be their weakest areas and discuss these at some length. Be sure they go home knowing *what* to

practice and *how* to improve their playing. By concentrating on one or two specific aspects of performance, much more will be accomplished than by asking them to go home and concentrate on their entire approach to the instrument. Continue to stress the weakest areas in succeeding weeks until reasonable improvement is in evidence. Then concentrate on another area which in the meantime has shown itself to be a major source of difficulty.

4. Do not try to teach everything you know to your students in the first few lessons. If you do, they will have no further need for your services. They will still need a teacher, yes, but you will not be that teacher. Remember that as old as you are now, you still have many performance problems. Some of these may have been with you for several years. Do not expect your nine- or ten-year-olds to accomplish any more—actually it should be less—than you do. Ideally you will see *some* improvement each week, but it is better to think on a long-term basis. How do your students sound now as compared to two months ago? Is their potential above average, average or below? Is their equipment of good quality? Are you, the teacher, doing a good job of getting down to their level and explaining proper concepts clearly? Make final judgments only after careful deliberation upon the many variables which enter into the picture.

G. CONCLUSION

Instrumental class lessons can be highly productive if organized properly and taught effectively. Ultimately their success or failure depends upon the teacher. Let us stop rationalizing that each student needs private lessons and our teaching schedule does not allow this. Let us stop making excuses about the inadequacies of the class lesson approach. Class teaching of instrumental music has been an accepted part of the music education scene since the 1920s. Instead, we should really learn the fundamentals of teaching all of the instruments and how to communicate this knowledge effectively to our students.

RECOMMENDED REFERENCES

Holz, Emil and Jacobi, Roger, *Teaching Band Instruments to Beginners.* Englewood Cliffs, NJ: Prentice-Hall, Inc., 1966.
Kohut, Daniel L., *Musical Performance: Learning Theory and Pedagogy.* Champaign, IL: Stipes Publishing Co., 1992. (Chapter Eight)

Chapter Eight

ENSEMBLE
REHEARSAL
PROCEDURES

The traditional design of a rehearsal is well known; it consists of tuning, warm-up, rehearsal of one or two works being prepared for performance, some sightreading, and a lively work like a march at the end so that everyone leaves the rehearsal in good spirits. On the other hand, specific objectives for each phase of the rehearsal period and effective methods for achieving them are not always as well defined in the minds of music directors. Discussion of these latter items is the principal focus of this chapter.

Before one is ready to conduct a good rehearsal, certain practical and philosophical questions need to be answered:

1. What are the basic purposes of the large ensemble rehearsal? Should the bulk of time be devoted mainly toward working on full ensemble problems, or should frequent attention be given to individual sections and individual players as well? Should the rehearsal involve teaching of fundamentals or should it be devoted primarily to refining ensemble precision, balance, blend, and the like?
2. What about the difficulty of the music to be used, not only for rehearsal but for concert and contest performances as well? Should music be chosen primarily on the basis of technical difficulty, or is musical difficulty a more valid criterion?
3. Should sectional rehearsals be scheduled on a regular basis? Should small ensembles be an integral part of the curriculum, or should they be organized only in the spring in preparation for solo and ensemble contests? And what about technique classes? Should these disband once students reach junior and senior high school?

All of the above considerations directly influence the objectives of a band or orchestra rehearsal, and consequently they determine what is to be rehearsed and how. In final analysis, these considerations largely determine the qualitative and quantitative outcome of the rehearsal, which in turn has a direct bearing on the musical education of the students. These matters are of sizeable consequence and should not be treated lightly.

A. PRELIMINARY CONSIDERATIONS

1. Basic Purpose of the Large Ensemble Rehearsal

Primary attention in full rehearsal should, quite obviously, be directed toward solving full ensemble problems rather than sectional or individual problems. This is assuming that some type of sectional, small ensemble, and/or technique classes are available in addition to the full ensemble rehearsal. If not, then every effort should be made to provide additional instruction of this type even if it means sacrificing some full rehearsal time in order to schedule it. Otherwise, the pace of the full rehearsal will tend to be slow and the efficiency of learning below what it should be. The complex technical problems of all the diverse instruments found in a full band or orchestra cannot be effectively taught when there are thirty to forty students in the room, certainly not when there are eighty to a hundred.

Some teachers have programs which include small ensembles, technique class, and/or sectionals, and still seem to find it necessary to spend considerable time rehearsing individual sections and players. This problem may be due to haphazard rehearsal planning or to an inability to establish objectives and/or priorities for each type of rehearsal; more often it is due to poor decisions concerning the difficulty of music chosen for the large ensemble which is the purpose of the following topic of discussion.

2. Selection of Music for Large Ensembles

If primary attention in rehearsal is to be directed toward full ensemble problems rather than sectional or individual problems, then two requisites are necessary: (1) The music being rehearsed should be challenging but not so difficult that rote teaching becomes necessary in order to "polish" the music; (2) students should be expected to take parts home after the first reading of a new piece and work out the hard spots on their own. This allows the director to concentrate on ensemble tone, balance, blend, intonation, precision, phrasing, and other items in full rehearsal which cannot be learned at home but must be acquired through actual ensemble experience. Persistent wrong notes, wrong rhythms, and the like are generally inexcusable after the first reading, unless, of course, the music is much too difficult to begin with.

Some directors make a practice of having their high school groups perform primarily Grade V and VI music, especially for contest. Even though the music may be above the heads of the players, these directors contend that students need considerable challenge in order to sustain their interest in performing. Moreover, they point out that students usually always rise to the occasion in the end and emerge from the experience being far better players than before. This philosophy has some merit and should not be dismissed entirely. But when carried to extremes or applied incorrectly, its effects can have far-reaching negative consequences, examples of which are given below:

1. What is sometimes considered "difficult" music is difficult mainly in terms of technical prowess. Students given a steady diet of this type of music often gain the false impression that good music means music which is technically difficult. They fail to realize that a composition by Bach or Mozart, erroneously listed in Grade III, is also good music, possibly far superior to the Grade VI piece they played for contest. Having received their challenge primarily in mastery of sheer technique, they fail to understand that the challenge of good tone control, phrasing, and expression can also be highly rewarding if taught properly. When this area of instruction is neglected, students graduate with minimal development of aesthetic sensitivity along with inadequate basis for judgment of quality in music and musical performance. One can only wonder if the same problem is not also shared by the director. If he lacks sensitivity to the expressive qualities of music, perhaps the only challenge the director sees is that found in music which is technically oriented.

2. Music which is excessively challenging almost always necessitates extensive drill in rehearsal, not only with individual sections but individual players as well. This inevitably results in boredom on the part of those players who must spend long periods of time sitting while the director works with other sections or players. When discipline becomes a problem, an authoritarian director can make them be quiet and finger their parts silently; but how much are these students really getting out of such rehearsals? No one, adults included, likes to spend a large part of a rehearsal period just sitting; the urge to play is very strong and there is seldom any valid reason for not meeting this need on a consistent basis. Extensive drill on sectional and individual problems can be done elsewhere, but the problem is best solved by choosing easier music to begin with.

3. Rehearsal of excessively difficult music literally forces the issue of rote teaching and frequently places unreasonable demands upon student embouchures and playing endurance as well as finger and tongue or bow control. Rote teaching of rhythm in particular fails to provide students with a functional means of learning to read music thereby stunting their sightreading ability. Students who are expected to play upper register tones prematurely, particularly brass players, tend to acquire poor playing habits which are frequently quite difficult to correct later. Students who are asked to finger and articulate passages far beyond their level of technical ability develop tension in the tongue and fingers. Clarity in tonguing and evenness in fingering is not only retarded but often deteriorates as well.

Why is it that some directors insist upon using music which is too difficult? One answer has already been given under item 1: It may be due to a lack of genuine musicianship on the part of the director. Another reason is that in the world of school music competition, lesser teachers continually strive to emulate their betters. The pressure from a neighboring school whose program is of high quality tends to become increasingly greater around contest time. Being unable to meet the same high standards through proper teaching of technical and musical fundamentals, the director decides to meet the challenge via other channels. He buys his music early and begins rehearsing it several months prior to the contest. Not only does he spend considerable full rehearsal time on it, but he also schedules numerous sectionals after school. If technique classes are offered, he also uses this time for additional drill on the same music. The result is, of course, much akin to a circus dog act when his group reaches the contest. Not only is the whole area of musical objectives seriously violated, but the gross misuse of student time and effort is also difficult to justify.

Surely the above example is somewhat exaggerated, but there are many degrees on the continuum between this and what is educationally sound and defensible. Frequent rote drill in full rehearsal, especially when devoted primarily to difficult technical passages, is open to serious question. Quality musical instruction should involve far more than this!

As a general rule, music should be chosen which is within the rhythmic, technical, and musical capabilities of a given organization. An appropriate balance between technical and musical difficulty should also be maintained. Despite opinions to the contrary, the musical demands of a good piece of music, even if it is easy technically, can be sufficient to challenge even the best players. Success or failure in this regard depends mainly on the musicianship of the director and his ability to communicate proper musical concepts and attitudes to his players.

3. Sectional Rehearsals

Not all students in a given organization or classroom will be of the same ability or be at the same level of proficiency. Instrumental music teachers, however, supposedly have a built-in solution to this problem in that the better players are assigned to play the first parts, lesser players assigned the second and third parts. But this does not solve the problem entirely. Second and third parts are also important musically and must be well played if the section is to meet its full measure of responsibility to the full ensemble. Wherever it is practical, strong and weak players should be distributed evenly throughout the section. This not only produces better results musically, but it also minimizes the need for frequent sectional rehearsals where players on the first part do a lot of sitting and listening while the director spends the bulk of time with players on the "lower" parts.

Even when strong and weak players are distributed rather evenly in a section, there will still be some sections which simply cannot meet the same high standard that others do. There will also be instances when the demands of a given score are greater for one section or group of instruments than they are for others. These are times when sectional rehearsals are both desirable and justifiable. If a sectional is not scheduled, rehearsal of these difficult passages will have to be done during the full rehearsal, and this should be avoided if at all possible.

If a sectional cannot be scheduled after school, then it might best be scheduled in lieu of one of the regular full rehearsals while the other players are excused to go to study hall. There is no point in having everyone there while three-fourths of the group just sits, and the one-fourth who really need work do not need to be inhibited by the presence of others in the room. Moreover, the director can also give his full attention to the problems at hand without feeling self-conscious about ignoring the rest of the organization.

Obviously, no strong case is being made here for the scheduling of regular sectional rehearsals for each section of the band or orchestra. The intent is that sectionals be scheduled only when necessary. One reason for this is that a number of situations have been observed in which sectionals turned out to be little more than rote drill sessions, with the students trained like seals to do their act with little emphasis on functional knowledge which could be transferred to future performance situations. If there is a need for frequent sectional rehearsals of several sections in the organization, this usually indicates that the music chosen for performance is too difficult. The solution, of course, lies on choosing easier music to begin with.

4. Technique Classes

Those teachers fortunate enough to have the available staff and time can schedule technique classes as a means for alleviating the problems inherent in the large sectional. Such a class might include the first clarinets alone, second and thirds together, or low clarinets, saxophones, or bassoons together. It is here that the fundamentals of performance can be most effectively taught. Fewer players to work with allows the teacher to provide students with more individual attention. Performance problems unique to the specific instruments and players can be also analyzed and worked on more effectively.

Some teachers use the technique class for challenges in seating and thereby motivate students to practice harder. This approach, properly used, can be effective, and those who fail to apply it to some degree are probably neglecting a useful, motivational technique. Those who disagree with fostering a spirit of competition among students will either temper the use of the challenge system or refrain from using it altogether. Each teacher must objectively consider its advantages and disadvantages. Ultimately the course he chooses must be the one that works best for him.

Some teachers feel that students need to study their instrument privately or in a technique class for at least a couple of years before being introduced to large ensemble participation. String teachers sometimes limit early orchestral experience to strings alone; full orchestra including winds and percussion is delayed until at least junior high school. Some even prefer to wait until junior high school before forming a string orchestra. In any case, student motivation, maintaining student interest and fostering the desire to work hard in home practice are important factors to be considered. Band directors as a group seem to favor the idea of forming beginning bands relatively early. Could this be one of the reasons why bands far outnumber orchestras in today's public schools?

5. Small Ensembles

Technique classes fill a very vital function in providing the means for teaching music reading and instrumental technique and in promoting individual musical growth. But since the music materials used are usually of a unison type, technique classes cannot provide the complete experience needed for good ensemble performance.

On first thought, it would seem that this experience could be acquired in the large group rehearsal, and it can be to a limited degree. But anyone who has ever played in an 80- to 100-piece band or orchestra as a clarinetist or violinist respectively knows how easy it is to become swallowed up in a full tutti section, how easy it is to be a "follower" or even a "chair warmer," learn very little from the experience, and contribute still less. Learning to play with independence and aggressiveness along with really hearing, evaluating, and improving one's musical contribution can be difficult in large ensemble situations. The answer then lies outside the full rehearsal; it is best accomplished through small ensemble experience.

Small ensemble experience is not something which should be offered only to a few students with rehearsals scheduled on a sporadic basis. Small ensemble experience of one type or another should be made available to all students at the junior and senior high levels (also at the elementary level where possible) and be included as an integral part of the curriculum the same as large ensembles. In order for this to be a reality, small ensembles ideally should be scheduled during the *regular school day.*

Small ensembles offer the following advantages:

1. They are the most effective medium for teaching music and musical performance, with the possible exception of private study with a good specialist teacher.
2. They provide a relevant environment for learning and applying concepts of balance, blend, intonation, rhythmic precision, and playing with confidence.
3. Probably most important, they are an excellent vehicle for getting students excited about performing, inspiring them to practice, helping them acquire a genuine love for and sensitivity toward music, and motivating them in general. All these things can be accomplished without inducing excessively strong competition, frequent challenges in seating, etc. In fact, good ensemble playing depends greatly upon exactly the opposite attitudes: cooperation, teamwork, and tolerance of the other players' problems. In a cornet trio or other ensemble involving several identical instruments, players can switch parts allowing everyone the experience of playing the first part as well as the lower parts. Everyone experiences the glamour of the first part and the importance of the lower parts, and becomes more tolerant of the other players' problems and appreciative of their responsibilities. This is one of the best ways of ensuring that the second and third parts in band or orchestra will be played well. These are also some of the same reasons why many students find jazz band participation so enjoyable and musically rewarding. Everyone has an independent part to play, and every part is important to the total sound of the group.

Few will deny that small ensemble experience is highly beneficial, and that it is at the heart of building a successful instrumental program. The problem, however, is one of finding sufficient student and teacher time for rehearsal. "How can I justify asking the administration for more student time? And even if this is granted, where do I find the time in my own schedule to meet with the students?"

The solution is not an easy one; mainly, it is a matter of personal philosophy and attitude. The director must ask himself, "How strongly do I believe in the value of small ensemble experience? Do I believe in small ensembles enough to sacrifice other regularly scheduled classes and even some large group rehearsals in order to make time for them?" If the answer to all of these questions is yes, then the problem is near its solution.

Many school bands and orchestras have as many as five one-hour rehearsals each week. Some believe that at least this much rehearsal time is necessary in order to see any worthwhile progress in an organization's performance level. But let us take a good, hard look at the situation. Is all of this time really used to best advantage? How often does the director come to rehearsal without having his scores fully prepared? How much time is actually wasted because of apathy on the part of the students? ("We have plenty of time; the concert is still four weeks away!") How much has actually been accomplished with regard to individual growth and resultant contribution to the overall sound of the group? Most important, could some of this time be used more efficiently in other types of instruction with more effective results? In the author's opinion, most large groups can operate quite effectively with three rehearsals a week, so long as the rehearsals are well organized and so long as they are supplemented by productive small ensemble training. Therefore, if the director is genuinely sold on the importance of small ensemble training, he will be willing to make this necessary sacrifice in order to make small ensembles an integral part of the instrumental curriculum.

B. TUNING AND WARM-UP

1. General Outline

Tuning and warm-up is the most important part of a rehearsal since this is the time when the proper atmosphere for the formal rehearsal is established. Too often directors either gloss over this phase of rehearsal as if it were of secondary importance, or else they seem uncertain as to exactly what should be accomplished and how to go about it. Good tuning and warm-up requires that the director have a clear set of objectives in mind, and that the means for achieving these objectives be well planned before the rehearsal, preferably outlined in writing.

Tuning

Initial tuning of the players should begin as soon as possible. There is no need to wait until everyone is present; it should start as soon as at least half the group is present.

While adherence to A-440 is preferable, this may not always be possible, particularly with a beginning group. If the double-reeds or clarinets are flat, they may force a lower pitch standard on the full ensemble temporarily until their pitch problem is solved elsewhere.

The recommended order of tuning for band is bass instruments, preferably tubas first, then tenor, alto, and soprano instruments afterward, in that order. In the orchestra the strings should be tuned first and the winds tuned last. This is so that individual strings which are quite flat can be brought up to pitch, allowed to stabilize, and be rechecked after the winds are tuned. Be careful not to tune the strings too high, however, or else the winds will never be able to get up to pitch. Be certain that the open strings are perfectly in tune.

Even though careful tuning is highly important, too much rehearsal time should not be devoted to this purpose; five minutes or so should be the usual limit. The conductor who spends half the period in tuning alone is wasting time as a rule and will find himself with little time left to accomplish anything else. Intonation, like balance, blend, and other areas of performance, should be stressed as needed *throughout* the rehearsal period; indeed, it must be if one really expects to reap any real benefits from the initial tuning period.

Warm-up

Warm-up is the time when the players and conductor should concentrate on one primary concept—listening. This should include intonation, balance, and blend as well as attacks and releases. The conductor should also seek the players' attention by varying tempo and dynamic gestures in conducting as well as have the ensemble perform in each of the three basic musical styles: *legato, staccato,* and *marcato.*

The usual vehicles for warm-up are major and minor scales. Concert C major for orchestra and Concert B-flat major for band are recommended as starting points. Various rhythms including repeated quarter notes, eighth notes, triplets, or quadruplets may be used along with varied articulations. When method books containing chord and ensemble studies are available, these also may be used. Experience has shown, however, that warm-ups based upon memorized material tend to be far more effective, since the players and conductor need not be distracted by reading notes.

The length of the warm-up period in a fifty-minute rehearsal should be approximately five minutes. Tuning and warm-up combined generally should not take more than ten to twelve minutes. More time may be needed if the rehearsal also serves the function of a large technique class as is unfortunately the case in a good many elementary and junior high school situations.

At some time during the warm-up period, attention should be given to proper seating arrangement and height of music stands. Flutists in particular tend to sit too close together and hang their right arms over the backs of their chairs. Percussionists often have their music stands too low to see the conductor properly. Such adjustments also can and should be made at any time during the rehearsal as the need arises. Teachers should also consider that quick reminders regarding such items as embouchure, poor posture, and instrument holding positions are in order when players obviously are being careless. Such brief comments can be especially effective to the extent that they reinforce the advice given by the regular class or private teacher.

Many contest judges agree that the quality of preliminary tuning and warm-up done by the director and his students is usually a clear indicator of the quality of the actual performance to follow. If this is true, then additional justification of this aspect of rehearsal procedure seems unnecessary.

2. Specific Procedures

Basic Tuning Notes

Concert A has become known as a standard tuning note for orchestra; Concert B-flat is the tuning note most often used by bands. These tuning notes are used today perhaps partially because of tradition, but also because they serve as the best compromise if one must choose a *single tuning note* for all of the diversely pitched instruments included in a given ensemble.

It is important, however, that the above compromise be understood for what it really is. If one takes the view that the orchestral A favors the strings and puts the winds at a real disadvantage, then the compromise is somewhat open to question. In the same way, perhaps the band B-flat favors some of the brasses at the expense of the woodwinds. In the case of the clarinetist, for example, Concert B-flat, which is his C in the third space, is sharp on almost all clarinets currently being manufactured. Add to this the student's rather common error of pulling out only the barrel to bring down the pitch of this note and we find that tuning to

Concert B-flat often causes intonation problems to become worse instead of better.

In order for a tuning note to be valid, it should indicate the *prevailing pitch* of the given instrument. Use of a "bad note" for tuning should be avoided especially with student musicians. The problems of intonation which exist because of relatively fixed laws of nature and currently unsolved problems in instrument manufacture and design are difficult enough to contend with. Complicating the matter still further by using bad notes for tuning purposes should be avoided.

Wind players can profit by taking a hint from string players who tune not one but four notes (strings) on their instrument. After the open strings are tuned, the string player is held responsible for adjusting the intonation of all the notes in between. Wind players would do well to develop a similar attitude in their approach to overall intonation in performance.

With beginning wind players, it is important that the tuning notes used be in the heart of their range—tones which are easily produced without forcing or undue strain. Initially this will be the starting note on their instrument. Eventually it will become the first note listed in the chart below. As soon as range and embouchure facility allow, additional tuning notes should be used to provide a more valid check of the instruments' outer ranges.

Chart 15

TUNING NOTES FOR BEGINNING PLAYERS

The first note used in each instance in the chart above favors the "Orchestral A," making it a compromise tuning note, but not as much a compromise as would be the case if the "Band B-flat" alone were used.

When all instruments play their first note together, a major triad (Concert F-A plus C in the F horn) will sound. Like instruments can use the second and third notes listed for tuning to each other and for checking against their first tuning note. All of these notes should also be checked periodically with a strobe, of course.

The author is fully aware that the tuning notes recommended above may seem quite unorthodox to some readers. On the other hand, there are several teachers who have used this approach and will vouch for its effectiveness. It is hoped that the reader will at least consider giving it fair trial in the tuning of beginning wind instrument ensembles.

The conductor should keep in mind the normal tuning tendencies of the various instrument sections to each other. Reed instruments as a group tend toward the flat side; flutes and upper brass in particular tend toward sharpness (this is true for advanced groups as well as elementary groups). In addition, special care should be given to the tuning of the low brass, especially the tubas. The tubas usually play the root of the chord thereby setting the pitch standard for all vertical sonorities.

In instances where rehearsal time is short, the teacher may be tempted to do all the tuning himself in order to save time. Particularly in tuning a large group, expediency in getting the job done accurately and quickly often becomes a prime consideration. In elementary orchestras, older string students fairly proficient in tuning themselves can assist the director immensely by tuning the younger players' instruments. Beyond this a final check by the teacher where needed should suffice. This final check is made by hearing all A strings together, then the D strings and G strings, the C strings of the violas and cellos, and finally the violin and string bass E strings.

The idea of a teacher going around the room tuning each player individually is considered to be wasted effort by some teachers. This is often true, but if the teacher uses this approach as a means for evaluating tone quality as well as pitch combined with on-the-spot suggestions for improving the tone, the procedure is not only helpful but serves to get at the root of most intonation problems—poor tone production. Without a doubt, frequent individual tuning of fifty or more players in a large ensemble rehearsal is time-consuming and difficult to justify, but it probably should be done periodically for the above reason. If technique classes and/or small ensembles are offered, it should be done as a matter of routine in these situations.

Intonation Drills

Once initial tuning of the ensemble has been completed, overall intonation should be further checked during the warm-up period. This can be accomplished by:

1. Playing scales in unison and octaves as a starting point. Octave "pyramids," built with bass, tenor, alto, and soprano instruments added in sequence, are also valuable.
2. Playing a series of major chords progressing upward chromatically and back down. Building a pyramid on those chords where intonation is poor helps players realize the direction and degree of adjustment required. The same procedures should be used with minor chords.
3. Memorizing a I-IV-V7-I chord sequence and playing it in various keys.
4. Altering a major chord by flatting the third to make it minor, raising the root to make it diminished, raising the fifth to make it augmented. This can be indicated by the conductor using one, three or five fingers and pointing the finger(s) downward to indicate lowering the pitch or pointing upward to indicate raising the pitch.
5. Probably the best and most advanced approach is to memorize an extended harmonic exercise or memorize an entire chorale. Since chorales probably offer the greatest challenge in intonation, what could be better for improving ensemble intonation than playing a chorale by memory where each player's prime objective is to listen and make his notes in tune so that he blends perfectly with the rest of the ensemble?

Ensemble Attacks

Poor attacks are often due to indecisive downbeats and confusing preparatory gestures. The conductor may need to practice in front of a mirror and to experiment during the rehearsal warm-up period in order to try solving the problem. A specific aid for students is to say *hot* at the beginning of the preparatory gesture and *tah* on the downbeat. The purpose of saying *hot* is to bring the tongue into position with breath support behind it in preparation for the downbeat *tah*. Repeated drill using this approach can help the conductor communicate his gestures more effectively as well as aid the students in performing their attacks together with assurance.

The above procedure must be done in a relaxed, almost continuous fashion; that is, there should not be a long wait between the *hot* and the *tah* or else undesirable player tension will result. Emphasis should be on a carefully synchronized preparation of the tongue and breath pressure, leading to a relaxed but precise attack at the moment the downbeat is given.

Ensemble Releases

In ensemble, players may release a tone either at the end of its normal duration or at a time specifically indicated by the conductor. If the former results in ragged releases, the conductor will need to indicate the release to ensure precise ensemble performance. This is especially the case in slow, sustained passages and in music where there are no written rests between phrases. Ultimately it is the conductor's responsibility to make certain that releases as well as attacks are performed together and to indicate these clearly and accurately through his conducting gestures.

Practicing Odd and Changing Meters

Probably the easiest way to practice odd and changing meters is to warm up on a scale at the beginning of rehearsal, asking the students to play five notes on each pitch. At a slow tempo this allows the conductor to practice beating five beats per measure rather than the usual four. As soon as this becomes easy, he can try increasing the tempo and do a 3-plus-2 combination of five eighth notes on each degree of the scale, gradually changing to two unequal beats per measure. He may then reverse the combination to 2-plus-3 and again increase the tempo until it feels comfortable to beat two unequal beats per measure. Next slow 7/4 meter may be tried, changing to fast 7/8 meter in its various permutations.

For those desiring still further challenge, interesting possibilities such as alternating a measure of eighth notes in 2/4 with three quarter notes in 6/8 can be tried. The secret is to begin slowly and increase the speed gradually. A feel for the rhythms must be developed through repetitive practice. Once this is accomplished, learning to sightread odd and changing meters is no more difficult than reading 2/4, 4/4, or 6/8.

Musical Style

The student of conducting knows that there are three basic styles he needs to master: *legato, marcato,* and *staccato.* Beyond this there are numerous variations and nuances which need to be learned and incorporated into one's baton technique, including dynamics, phrasing, *rubato,* and other subtleties. Unless the conductor is capable of indicating these nuances via his gestures, his ensemble will not be able to play well musically. This point is of great importance and can hardly be overemphasized!

One means of awakening student sensitivity to the three basic styles is to include them as an integral part of the regular rehearsal warm-up. If memorized warm-up materials are used, students will be more conscious of what the conductor is doing with his baton and/or hands since they will not need to divide their attention between note reading and watching the conductor. Likewise the conductor can practice and refine his conducting technique with a live group without the burden of watching a score. Students eventually need to be able to change styles, tempo, dynamics, and interpret accents and phrasing without verbal directions from the conductor.

C. THE REHEARSAL PROPER

1. General Outline

Preparing the Score

"The score should be in your head, not your head in the score" is a suggestion frequently made by conducting teachers. In order to achieve this goal in its most ideal application, the score should be memorized. A general outline for preparing a score for rehearsal leading toward eventual memorization is given below:

1. Solfeggio or in some way sightsing all parts beginning with melody parts down through each succeeding lower voice.
2. To the extent that you are capable, play from score at the piano by sections all string parts, woodwind parts, etc.
3. Practice conducting in front of a mirror while singing the melody line, and also have a colleague observe you if possible to make suggestions for improvement.
4. Mark in red pencil all difficult passages, abrupt changes of key, important phrasing, etc.

Rehearsing the Score

1. Synthesis-Analysis-Synthesis: First, read through the entire work so that the players can get a concept of the whole. Avoid rehearsing individual phrases and single sections of instruments until after the first playing. At the end try to play through the work once again without stopping.
2. As a result of studying the score prior to rehearsal, be prepared to anticipate the hard spots in the score. During the first play-through, listen carefully to see if these spots were in fact as difficult as you anticipated. You will be correct in your assumption on some sections but probably incorrect on others which the players nevertheless play poorly. Be prepared to rehearse these passages also.
3. Unless the conductor knows his score very well, he will not hear half of the major problems during the first play-through. Therefore, in order to conduct a first-rate rehearsal, study the score very carefully before rehearsal, memorize as much of it as possible, and be prepared to "keep your head out of the score" so that your eyes and ears are free to see, hear, and evaluate what is really going on. This can hardly be over-emphasized!

4. There is a tendency among novice conductors to spend most of the rehearsal time stressing elements such as dynamics and phrasing while wrong notes and incorrect rhythms go by seemingly unnoticed. Below is a suggested list of priorities to be used in conducting rehearsals of public school instrumental groups in particular. Certainly this list will not apply to every situation. Each conductor must use his good judgment as to when a given problem needs attention. The list below is intended to serve only as a starting point—a general guideline.
   a. Rhythmic accuracy.
   b. Correct notes, key changes.
   c. Tone quality and intonation.
   d. Bowing and articulation.
   e. Precision, including rhythmic interpretation, attacks and releases.
   f. Melodic phrasing and expression.
   g. Dynamic contrast.
   h. Tonal balance and blend.

5. One should not expect to solve all of the performance problems in one rehearsal. Excessive emphasis on one specific area should also be avoided. Go on to something else in the piece, or even to another piece, when things get bogged down. Work on that "problem section" again in the next rehearsal. If the piece is obviously above the heads of your group, store it in the library for use at a later date. Substitute another piece which is challenging but not so much so that it has to be taught by rote in order to achieve satisfactory performance results.

   But the problem with some school conductors is just opposite to that cited above. The tendency it to play through the music, check out a couple of the worst sections and leave it. A good conductor knows what he wants and gets it. A good conductor also knows when his players have reached the point where they will refuse to give any more, and the only reasonable recourse is to go to something else for relief.

2. Specific Procedures

Memorizing the Score

The conductor's job of listening, evaluating, and recommending corrections toward improvement of an ensemble's performance is indeed a most difficult one. Not all of the problems can be heard at once nor can they be solved at once. One thing is for certain: If the conductor has his head buried in the score, he will hear very little of what is going on, and will consequently be ill-equipped to improve his group's performance rapidly and efficiently. One good rehearsal is worth far more than ten poor ones.

One way of helping ensure a good rehearsal is for the conductor to study his score with an effort toward memorizing it. If a work is to be used for public performance, then memorization is especially recommended. The purpose is not to impress the players and the audience, but to rid the conductor of the shackles imposed by the score on his senses of sight and hearing. Once this is done, the conductor is able to give his full attention to watching and listening to his group. Only then can he be in the best position to hear what is actually being played. The continued eye contact he is able to maintain with his players is also important in helping them feel more confident.

Establishing Intonation Priorities

As a teacher, one must establish a logical, sequential procedure in trying to solve intonation problems with performing groups. The place to start is where intonation problems are the most obvious. Listed below are problems which should be solved before tackling the more involved aspects of intonation adjustment.

1. Thinly scored passages using long tones in unison, in octaves or in open fourth and fifths.
2. High register lines in instruments such as first violin, flute-piccolo and/or first clarinet.
3. *Pianissimo* flute passages and phrase endings which are apt to be quite flat.
4. High range *forte* or *fortissimo* passages in upper brass which are apt to be sharp in pitch and pinched in tone quality.
5. Starting notes for strings which use the fourth finger in particular—usually flat.
6. Phrase releases which are not together, in *tutti* as well as thinly scored passages. These particularly expose out-of-tune playing. Clean up the releases first and work toward solving individual intonation problems later.
7. Muddy low brass caused by lack of proper breath support. Clean this up so that treble instruments will have a valid fundamental on which to place their thirds, fifths and octave doublings.
8. Eliminate the low pitched rumble of the cellos and basses caused by poor tuning.
9. Tune long *tutti* chords by building from the bottom up. Be sure again that the fundamental in the string basses or tuba is in tune.
10. In contrapuntal music check imitative passages at the unison or octave to see that at least the starting tone is reasonably well in tune.

From here on, good intonation depends primarily upon the degree of knowledge students have regarding the deficiencies of their own instrument in general and specific terms, and the level of competence they have achieved in personally solving these deficiencies.

Using the Tape Recorder

Hearing music is quite different from looking at a painting or piece of sculpture. When one views a painting, he has time to study its lines, analyze its colors, and make a value judgment based upon deliberate, calculated analysis. Musical performance, on the other hand is very fleeting; a musical idea is heard only briefly and then it is gone, gone forever unless, of course, it is recorded. Some directors frequently record their rehearsals. Others do so infrequently, while still others practically never use this valuable teaching aid. Not only is a tape recording helpful to the director when he studies it prior to the next rehearsal; it can often illuminate performance problems to students in a way that no amount of verbal discussion could ever accomplish.

Setting up a tape recorder for each rehearsal is admittedly time-consuming and frustrating, especially if one has to borrow one from a teacher down the hall and/or return it to the audio-visual room afterward. Also, if the recorder is of mediocre quality and the microphone even worse, the resultant quality of the recording will no doubt be quite discouraging. Probably the only way to obtain worthwhile results is to purchase a professional type recorder with a quality microphone for the exclusive purpose of music ensemble recording. The apparatus can then be left set up and preferably be built-in somehow so that interested colleagues cannot conveniently borrow it. Once optimum recording level and microphone placement have been established, extensive preparation time for recording a given rehearsal can be virtually eliminated. On the other hand, the quality of the director's preparation for the next rehearsal should be greatly enhanced along with his ability to conduct a more efficient, productive rehearsal.

Teacher Self-Evaluation

Evaluation involves sincere, critical analysis. Were rehearsal instructions clearly understood by the players? Did the conductor achieve all that he could reasonably expect or did the students leave the rehearsal confused in general? The list of questions is endless, but the final responsibility lies with the teacher-conductor. He must avoid blaming only the players for poor results; primary if not total blame should be accepted by the conductor. Those who subscribe to the latter philosophy usually are in a far better position to improve themselves far more quickly.

D. WIND-PERCUSSION TONE COLOR

A frequent criticism of bands is that they play too loudly. Another fault voiced by some musicians is that bands allegedly project very little variety in tonal color; consequently it is concluded that this is one of the main reasons why bands can never compete with the sound of an orchestra. There can be no doubt that the full-bodied richness and resonance of a good string section is a beautiful thing, but the potential of tonal color inherent in wind and percussion instruments is also considerable. Realizing this potential requires imaginative scoring on the part of the composer including the presence and appropriate use of so-called odd instruments which can add new color to the ensemble sound.

The scores of Percy Grainger undoubtedly represent one of the greatest achievements in the utilization of wind-percussion color potential. It is important to note that much of this color is obtained through imaginative use of the so-called odd instruments. The average piccolo player, bass clarinetist, and English horn player becomes ecstatic when one of Grainger's works is about to be rehearsed or performed, and for good reason: he will usually have an interesting, a functional, and perhaps even a soloistic part to play.

Not every band composition or arrangement will be as well-written or functional for the odd instruments as those of Grainger; however, much richness and variety can be added to overall ensemble color if only these instruments are included and the parts played with competence and assurance. The contrabass clarinet may not be the greatest solo instrument, but the sonority it can add to a group is well worth the expense involved. Directors who have enjoyed the presence of one or two good string basses as part of their instrumentation will agree that these instruments can also add a great deal. When parts are available, the fluegelhorn can also be a desirable color addition to the instrumentation.

Some directors go to the trouble of writing or rewriting parts so that instruments such as those above can contribute to the ensemble color more effectively. A few have gone so far as to rearrange entire works so that a full-sized clarinet choir concept can be more effectively utilized within the regular band instrumentation. Such projects take considerable time and effort and are not necessarily recommended as the most practical solution. It is recommended, however, that directors include these instruments in their groups and try to use them to best advantage. When enough bands use them as part of their basic instrumentation, composers, and arrangers will surely respond by writing better, more functional parts for them.

E. LEARNING ABOUT MUSIC IN REHEARSAL

In many schools, students participate for several years in instrumental groups, play a rather extensive body of literature, graduate, and sometimes attend concerts later on only to realize that they cannot meet the criteria of an intelligent listener or consumer of music. This is a frequent outcome of performance-oriented school groups. Students who merely push valves and finger keys during the course of countless practice hours and rehearsal periods do not always acquire the understanding and appreciation required to listen to a good piece of music and enjoy it for its own sake.

In an effort to alleviate this problem, some directors have tried devoting portions of individual rehearsal periods or even certain rehearsal days to the study and analysis of musical form, style, composers' lives, and other areas of musical information. Although this would seem to be the answer to an important phase of musical instruction, any director who has tried this approach soon realizes that students soon tend to become bored and restless. While they may agree that knowledge of this type is probably important, they soon make it known that the main reason why they are in the band or orchestra is to play. When they are repeatedly denied this opportunity, many of them lose interest and quit entirely.

And yet we must ask ourselves the question: Why did they discontinue? Were the lectures really boring? Or maybe the students weren't really that serious about music in the first place—just along for the ride, out-of-town trips, and free admission to athletic events? In all probability, extended music history and theory lectures have no place in the band or orchestra rehearsal, but some time should be devoted to this type of instruction at all grade levels. Students as a group are curious about the music they play, but the information given needs to be relevant. A brief discussion about the formal design of a fugue can be both interesting as well as informative if it is related directly to a fugal piece they have just rehearsed. A comment or two about "the suspension used in the seventh measure" not only makes students aware that it exists but can also help them perform the music more effectively.

Original compositions, arrangements, and transcriptions done by the students, from small ensembles involving their own instrument to full band and orchestra, is also recommended for those capable and interested. Original student writing can be both rewarding and revealing at all levels.

In final analysis, good performance and theoretical musical instruction should go hand in hand. The astute director who knows his score well will usually teach his players a great deal about the structure and content of the music being rehearsed. In doing so he will have led them toward a more intelligent and sensitive performance of the music as well as having taught them something about music.

F. MISCELLANEOUS CONSIDERATIONS

Tonal Resonance

Strive to develop a solid core of sound in the bass and tenor range instruments. This means emphasis on centering the tone and developing resonance (upper partials) through proper breath support and throat opening (controlled largely by the use of proper vowels). Then use the upper voice instruments for color, and blend their tones into the fabric of overtones produced by the lower voice instruments.

Tonal Blend

Listen for differences in tonal color between sections and between individual players. High flutes or first clarinets which sound excessively bright in contrast to other sections of instruments will prevent proper blending of tones. Think of the combined colors of several instruments as resulting in an entirely new color creation rather than a combination of individual instrumental colors. Good blend consists in the tones fusing together and forming a new color rather than sounding as separate layers of sound, each retaining its own unique character.

Balance

Listen carefully for proper balance not only between the root, third, and fifth of a chord but also between families of instruments in particular. There may be some justification for allowing the brass section to "play out" when marching outdoors, but this is inexcusable indoors even in *fortissimo* passages. Balance of instrumentation is a factor, and so is the scoring of the arrangement, but the ultimate responsibility for control of ensemble balance lies with the conductor.

Sometimes poor balance is due to the brass section being too large. More frequently, the real problem lies with the woodwinds. Woodwind players, flutists included, must develop their dynamic range to include all degrees of the dynamic spectrum. Learning to play with a good tone beyond *mezzoforte* is not always easy, but it can be done. Conductors need to teach woodwind players how to attain this goal properly and then insist that they meet it when the music calls for it.

Colwell, Richard J., and Thomas Goolsby, *The Teaching of Instrumental Music*. 2nd ed., Englewood Cliffs, NJ: Prentice-Hall, Inc., 1992. (Chapter 7)

Green, Elizabeth A. H., *The Dynamic Orchestra: Principles of Orchestral Performance for Instrumentalists, Conductors and Audiences*. Englewood Cliffs, NJ: Prentice-Hall, 1987.

Hovey, Nilo, *Efficient Rehearsal Procedures for School Bands*. Elkhart, IN: H & A Selmer, 1982.

Kinney, Richard, *Handbook of Rehearsal Techniques for the High School Band*. West Nyack, NY: Parker Publishing Co., 1976.

Kohut, Daniel L. and Joe W. Grant, *Learning to Conduct and Rehearse*. Englewood Cliffs, NJ: Prentice-Hall, Inc., 1990.

Long, R. Gerry, *The Conductor's Workshop*. Dubuque, IA: Wm. C. Brown, 1977. (Part I)

McBeth, Francis, *Effective Performance of Band Music*. San Antonio, TX: Southern Music Co., 1972.

SELECTED
BIBLIOGRAPHY
ON
INSTRUMENTAL MUSIC

A. GENERAL INSTRUMENTAL TEXTS

Butts, Carrol M., *Troubleshooting the High School Band: How to Detect and Correct Common and Uncommon Performance Problems*. West Nyack, NY: Parker Publishing Co., 1981.

Colwell, Richard J., and Thomas Goolsby, *The Teaching of Instrumental Music*. 2nd ed., Englewood Cliffs, NJ: Prentice-Hall, Inc., 1992.

Duerksen, George L., *Teaching Instrumental Music*. Washington, D.C.: Music Educator's National Conference, 1972.

Green, Elizabeth, *The Dynamic Orchestra*. Englewood Cliffs, NJ: Prentice-Hall, Inc., 1987.

Holz, Emil, and Roger Jacobi, *Teaching Band Instruments to Beginners*. Englewood Cliffs, NJ: Prentice-Hall, Inc., 1966.

Kinyon, John, *The Instrumental Music Director's Source Book*. Sherman Oaks, CA: Alfred Publishing Co., 1982.

Kohut, Daniel L., *Musical Performance: Learning Theory and Pedagogy*. Champaign, IL: Stipes Publishing Co., 1992.

Pizer, Russell A., *Evaluation Programs for School Bands and Orchestras*. West Nyack, NY: Parker Publishing Co., 1990.

Schleuter, Stanley L., *A Sound Approach to Teaching Instrumentalists*. Kent, OH: The Kent State University Press, 1984.

Walker, Darwin E., *Teaching Music: Managing the Successful Music Program*. New York: Schirmer Books, 1989.

B. WOODWINDS

General References

Bartolozzi, Bruno, *New Sounds for Woodwinds*. 2nd ed., London: Oxford University Press, 1982.

Westphal, Frederick, *Guide to Teaching Woodwinds*. 4th ed. Dubuque, IA: Wm. C. Brown, 1985.

Woodwind Anthology, Vols. I & II, Northfield, IL: The Instrumentalist Co., n.d.

Individual Instruments

Berman, Melvin, *The Art of Oboe Reed Making*. Toronto: Canadian Scholars' Press, 1988.

Galway, James, *Flute*. New York: Schirmer Books, 1982.

Hemke, Frederick, *Teacher's Guide to the Saxophone*. Elkhart, IN: H & A Selmer, Inc., 1977.

Mazzeo, Rosario, *The Clarinet*. Sherman Oaks, CA: Alfred Publishing Company, Inc., 1981.

Putnik, Edwin, *Art of Flute Playing*. Evanston, IL: Summy-Birchard, 1970.

Spencer, William G., *The Art of Bassoon Playing*. 2nd ed., rev. by Mueller. Evanston, IL: Summy-Birchard, 1969.

Sprenkle, Robert and David Ledet, *The Art of Oboe Playing*. Evanston, IL: Summy-Birchard, 1961.

Stein, Keith, *The Art of Clarinet Playing*. Evanston, IL: Summy-Birchard, 1958.

C. BRASSES

General References

Brass Anthology, new rev. ed., Northfield, IL: The Instrumentalist Co., 1991.

Stewart, M. Dee, *Arnold Jacobs: The Legacy of a Master*. Northfield, IL: The Instrumentalist Co., 1987.

Whitener, Scott, *A Complete Guide to Brass: Instruments and Pedagogy*. New York: Schirmer Books, 1990.

Individual Instruments

Bowman, Brian, *Practical Hints for Baritone (Euphonium)*. New York: Columbia Pictures, Inc., 1983.

Cummings, B., *The Contemporary Tuba*. New London, CT: Whaling Music, 1984.

Dale, Delbert, *Trumpet Technique,* 2nd ed. New York: Oxford University Press, 1985.

Farkas, Phillip, *The Art of French Horn Playing*. Evanston, IL: Summy-Birchard, 1956.

Fink, Reginald, *The Trombonist's Handbook*. Athens, OH: Accura Music, 1977.
Johnson, Keith, *The Art of Trumpet Playing*. Ames, IA: The Iowa State University Press, 1981.
Little, Donald, *Practical Hints on Playing the Tuba*. Melville, NY: Belwin-Mills, 1984.
Tuckwell, Barry, *Horn*. New York: Schirmer Books, 1983.

D. STRINGS

General References

Applebaum, Samuel, *The Art and Science of String Performance*. Sherman Oaks, CA: Alfred Publishing Co., Inc., 1986.
Klotman, Robert H., *Teaching Strings*. New York: Schirmer Books, 1988.

Individual Instruments

Bunting, Christopher, *Essay on the Craft of Cello Playing*. Cambridge: Cambridge University Press, 1982.
Galamian, Ivan, *Principles of Violin Playing and Teaching*. Englewood Cliffs, NJ: Prentice-Hall, Inc., 1962.
Krolick, Edward, *Basic Principles of Double Bass Playing*. Washington, D.C.: Music Educator's National Conference, 1957.
Potter, Louis, *The Art of Cello Playing*. Evanston, IL: Summy-Birchard Co., 1964.

E. PERCUSSION

Bartlett, Harry R., *Guide to Teaching Percussion*. 4th ed., Dubuque, IA: Wm. C. Brown, 1983.
Cook, Gary D., *Teaching Percussion*. New York: Schirmer Books, 1989.
Percussion Anthology, Northfield, IL: The Instrumentalist Co., 1977.
Percussion Education: A Source Book of Concepts and Information. Urbana, IL: The Percussive Arts Society, 1990.

INDEX